AF101587

Compiler Construction

A Practical Approach

JAMES E. MILLER

The Clark Group

Lexington, Kentucky

Copyright © 2009 by James E. Miller.

All rights reserved. No part of this book may be reproduced in any form or by any electronic or mechanical means, including information storage and retrieval systems, without permission in writing from the publisher, except by a reviewer who may quote brief passages in a review.

Clark Publishing
dba The Clark Group
250 East Short Street
Lexington, KY 40507
800 944 3995 info@theclarkgroupinfo.com

Visit our Web site at www.TheClarkGroupInfo.com

Printed in the United States of America.

ISBN: 978-0-9825057-3-1

For my students

Table of Contents

PREFACE

There are many good compiler texts available; however, most of them concentrate more on theory than on actual implementation of a working compiler. Because of this, a student must be advanced in his undergraduate study of computer science or be at the graduate level before he/she can sufficiently grasp the material. In many of these compiler texts a theory of programming languages is essentially a prerequisite. Since most texts concentrate more on theory, it is rare that a student will complete the actual programming project to see the true fruits of their labor.

The purpose of this text, is to give the undergraduate level student an understanding of what a compiler is, sufficient theory to understand how it is developed, and actually complete the task of writing a compiler in a one semester course. The development and completion of a working compiler is a first priority and sufficient theory is presented to assist in this project. I have seen students, after completing this one-semester course, able to write elaborate programs in their new language. In this course the student has an opportunity to develop a large programming project which I consider essential for all undergraduate computer science majors. Even though this text is designed as a compiler construction text, it also could be used in a software design and development course, or a software engineering course.

In this text, a complete computer programming language (Transy_source) equivalent to the early versions of translating languages (FORTRAN, BASIC, and Pascal) is developed. However, due to time constraints and the fact that a working compiler by the semester's end is the objective, the student will often use the language as presented with few, if any, modifications. Also, a complete object language (Transy_object) consisting of numbers (operators and memory locations) is developed. A student with a good working knowledge of any modern programming language (C, C++ or Perl) and basic data structures can sufficiently understand the material to complete the course in one semester. Students are free to select the language to code their compiler but most will use C, C++, or even Perl. The code given in this text will be in C++.

The text starts with the what and why of a compiler. Some history of languages is given by looking at what languages were available in the earliest days of computing (1937–1940s): machine (pseudo code). The main purpose of presenting the machine language is to understand its necessity and to understand its simplicity. The second and third steps in the development of programming languages, assembly language and translating languages are reviewed and contrasted with the machine language. Some basics of a compiler are presented and the big C notation is used to illustrate the conversion of a translating language to an object language.

A language in binary (machine language) and a pseudo assembly language are described and programs are written to contrast the two languages and give the student a familiarity with each. Graphics are presented to show how the contents of the accumulator (A), location counter (LC), and instruction address register (IAR) change as a program is executed.

Translating languages BASIC, FORTRAN, Pascal, C, C++, and Java are introduced. The five basic types of statements (Input/Output, Assignment, Control, Specification, and Subprogram) are contrasted for each language. The syntax of each language is presented and some simple programs in each language are given. These languages are presented for the purpose of giving the student a better understanding of the source language to be developed–Transy_source.

The alphabet, syntax, data types and statements representing each of the five basic types of statements in Transy_source language are presented. Since this is very similar to other translating languages, students will quickly learn to write programs in this language. Several programming examples will be given and students will be asked to write programs in this new language. Hopefully, students will become skilled programmers in this language as they will be writing a program (compiler) that will translate this language to an object language (Transy_object).

A chapter is presented on the object language (Transy_object).

The object language for each source statement in the Transy_source language is developed. Several programming examples are presented and students will be asked to write programs in this language. It is essential that this language be well defined just as the Transy_source must be well defined. Students must have a good understanding of this language as their translation phase of the compiler will translate the Transy_source to this Transy_object language.

A chapter is developed on automata theory and the basic theory of how a compiler works. The two basic components of the translation phase, the lexical scan and the syntactic scan, are presented. The automata theory analysis gives the student the basic ideas on how to take a string – a statement in a programming language – and determine its type. Is the string an input, output, control, or does the string match any of the language key-words? Later in the translation phase chapter, a token number will be assigned to each token word that determines the statement type. The syntax analysis phase discusses how the input string, once its type is determined (read, write, etc.), is broken into individual atoms – variable names, constants, math operators, relational operators, etc. Unique numbers are then assigned to each atom. A symbol table (to equate variable names with core addresses) is developed and can be developed through a simple array type structure or through a binary tree structure. Here again, due to time constraint, the student is given the option of which data structure to use.

A chapter on the translation phase is presented. This chapter is the heart of the compiler and consists of taking the Transy_source language to the Transy_object language. There are thirteen (13) programming projects, each of which is independent that come together to form the translation phase of the compiler. One project removes all blanks from each source input, thereby making it easier to examine the string and turn it into a set of atoms. One project is the lexical scan and determines the type of statement – i.e., it determines which keyword, if any, is found in the input string. Here, the chapter on automata theory is applied. One project constructs a symbol table and other projects take each string, source line, and create an object line–a line of numbers.

A chapter is presented on the execution phase. The execution phase of the compiler again is a program (a segment of the compiler) that takes as input the Transy_object statements and executes each as directed by the object code. More specifically, an input statement in the Transy_source has form READ A,B,C and the corresponding Transy_object statement has form 1 3 0 1 2, the first 1 tells the execution phase that this statement is an input statement, the 3 signifies that 3 values are to be entered, and the 0 1 and 2 tell where in the memory the 3 values are to be stored.

A chapter is devoted to testing the compiler. Several programs are written in the Transy_source language, translated, and then executed. The compiled and executed programs show the Transy_source code, the Transy_object code, the core file, the literal file, and the output after execution.

I am grateful to my former colleague Dr. Kenny M. Moorman, Associate Professor of Computer Science at Transylvania University for the technical review of the book. The material in this book has evolved over the past 25 years from my teaching a Compiler Construction class at Transylvania University. My students have played a large role in testing the material and have assisted me in making this an enjoyable and cumulative experience for the computer science major.

Finally, I am most grateful to my wife Betty, for being so understanding during the time that I have spent working on this project.

James E. Miller
jmiller@Transy.edu

CHAPTER 1

The Basics of Compiler Writing

INTRODUCTION

The purpose of this text is to give the undergraduate level student an understanding of what a compiler is, how it is developed, and actually complete the task of writing a compiler for a fairly extensive language in a one-semester course. Some basic theory is given but this is not the main focus. A complete computer programming language (Transy_source) equivalent to the early versions of translating languages (FORTRAN, BASIC and Pascal) is developed. Also, a complete object language (Transy_object) consisting of numbers (operators and memory locations) is developed. A student with a good working knowledge of any modern programming language (C, C++, or Perl) and basic data structures can complete this course. The text starts with some history of languages available in the early days of computing (1937 – 1940s), machine and assembly (pseudo of each). The syntax of each language is presented and students will be asked to write basic programs in each. The main purpose of presenting the machine language is to understand its necessity and to actually understand its simplicity. Graphics will be presented to show how the contents of the **accumulator** (A), **location counter** (LC), and **instruction address register** (IAR) change as a program is executed. Translating languages are reviewed and contrasted and programs are written in the languages FORTRAN, BASIC, Pascal, C, C++, and Java. Short courses on FORTRAN, BASIC, Pascal, C, C++, and Java are available.

1.1 Computer Hardware and Software

The study of the computer is classified as the study of **computer hardware** and the study of **computer software**. The hardware being the essential physical components of the computer that perform the functions prescribed by the software, and the software being the **instruction set** and necessary logic that tells the computer how to understand the original algorithm of the problem. In the early days of the computer (pre-1945), the programmer or algorithm coder could relate to the computer only in binary software. Today, programs called **compilers** are written which makes it possible to relate to the computer in a natural or **formal language**.

1.2 What is a Compiler?

Simply stated, a **compiler** is a program that reads a program written in one language–the source language–and translates it into an equivalent program in another language–the target (object) language. As an important part of this translation process, the compiler reports to its user the presence of errors in the source or original language.

At first glance, the variety of compilers may appear overwhelming. There are hundreds of source languages, ranging from traditional programming languages such as **BASIC**, **FORTRAN**, **Pascal**, **C**, **C++**, and **Java** to specialized languages that have arisen in virtually every area of computer application. Target languages are equally as varied; a target language may be another programming language, or the machine language of any computer between a microprocessor and a supercomputer. Compilers are classified as single-pass, multi-pass, load-and-go, debugging, or optimizing, depending on how they have been constructed or what function they are supposed to perform. Despite this apparent complexity, the basic tasks that any compiler must perform are essentially the same. By understanding these tasks, we can construct compilers for a wide variety of source languages and target machines using the same basic techniques. Our knowledge about how to organize and write compilers has increased greatly since the first compilers started to appear in the early 1950s. It is difficult to give an exact date for the first compiler because initially a great deal of experimentation and implementation was done independently by transforming arithmetic formulas into machine code. Throughout the 1950s, compilers were considered notoriously difficult programs to write. We have since discovered systematic techniques for handling many of the important tasks that occur during compilation. Good implementation languages, programming environments, and software tools have also been developed. With these advances, a substantial compiler can be implemented even as a student project in a one-semester compiler-design course.

Normally, the program to be converted is written in a high-level language (a language easy for the programmer to understand), and the compiler converts this to a low-level language (a language easy for the computer to understand). The program written in the high-level language is spoken of as the **source code** (program) and the program written in the low-level language as the **object code** (program).

Computer languages for the modern day computer have been around since the late 1930s. Today, there are many computer languages and new languages are still evolving. There are three basic types of computer languages: **machine**, **assembly**, and **translating**. However, the machine language (ML) is the only language the computer understands and is in binary code. The ML, like all computer languages, consists of a set of instructions. Here each instruction has two parts, the **operator** and the **operand**. The operator tells the computer what to do and the operand what to do it on. The assembly language (AL) is machine oriented and easy to convert directly to ML. The translating language (TL) is easier for the programmer to understand but requires an extensive task or program to prepare the language so that the machine can understand it.

1.3 The Phases of a Compiler

The compiler developed in this course will consist of two phases. One phase will be spoken of as the **translation phase** and one spoken of as the **execution phase**. The translation phase will take the high-level language and convert to a low-level language. The execution phase will take the low-level language or code and execute or perform the tasks of the original code.

A language consists of a group of statements, each performing specified tasks and each abiding by specified syntactic rules. The purpose of this course is to develop a program (compiler) that takes a TL to a ML (pseudo) and then execute the actual program by processing the ML code. This course can be considered as a typical compiler construction course, more applied than most, or as a software engineering project.

The two steps of translation and execution necessary for high-level languages is spoken of as **executing a program**. The source program is translated to object then the resulting object program is loaded into memory and executed. Compilers were once considered almost impossible programs to write. In fact, the first and possibly the most important compiler ever written, FORTRAN, required years to implement. Today, compilers can be built in much less time. In fact, the object of this course will be to develop a translating language as well as an object language and then write the compiler to implement this language all in a one semester effort.

The first attempts toward the development of a high-level language were in the early 1950s. The hardware at this time was expensive and much less sophisticated than today. Hence, the machine requirement for speed of program execution and efficiency in storage was a major priority. Today, being able to have essentially unlimited memory space as well as a high speed computing machine, the writing of compilers has less time spent on code optimization or efficiency in storage and execution than in the past.

1.4 Computer Software/Basic Computer Hardware Components

A digital computer cannot work without **computer software**–i.e., a program–which controls the different **hardware components** of the computer in a sequence specified by the user. By simply changing the program, the computer can be made to work in a different manner. In other words, software provides a digital computer with general-purpose computing capability. The software makes it possible for the programmer to interact with the five basic functional units of a computer. Through this interaction, the programmer is able to make the digital computer a general purpose machine rather than just a special purpose machine. The five (5) functional units are **Input** (I), **Output** (O), **Memory** (M), **Arithmetic Logic Unit** (ALU), and the **Control Unit** (C). The **input** unit allows for information to be entered into the computer. In the early days of computing, the main input device was a card reader. Today, one machine may have many input devices – magnetic disk, keyboard, etc. The **output** device is used to display information to the user. Again, in the early days cards would be punched or output would be printed to paper. A little later, a much faster form of output was the magnetic tape or magnetic disk. Today, the terminal screen is the main way of viewing output. Multiple storage devices with almost unlimited storage capacity are available. The **memory** of a computer (primary memory as opposed to secondary memory–such as a magnetic disk) is the main reason the computer is such a fantastic tool. We think of the primary memory as being hard wired as opposed to rotational or tape-type memory. The memory allows us to store information and then retrieve it at will. Charles Babbage, in the 19th century, envisioned such a machine that would allow the user to store information, data and instructions, and then carry out the instructions without continuous interaction from a user. Although he was not able to carry his idea to completion, the idea did play a large role in the development of the modern day computer. The memory of the computer is broken into cells or compartments with each cell capable of storing one unit of information – a byte (8 bits) or multiple bytes. Each cell will also have an address. This address is the same as a street address – it tells us where something is located. The **arithmetic logic unit** (ALU) is a portion of the central processing unit and contains the logic circuits necessary to tell the computer how to perform basic operations – add, subtract, etc. As illustrated later in the text, the ALU will be displayed as a single register: the **accumulator** (A) – a set of bits that can change from one state to another state at a very rapid rate. The **control unit** (C) will be displayed as consisting of two registers: the **location counter** (LC) and the **instruction address register** (IAR). The LC will contain the address of the next instruction to execute and the IAR will contain the instruction currently being executed. See diagram below:

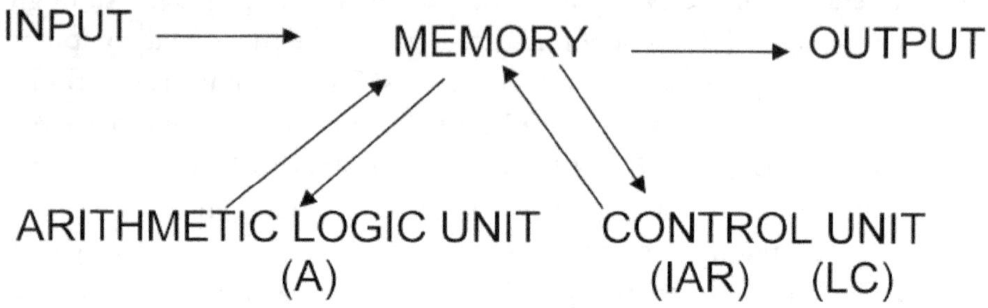

1.5 Types of Computer Languages

The three basic types of computer languages – **machine, assembly, and translating** evolved from the 1930s through the 1960s and even today major computing efforts are devoted to making a better computer language. The **machine language** is the only language the computer understands and is in **binary** (two basic devices or symbols used to represent the language). The machine language was the only language used to code programs until the early 1940s. Individuals became proficient at coding programs in machine language; however, the coding was slow and tedious. A better way to communicate to the computer was developed and a new language or way to communicate with the computer was developed in the early 1940s. This new way was called **assembly language** as symbols were used to represent strings of 0s and 1s. As detailed on the following page a string of zeros and ones such as 0010 which could signal the computer to add something to the accumulator may now be represented by the symbol ADD. The new language greatly enhanced the process of communicating with the computer and was used extensively through the 1940s and 1950s. Again, a better and faster way to communicate was sought and in the mid-1950s **translating languages** were developed. Translating languages used methods similar to those already being used by mathematicians in problem solving, and were easier to implement or code algorithms than assembly or machine languages.

To illustrate a comparison of the three languages, consider the simple computational task of adding the number X stored in memory address 8 to the number Y in memory address 10 and then storing the result in memory address 5. This can be written as the following program consisting of only three instructions, although a program in general can consist of any number of instructions:

Machine:	0011 1000 0010 1010 0100 0101
Assembly:	LOAD 8 ADD 10 STORE 5
Translating:	Z = X + Y

The first instruction, 0011 1000 or LOAD 8, reads the number X from memory address 8 and places it into the arithmetic logic unit (ALU) or accumulator (A), clearing any number previously placed there. The second instruction adds number Y stored in memory address 10 to X in the ALU. The third instruction stores the sum held in the ALU into memory address 5. The numbers X and Y need not be mentioned explicitly in this program because it is assumed that they have been stored in their respective addresses by previous instructions that are not shown here. The first part of each instruction, such as 0011 or LOAD, is called the operation code (**op-code**), and the second part, such as 8, is called the **operand.**

Some computers have instructions containing two or three operands. An example is ADD 8 10, which means the addition of the numbers stored in memory addresses 8 and 10 and store the result in the accumulator. The instructions in a program are collectively called **code**.

A computer can directly understand only machine language, which is unique to each specific computer. Machine language instructions are written in binary form–i.e., strings of 0s and 1s (e.g., 01011101)–because electronic circuits inside computers (including memories) work only with the signals 0 and 1. Thus LOAD 8, an instruction in the previous example, might be written as 001100001000 in a machine code, where the initial 0011 means the LOAD operation and where the remaining 00001000 means the decimal number 8. Although computers work easily with machine language, such code is tedious for humans to write and read. Thus, programmers use languages that are readable for them but not for computers. For example, the **mnemonic code** LOAD in a human-readable language is far easier to understand than 0011 in machine language. Such a human-readable language must be translated into machine language by special-purpose programs called **language processors**. In our study, the language processor will be the translation phase of the compiler.

Programming languages can be classified from the viewpoint of readability. A language whose readability is close to machine languages is called a **low-level language**. Assembly languages are examples. Those whose readability is close to human languages are known as **high-level languages**. Pascal, C, C++, and Java are examples of high-level languages. Programs written in low-level languages can make more efficient use of the hardware and often execute faster and require less memory space in a computer than those written in high-level languages.

COBOL, a high-level language, has been used extensively for business applications. COBOL was written so that people with a business background could easily understand. The following is an example of a COBOL program:

```
IF ITEM--COUNT = 0

THEN

NEXT SENTENCE

ELSE

COMPUTE AVERAGE--PRICE =

AVERAGE--PRICE / ITEM--COUNT.

MOVE AVERAGE--PRICE TO

PRINT--AVERAGE--PRICE.

PERFORM 300--PRINT--DETAIL--LINE.
```

Keywords in the COBOL language like COMPUTE are easily understood by users without technical backgrounds.

Programming languages are further classified from different viewpoints, such as their main applications or the manner of solving problems. FORTRAN and ALGOL are classified as programming languages with scientific or engineering applications; COBOL and RPG are used mainly for business problems. FORTRAN was originally written as a scientific compiler or formula translator but has evolved over the years and today can be considered a general-purpose language suited for business problems as well as scientific problems. Languages such as PL/I, BASIC, C, C++, and Pascal are also considered to be general-purpose languages.

Instructions as described previously are actually steps of programs written in assembly or machine languages. Each step of a high-level language is called a **statement**. Each instruction in a machine language specifies an operation of the ALU, memory, or other hardware. Each statement in a high-level language specifies a computational task, which may not be directly related to hardware operations and which generally translates into many instructions when converted into assembly or machine language.

1.5a Machine Language

Machine language–The lowest-level programming language is machine language which is in binary. While easily understood by computers, machine languages are difficult for humans to use because they consist entirely of numbers. Programmers, therefore, use either a high-level programming language or an assembly language. An assembly language contains essentially a 1 – 1 correspondence to the machine language, but the instructions and variables have names instead of being just numbers.

Programs written in high-level languages are translated into assembly language or machine-like language or machine language by a compiler. Assembly language programs are translated into machine language by a program called an **assembler**. Every CPU has its own unique machine language. Therefore, programs must be recompiled to run on different types of computers.

An example of a machine language program is given below:

Operation Codes: 0001—Clear Accumulator
0010—Add to Accumulator
0100—Store to Accumulator

Program Segment: 0000 / 0001 / xxxx
0001 / 0010 / 0110
0010 / 0010 / 0111
0011 / 0100 / 0110
0100 / 0100 / 1011

The **operation codes (op-codes)** are hard wired and specify the operation to be performed; such as 0001 for a particular computer could mean "clear accumulator" and 0010 could mean "add to accumulator" and 0100 "store to or in accumulator." The first column of binary numbers in the program segment tells the computer where to store the given instruction; such as 0001/0010/0110 tells the computer to store the instruction 0010 0110 in address 0001 of memory. The programmer writing a machine language program must keep track of where to store the instructions and where to store the data.

1.5B Assembly Language

Assembly Language–In computer **assembler** (or assembly) language, a mnemonic is an abbreviation for an operation or op-code. It is entered in the operation code field of each assembler program instruction. For example, in the above **machine language program** the op-code 0001 (clear accumulator) could be replaced with the mnemonic CLA and the op-code 0010 (add to accumulator) could be replaced with ADD. The above program when written in assembly language will have the more readable form:

```
CLA
ADD X
ADD Y
STO Z
STO P
```

Here the assembler will keep track of where to store the instructions and also where to store the data.

Mnemonic–In general, a **mnemonic** (from Greek *mnemon* or mindful; pronounced neh-MAHN-ik) is a word, abbreviation, rhyme, or similar verbal device one learns or creates in order to remember something. The technique of developing these remembering devices is called "mnemonics." Mnemonics are often used to remember information such as phone numbers. In programming, they are used to represent a specific set of 0s and 1s.

1.5c Translating Languages

Translating Languages – syntax, grammar, and symbols or words are used to give instructions to a computer. Because computers work with binary numbers, the first-generation languages or machine languages required the writing of long strings of binary numbers to represent such operations as add, subtract, and compare.

Later, improvements allowed octal, decimal, or hexadecimal representation of binary strings. It is difficult to write error-free programs in machine language; hence, languages have been created to make programming easier and faster. Symbolic or assembly languages (second-generation languages) were introduced in the 1940s. They use simple mnemonics which were translated into machine language by a computer program called an **assembler**. An extension of such a language is the macro instruction, a mnemonic (such as READ) for which the assembler substitutes a series of simpler mnemonics.

In the mid-1950s, a third generation of languages called high-level languages came into use. These languages are largely independent of the hardware and are classified as algorithmic, or procedural languages and are designed for general purpose problem solving. Unlike machine or symbolic languages, these high-level languages are essentially the same for all computers. Remember, they must be translated into machine code by a program called a compiler or interpreter.

The machine program given earlier can be written in a translating language with the two statements $Z = X + Y$ and $P = Z$. The first such high-level language was **FORTRAN** (FORmula TRANslation), developed in the late 1950s and best used for scientific calculation. The first commercial language, **COBOL** (COmmon Business Oriented Language), was developed in the early 1960s. It was developed so that computer processing could also be available for the business person. **ALGOL** (ALGOrithmic Language), developed in Europe about 1958, is used primarily in mathematics and science, as is **APL** (A Programming Language), published in 1962. **PL/I** (Programming Language 1), developed in 1964, and **ADA** (for Ada Augusta, Countess of Lovelace, biographer of Charles Babbage), developed in 1981, are designed for both business and scientific use. For early day **personal computers**, the most popular language was **BASIC** (Beginners All-purpose Symbolic Instruction Code). BASIC was developed in 1964 and is similar to FORTRAN. **Pascal** (named for Blaise Pascal, who built the first successful mechanical calculator), was introduced in 1971 as a teaching language. The **C** language (introduced in 1972 to implement the **UNIX** operating system) has been extended to **C++** to deal with the rigors of object-oriented programming. The language **Java** was introduced in the early 1990s as a web-based language.

Computer Programs–Computer programs are made to do many different things and range in size from a simple 2 line program in BASIC that prints Hello World:

```
10 print "Hello World"
20 end
```

to rather large programs in the language C++. A C++ program that checks the numerical accuracy of a 3 x 3 stencil and the accuracy of a 5 x 5 stencil for the Laplacian operator on the function $x^2 + y^2$ is given below:

(The Laplacian operator is defined as $\partial^2 u / \partial x^2 + \partial^2 u / \partial y^2$)

```
#include <iostream.h>
#include <stdlib.h>

float l3( int , int );
float l5( int , int );
float tb1[3][3];
```

```
float tb2[5][5];
int main(void)
{
        int j,k;

        float temp1, temp2;

     for(j=0; j<3; ++j) for(k=0; k<3; ++k)
            tb1[j][k] = (.5*j)*(.5*j) + (.5*k)*(.5*k);
     for(j=0; j<5; ++j) for(k=0; k<5; ++k)
            tb2[j][k] = (.5*j)*(.5*j) +(.5*k)*(.5*k);

     temp1=l3(1,1);
     cout << "This is 3 by 3 value:" << temp1 << endl;

     temp1=l5(2,2);
     cout << "This is 5 by 5 value:" << temp1 << endl;
}
float l3(int h, int k)
{
   const float c[3][3] = {
   {1, 4, 1},
   {4,-20,4},
   {1, 4, 1}};
   int x, y;
   float w, sum=0;
   w = .5;
   for (x=-1; x<=1; ++x)
    for (y=-1;y<=1;++y)
     sum = sum + (t[h+x][k+y] * c[x+1][y+1]);
   sum = 1./(6.0*w*w)*sum;
   return sum;
}
float l5(int h, int k)
{
   const float c[ 5][5] = {
   { -83, -601, -1677, -601, -83},
```

```
  { -601, 6136, 37650, 6136, -601},
  {-1677, 37650, -163296, 37650, -1677},
  { -601, 6136, 37650, 6136, -601},
  { -83, -601, -1677, -601, -83}};
  int x, y;
  float w, sum=0;
  w = .5;
  for (x=-2; x<=2; ++x)
   for (y=-2;y<=2;++y)
    sum = sum + (t[h+x][k+y] * c[x+2][y+2]);
  sum = 1./(36540.*w*w)*sum;
  return sum;
}
```

The input to a compiler is just a character string. The compiler must be smart enough to determine the type of statement – **Input/Output**, **Assignment**, **Control**, **Specification** or **Subprogram**–then break the string into **tokens**, (a group of characters that have a specific meaning such as READ or WRITE, etc.). Once the statement type is determined, the statement is further dissected into variable names, operators, and constants. A **symbol table** is used at this time to assign variable names addresses in memory.

The compiler process presented here will develop in phases with the **Lexical Analysis Phase** being used to determine the type of statement and the **Syntax Analysis Phase** used to get tokens from the assigned statement. The Syntax Analysis Phase will also assign addresses to the tokens and determine if the rules of the language for the given statement have been obeyed.

1.6 The Big C Notation

The writing of a compiler involves optimization and the inclusion of other desired features needed to make it competitive in the vast array of languages. Even today, with modern software and hardware, it could take a programmer(s) years to complete such a project for an extensive language. That being the case, the programmer is always looking for shortcuts. A shortcut is often obtained by using components of the total project that have been developed and tested. A simple example of this is the effective use of the many pre-defined functions found in most languages. Today, if someone is developing a new compiler and the main goal is the development of the software and not as a course project to learn how software is developed, they may by "**boot-strapping**" make use of compilers already available for their computer.

The **big C** notation is used below to illustrate how a new compiler can be developed assuming you already have at least the machine language and possibly the assembly language for a particular machine.

FORTRAN → IBM 1130 Assembly

C

IBM 1130 Assembly

The above symbolism illustrates a compiler written in IBM 1130 assembly language that takes the FORTRAN language to IBM 1130 assembly. The thinking behind this is that you already have an assembly language compiler and the assembly language is friendlier than machine language. After writing the code to take FORTRAN to 1130 Assembly then the existing program – 1130 assembly compiler (written in machine language) – can be used to take the output from your compiler (1130 Assembly) to machine code.

IBM 1130 Assembly → Machine

C

Machine

The **big C** notation to illustrate a compiler written in the FORTRAN language which converts the language C to C++ is given by

C → C++

C

FORTRAN

Again, this assumes that you have the FORTRAN compiler and the C++ compiler and you want to develop a C compiler for your machine. So the task is to write the code in FORTRAN that converts C to C++ code and then use the C++ compiler to complete the task. The next steps in the above process might look as follows:

C++ → Assembly	Assembly → Machine
C	**C**
Assembly	Machine

But here we are assuming that you already have the C++ as well as the assembly compiler so the two steps above are already written for you.

Consider the FORTRAN assignment statement:

A = B + C * D

If the IBM 1130 assembly language had the statements LOD, MUL, ADD, and STO; then the above FORTRAN statement would be translated into the statements given below:

L1: LOD R1, C—Load register 1 with contents of memory C
MUL R1, D—Multiply R1 by the contents of D
ADD R1, B—Add the contents of B to R1
STO R1, A—Store R1 in A

The compiler writer for the FORTRAN compiler would need to write the code in IBM 1130 assembly to generate the assembly code above. Note that the compiler must be smart enough to know that multiplication takes place before addition. The compiler must also check to see that the expression is correctly formed, i.e., has proper syntax. High-level languages have many advantages, possibly the most important being the ease of coding algorithms. High-level languages also have disadvantages such as the programmer not having complete control of the hardware.

1.7 Interpreters vs. Compilers and Error Types

Interpreters differ from compilers in that the output of the interpreter is the compilations specified by the source code and not an object language.

Compiler:	Interpreter:
A = 2; B = 3;	A = 2;
Print (A * B);	B = 3;
-----------------	Print(A * B)
MOVE A, 2	-----------------
MOVE B, 3	6
LOD R1, A	
MUL R1, B	
STO R1, Temp	
OUTP Temp	

Today, it is easy to confuse a compiler and an interpreter as the programmer often clicks the **compile/run** rather than just the **compile** button. Today, since computers are very fast, the programmer will not notice the difference. In earlier days this was not possible. In many cases the computer was not large enough to allow both the translation phase and the execution phase to reside in the machine at the same time.

In compiler writing it is necessary to check for **translation errors** as well as **execution errors** – compile time and run time errors.

Example:

Compile time error:	**Run time error:**
a = (b + c) * d);	x = 0;
	y = a / x;

The compile time error is the extra ')' and would be detected in the translating phase as a syntax error. The run time error would be a 'divide by zero' and would be detected during the execution phase.

The **source language** is the input to a compiler, the **object language** is the output of the compiler, and the **implementation language** is the language the compiler is written in.

As stated earlier, the **Lexical Analysis** phase takes the input string and determines the type of the statement, whether **READ**, **WRITE**, **ASSIGNMENT**, or other type. The **Syntax Analysis** phase checks for proper syntax and outputs **atoms** or **tokens**, **variable names**, **operators**, and **constants**, as well as builds the **symbol table**.

The syntax analysis would use a **transducer** or **syntax tree** to convert the source statement

A = B + C * D;
to object code.

Given the statement:
S = Sum + Unit * 1.2E-12;

show tokens and type

Tokens	Type	How treated
S	Identifier (variable name)	Place in symbol table and give address
=	Assignment Operator	Assign a #
Sum	Identifier	Place
+	Operator	Assign a #
Unit	Identifier	Place
*	Operator	Assign a #
1.2E-12	Constant	Place, store

Consider the statement

A = B + C * D

To get the compiler to understand, we must place the statement in **reverse Polish notation**, an easier form for the compiler. To perform this, a tool or table such as a transducer is needed.

With the token legend given below:

= is -1
+ is -6
- is -7
* is -4
/ is -5

The statement: A = B + C * D

Address A = address B + address C * address D

becomes:

A B C + D * = in reverse Polish notation

with addresses assigned to variable names and operator tokens assigned to math operators, the assignment statement as written in object code becomes

0 1 2 -6 3 -4 -1

where A is stored in memory address 0, B in memory address 1, C in memory address 2, and D in memory address 3.

1.8 The Compiler Development Process

Chapters will be presented that develop a unique "high-level language," the Transy_source language, and a unique "low-level language," the Transy_object language. The basic statements in six other high-level languages will be contrasted and a general low-level language – assembly language – will be studied. Examples will be given to illustrate how a program can be coded in a binary language (machine language), loaded and executed. The theory will be presented to assist in taking statements in the Transy_source language and converting to statements in the Transy_object language. A transducer will be used to take an infix notation expression to reverse Polish notation. The computer code (compiler) will then be written that takes the Transy_source language to the Transy_object language (translation phase of the compiler) and then a segment written (execution phase of the compiler) that will execute the Transy_object language. Programs will be written in the Transy_source language and executed using the developed compiler.

Chapter 1 Exercises

Exercise 1. Develop a machine-language program similar to the one found in the text to add the numbers stored in memory positions 1001 through 1111 and store the result in memory 0000. Use 5 bits for memory addresses if necessary.

Exercise 2. Develop a machine language program to add the set of instructions created for exercise 1 and store the result in memory 00000000.

Exercise 3. Repeat exercise 1 using the pseudo assembly code given in this chapter.

Exercise 4. Discuss any problems you may encounter while repeating exercise 2 using pseudo assembly code.

Exercise 5. Discuss the following statement: Someday compilers will no longer be necessary.

Exercise 6. Use the big C notation to illustrate a compiler written in ML that converts C++ to C.

Exercise 7. Discuss why assembly language programmers in the late 1950s were reluctant to write programs in FORTRAN.

Exercise 8. Describe the differences between an interpreter and a compiler. When might an interpretive language be preferred over a compiled language?

Exercise 9. Discuss the difference between a translation error and an execution error.

Exercise 10. What programming languages were available for Nicklaus Wirth to write the Pascal compiler? Use the big C notation to illustrate how this might have been accomplished.

Exercise 11. Would it be possible to write the C++ compiler using the C programming language? If yes, use the big C notation to illustrate how it can be accomplished.

Exercise 12. For the statement Z = A + B/C – 1476 / X; identify the tokens and type.

Exercise 13. Code the algorithm given below in the language of your choice and describe its output.

Algorithm:

1. Input a,b,c
2. Let la = a
3. Compare b with la if greater than, let la = b
4. Compare c with la if greater than, let la = c
5. Output la
6. Stop

Exercise 14. Devise an algorithm and code in the language of your choice that inputs 10 numbers, one per line, then find and output the largest of the ten.

Exercise 15. Try your skills. A prime number is a number that has no divisors other than 1 and itself. Examples are 2, 3, 5, 7, 11, 13, and 17. Devise an algorithm (code in the language of your choice), that finds and outputs all prime numbers less than 10,000.

Exercise 16. Try your skills. A perfect number is a number that is equal to the sum of its divisors, not including itself. Example of a perfect number is 28, i.e., 1 + 2 + 4 + 7 + 14 =28. Devise an algorithm (code in the language of your choice) that finds and outputs all perfect numbers less than 30,000.

Exercise 17. Suppose you want the Ada compiler for your HP machine and you already have the Pascal compiler for the HP. You can also assume you already have the assembly language and machine language compiler for the HP machine. Show symbolically how this can be accomplished.

CHAPTER 2

Programming Languages—Machine and Assembly

INTRODUCTION

A programming language is a set of instructions that can be used to construct a self-contained set of commands used to operate a computer to produce a specific result. It is through these languages that we talk to the computer and give the computer the ability to "think." Blaise Pascal, the namesake of one popular language, as well as a mathematician who invented the first computing machine in the 17th century, said:

All our dignity consists then in thought. By it we must elevate ourselves and not by space and time, which we cannot fill. Let us endeavor to think well; this is the principle of mortality.

Though it is certain Pascal wasn't speaking of computers at the time, the passage relates to the progress of programming languages throughout history. His namesake language indeed was one of the first languages to allow the computer to "think well" according to modern standards.

2.1 MACHINE LANGUAGE

Machine languages are the only languages understood by computers.

They are the lowest-level programming languages except for computers that utilize programmable microcode. They are easily understood by computers, but difficult for humans to use because they consist entirely of numbers. Programmers, therefore, use either a high-level programming language or an **assembly language**. An assembly language contains essentially the same instructions as a machine language, but the instructions and addresses have names instead of numbers.

Programs written in high-level languages are translated into assembly language or machine language by a **compiler**. Assembly language programs are translated into machine language by a program called an **assembler**. Every **central processing unit** (CPU) has its own unique machine language. Programs must be rewritten or recompiled, therefore, to run on different types of computers.

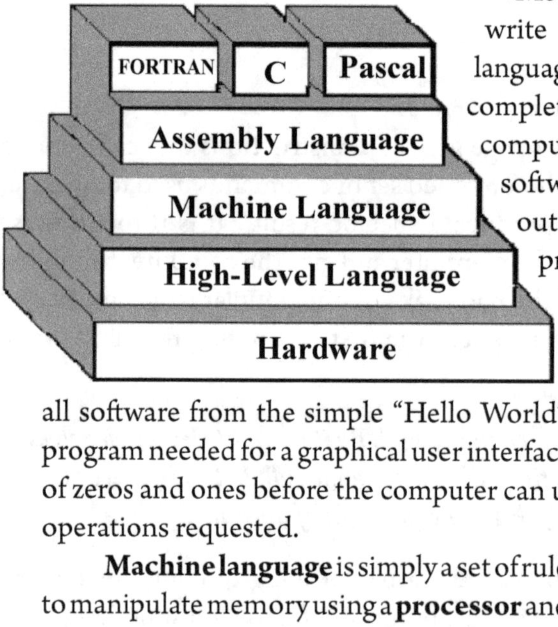

Most programmers will never write programs in machine language. However, to have a complete understanding of how computer hardware and computer software work together to carry out the instructions of the programmer, it is essential to have some knowledge of machine language. Also, it is amazing to realize how all software from the simple "Hello World" program in BASIC to the program needed for a graphical user interface eventually become a series of zeros and ones before the computer can understand and perform the operations requested.

Machine language is simply a set of rules and conventions designed to manipulate memory using a **processor** and a set of **registers**. **Memory** is a set of hardware devices that are used to simulate the zeros and ones used to represent information. All memories have the same structure – a continuous array of cells (a compartment to store information) with each having a unique address. An individual word (representing either a data item or an instruction) is specified by supplying its address.

The processor, normally called the CPU, is a device capable of performing a fixed set of operations, such as arithmetic and logic operations, memory access operations, and control (also called branching) operations. An individual instruction consists of an **operator** and an **operand**. The operator of the instruction specifies which operation is to be performed (e.g., store, add, multiply, etc.) and the operand of the instruction specifies the addresses of the **registers** (high speed local memory) or selected memory location on which the operation is to be performed. Likewise, the results of the operation can be stored either in registers or in selected memory locations.

Instructions can be a long string of zeros and ones, with an op-code, operand and instruction address. The total instruction can require as much as 64 bits. Most processors will contain several storage devices called registers. Each register is capable of holding a single value. Located in the processor's immediate proximity, the registers are high-speed local memory, allowing the processor to quickly store and retrieve the data. The registers are normally labeled as R0, R1, R2, etc.

Programming languages began as fundamental low-level languages consisting solely of instructions in binary code which only the programmer and the computer that the programmer was operating could understand. A little later **assembly languages** were instituted which substituted word-like symbols (ADD, SUB, MUL) for binary operation codes. These (as do all programming languages aside from machine languages) need a translator or "assembler" to allow the computer, being used, to understand the instructions. The assembly language added simplicity to the writing of programs. The instruction given as:

001000000 00000000001 00000000010

in machine language becomes:

ADD R1, A

in assembly language. Here the contents of memory position A at address (00000000010) will be added to register 1.

The following illustrates a machine language program starting from loading into memory through the execution. The program first clears the accumulator, adds to the accumulator the contents of memory position

6, adds the contents of memory position 7, then stores the accumulator in memory 6 and stores the accumulator in position 11. The first set of 0s and 1s tells the computer where to store the 8 bit instruction which follows. The second set of 0s and 1s is the **operation** (op) code and the third set of 0s and 1s is the memory address or **operand**. The basic computer with the five functional units – **Input** (I), **Output** (O), **Memory** (M), **Arithmetic Logic Unit** (ALU) and **Control Unit** (C) is displayed. The ALU contains the logic necessary to perform basic arithmetic and as presented here will consist of the single register, the **Accumulator**. The Control Unit interprets and executes instructions and consists of the two registers: **Instruction Address Register** (IAR) and the **Location Counter** (LC). The instruction address register contains the instruction being executed and the location counter contains the address of the next instruction to be executed. The program as well as data could be entered through toggle switches provided by early computer systems such as the IBM 1620 and IBM 1130. The output would be displayed through LEDs.

The machine illustrated here will have 16 memory cells or positions (addressed as 0000 ... 1111) and at most 16 operation codes.

2.1A Machine Language Example

Machine Language Program

Operation Codes: 0001—Clear Accumulator
0010—Add to Accumulator
0100—Store to Accumulator

Program Segment: 0000 / 0001 / xxxx
0001 / 0010 / 0110
0010 / 0010 / 0111
0011 / 0100 / 0110
0100 / 0100 / 1011

Memory before program execution starts

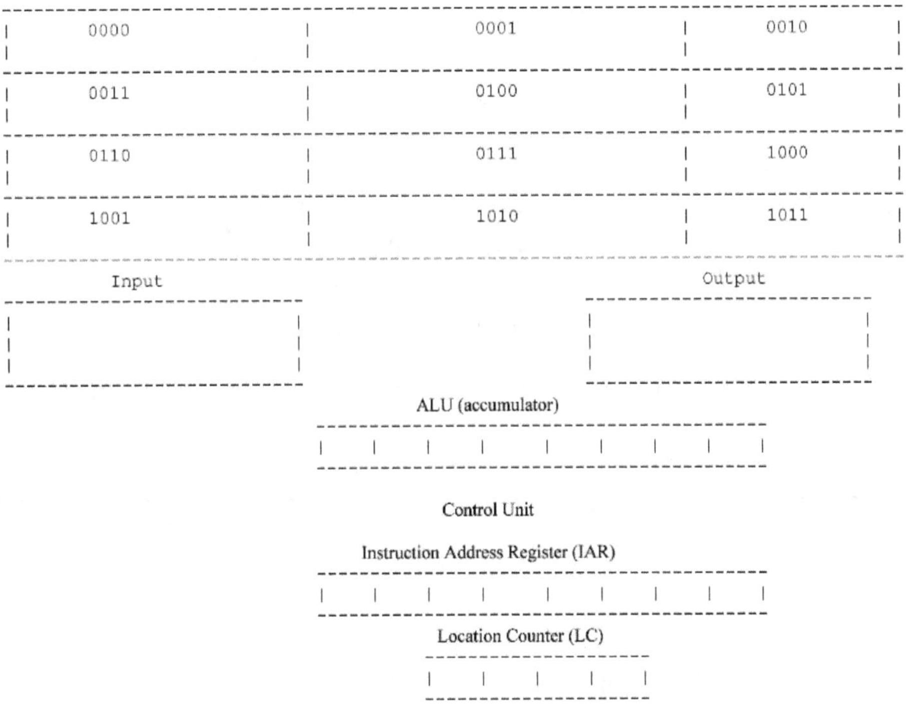

A view of the basic computer before the program is loaded.

Machine Language Program

Operation Codes:	0001—Clear Accumulator
	0010—Add to Accumulator
	0100—Store to Accumulator
Program Segment:	0000 / 0001 / xxxx
	0001 / 0010 / 0110
	0010 / 0010 / 0111
	0011 / 0100 / 0110
	0100 / 0100 / 1011

With 3 in memory position 0110 and 4 in memory position 0111

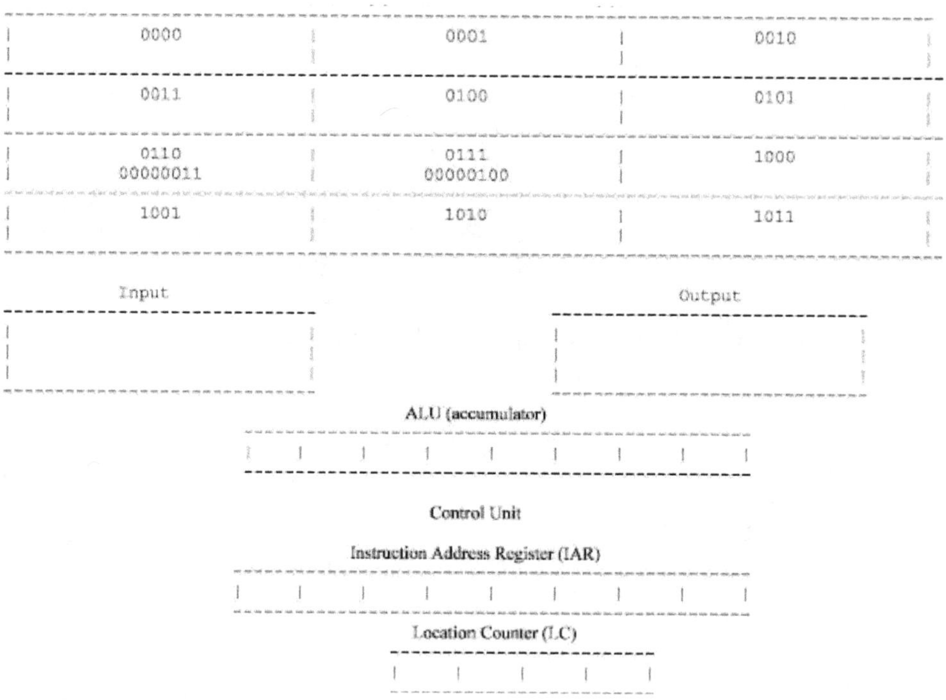

Basic computer with the number 3 stored in memory position 6 and the number 4 stored in memory position 7.

Operation Codes: 0001—Clear Accumulator
0010—Add to Accumulator
0100—Store to Accumulator

Program Segment: 0000 / 0001 / xxxx
0001 / 0010 / 0110
0010 / 0010 / 0111
0011 / 0100 / 0110
0100 / 0100 / 1011

Computer Memory—With Loaded Program

0000 00010000	0001 00100110	0010 00100111
0011 01000110	0100 01001011	0101
0110 00000011	0111 00000100	1000
1001	1010	1011

Input

Output

ALU (accumulator)

Control Unit

Instruction Address Register (IAR)

Location Counter (LC)

0	0	0	0

The program is loaded and the location counter now points to the first instruction to execute.

Operation Codes: 0001—Clear Accumulator
0010—Add to Accumulator
0100—Store to Accumulator

Program Segment: 0000 / 0001 / xxxx
0001 / 0010 / 0110
0010 / 0010 / 0111
0011 / 0100 / 0110
0100 / 0100 / 1011

Computer Memory—With Loaded Program—First Step Execution

0000 00010000	0001 00100110	0010 00100111
0011 01000110	0100 01001011	0101
0110 00000011	0111 00000100	1000
1001	1010	1011

Input	Output
00010000	00000000

ALU (accumulator)

0	0	0	0	0	0	0	0

Control Unit

Instruction Address Register (IAR)

0	0	0	1	0	0	0	0

Location Counter (LC)

0	0	0	1

The necessary logic is hard wired into the computer and the contents of the memory pointed to by the location counter are copied into the IAR. The instruction identified by the op-code is now performed. The location counter is then incremented by 1 and now points to the next instruction to execute.

Operation Codes:	0001—Clear Accumulator
	0010—Add to Accumulator
	0100—Store to Accumulator

Program Segment:	0000 / 0001 / xxxx
	0001 / 0010 / 0110
	0010 / 0010 / 0111
	0011 / 0100 / 0110
	0100 / 0100 / 1011

Computer Memory—With Loaded Program—Second Step Execution

0000 00010000	0001 00100110	0010 00100111
0011 01000110	0100 01001011	0101
0110 00000011	0111 00000100	1000
1001	1010	1011

Input	Output
00100110	00000011

ALU (accumulator)

0	0	0	0	0	0	1	1

Control Unit

Instruction Address Register (IAR)

0	0	1	0	0	1	1	0

Location Counter (LC)

0	0	1	0

Again, the instruction pointed to by the location counter is copied into the IAR and executed. Then the location counter is incremented by 1.

Machine Language Program

Operation Codes: 0001—Clear Accumulator
0010—Add to Accumulator
0100—Store to Accumulator

Program Segment: 0000 / 0001 / xxxx
0001 / 0010 / 0110
0010 / 0010 / 0111
0011 / 0100 / 0110
0100 / 0100 / 1011

Computer Memory—With Loaded Program—Third Step Execution

```
---------------------------------------------------
|    0000        |     0001       |     0010       |
|  00010000      |   00100110     |   00100111     |
---------------------------------------------------
|    0011        |     0100       |     0101       |
|  01000110      |   01001011     |                |
---------------------------------------------------
|    0110        |     0111       |     1000       |
|  00000011      |   00000100     |                |
---------------------------------------------------
|    1001        |     1010       |     1011       |
|                |                |                |
---------------------------------------------------

           Input                                  Output

-----------------------------          -----------------------------
|                           |          |                           |
|         00100111          |          |         00000111          |
|                           |          |                           |
-----------------------------          -----------------------------

                                  ALU (accumulator)

                                     Accumulator
                       ---------------------------------------
                       | 0 | 0 | 0 | 0 | 0 | 1 | 1 | 1 |
                       ---------------------------------------

                                     Control Unit

                           Instruction Address Register (IAR)
                       ---------------------------------------
                       | 0 | 0 | 1 | 0 | 0 | 1 | 1 | 1 |
                       ---------------------------------------

                                Location Counter (LC)
                              ---------------------
                              | 0 | 0 | 1 | 1 |
                              ---------------------
```

The process described on the previous screen is continued.

Machine Language Program

Operation Codes: 001—Clear Accumulator
0010—Add to Accumulator
0100—Store to Accumulator

Program Segment: 0000 / 0001 / xxxx
0001 / 0010 / 0110
0010 / 0010 / 0111
0011 / 0100 / 0110
0100 / 0100 / 1011

Computer Memory—With Loaded Program—Fourth Step Execution

0000 00010000	0001 00100110	0010 00100111
0011 01000110	0100 01001011	0101
(2) 0110 00000111	0111 00000100	1000
1001	1010	1011

(2) Store the contents of the Accumulator in location 0110

Input	Output
01000110	00000111

ALU (accumulator)

0	0	0	0	0	1	1	1

Control Unit

Instruction Address Register (IAR)

0	1	0	0	0	1	1	0

Location Counter (LC)

0	1	0	0

The process continues.

Machine Language Program

Operation Codes: 0001—Clear Accumulator
0010—Add to Accumulator
0100—Store to Accumulator

Program Segment: 0000 / 0001 / xxxx
0001 / 0010 / 0110
0010 / 0010 / 0111
0011 / 0100 / 0110
0100 / 0100 / 1011

Computer Memory—With Loaded Program—Fifth Step Execution

0000 00010000	0001 00100110	0010 00100111
0011 01000110	0100 01001011	0101
0110 00000111	0111 00000100	1000
1001	1010	1011 (2) 00000111

(2) Store the contents of the Accumulator in location 1011

Input	Output
01001011	00000111

ALU (accumulator)

0	0	0	0	0	1	1	1

Control Unit

Instruction Address Register (IAR)

0	1	0	0	1	0	1	1

Location Counter (LC)

0	1	0	1

The process is carried to completion. The two numbers are added and their sum is stored in addresses 6 and 11.

2.2 Assembly Language

Early programming languages gave the programmer complete access to the computer. These languages were designed only with the operator and the computer in mind. They were used to manipulate data, through stored program capability, and made the computer the fantastic machine that it was in the early days of computing. It was necessary for the programmer to determine where the data, as well as the instructions, were to be stored and to be careful not to store data and instructions in the same memory position. The early computers (1937) made it possible for the programmer to store the program code in the computer's memory and then the program to be executed independent of the programmer executing the code, step by step. It was soon realized that a truly utile, efficient language could be easily writeable and readable and even be transferable among different computer systems. This realization led to the development of a machine-oriented language (assembly language) where the op-code of the instruction was replaced with a mnemonic code and the operand or address of an instruction was replaced with a meaningful name. Each statement in the machine language was basically replaced with a statement in this new language called **assembly language**. Rather than using the binary code 0001 to clear the accumulator, a much easier code CLA was used. Similarly, the code 0010 (used to add) was replaced with ADD and the code 0100 (used to store the contents of the accumulator) was replaced with STO. Also, the assembly language programmer was able to give names to data and let the software program (**assembler**) keep track of where the data was to be stored. However, to be able to write programs in this new **assembly language,** it was necessary for a programmer to write a machine language program that would take the assembly language program and convert it to binary code. Once this was done, it was no longer necessary for the programmer to understand machine language for the machine he/she was using. In the initial days of assembly language programming (1944), it was debated as to whether or not an assembly language programmer could use the computer as efficiently as a machine language programmer. At this time the computer was small and slow in comparison to today's machine so it was critical to best utilize the computer's capability.

In the example below, R1 (register 1) serves the role of the accumulator. A program to perform the operation A = B + C / D would look as follows (assuming numbers have been stored in the memory positions assigned B, C and D, and we want to store the result from the operation in memory position assigned to A):

```
LOD R1, C  {Load the contents of memory assigned to C into register 1}
DIV R1,D   {Divide the contents of register 1 by the contents of memory
           assigned D}
ADD R1,B   {Add the contents of memory assigned to B to contents of
           register 1}
STO R1, A  {Store the contents of register 1 in memory address assigned
           to A}
```

A more complicated statement such as a looping statement given below could be programmed in assembly using the following code:

```
for( i = 1; i<= 4; ++i)
   x = x + i;
```

```
     MOV x, '0'
     MOV temp1, '4'
     MOV i, '1'
L1: CMP i, temp1
     BH  L2  {Branch if i > temp1}
     LOD R1, x
     ADD R1, i
     STO R1, x
     LOD R1, i
     ADD R1, '1'
     STO R1, i
     B   L1
L2:
```

The assembly language program above could be part of a compiler or assembler that translates the C++ looping statement to assembly language. The programmer could code an **algorithm** in C++ code then a compiler written in assembly language could be used to take the C++ code to assembly code and then a program written in machine language could be written to take the assembly code to machine code. In Big C notation, it would look as follows:

C++ → Assembly

C

Assembly

Assembly → Machine

C

Machine

Here the **source program**, (the program the programmer writes), is converted to the **object program**, i.e., the program the compiler writes.

As stated earlier, the machine language is the only language the machine understands and consists of 0s and 1s. Even a program as simple as adding numbers stored in memory and then storing the result in another memory position can get extensive in machine language.

Even though the assembly language was much easier for the programmer than machine language, it wasn't long (early 1950s) until an even easier language for the programmer was being sought. As a result a more human oriented language, a translating language, was developed. Today, we have the three basic types of **programming languages**: **machine** (binary), **assembly** (mnemonic) code, and **translating** (human oriented) language.

Below is an example of the three languages used in coding a simple program:

Example: Using machine, assembly, and translating language programs, take two numbers stored in memory and form their sum then store the sum in another position of memory.

First consider the following machine language program with the op-codes defined as given:

Clear accumulator	0001
Add to accumulator	0010
Store accumulator	0100

Program:

op-code	operand
0001	xxxx
0010	0100
0010	0101
0100	0110

In the above machine language program, numbers are stored in machine addresses 0100 and 0101. The program will add the two numbers and store the sum in address 0110. The programmer must designate the instruction addresses telling the computer where to store the instructions. Once the instruction address has been assigned, the above program segment becomes:

Instruction address	op-code	operand
0000	0001	xxxx
0001	0010	0100
0010	0010	0101
0011	0100	0110

If we use the mnemonic code of CLA to clear accumulator, ADD to add to accumulator and STO to store accumulator and use symbols A, B and C to represent addresses, the assembly language program for the same task will look as follows:

CLA xxxx

ADD A

ADD B

STO C

Here, one can see that mnemonics have replaced the machine operator codes and labels A, B and C have replaced the machine addresses. Also, a program, the assembler (possibly written in machine language -ML), takes the assembly language (AL) program and converts it to a machine language program. The assembler must also decide where to store the instructions and where to store the data. The big C notation for the process that completes this task becomes:

$$\underset{ML}{\overset{AL \rightarrow ML}{C}}$$

One translating language statement, given below, can perform the same task as the ML and AL illustrated above:

C = A + B

This one translating language (TL) statement tells the computer to take the information stored in memory address A, add to this the information stored in address B, and then store the sum in memory address C. Again, a program, the compiler, takes the one statement and converts it to machine language. The process may consist of two steps as indicated by the big C notation below:

$$\underset{AL}{\overset{TL \rightarrow AL}{C}} \qquad \underset{ML}{\overset{AL \rightarrow ML}{C}}$$

Note that the machine code and assembly code listed above could be part of the process of converting the TL statement to ML statements.

2.2A Assembly Language Examples

To better illustrate the workings of assembly language, some statements are coded below in Pascal and C++ with corresponding assembly code (pseudo-assembly)

The Assignment statement
Pascal:

```
VAR
 x, y : INTEGER;

BEGIN
 x := 10;
 y := x;
END;
```

C++:

```
main () {
 int x, y;
 x = 10;
 y = x;
}
```

Assembly:

```
SET R1,10        ; set R1 to immediate value 10
STORE x,R1       ; store R1 into variable x

LOAD R1,x        ; load variable x into R1
STORE y,R1       ; store R1 into variable y

.DATA
x: 0             ; declare a memory location for variable x
y: 0             ; declare a memory location for variable y
```

The Control statement, IF

The **IF** statements can be coded by using JMP instructions. Multiple conditions can be tested by using several JMP instructions.

Pascal:

```
IF (x = 10)
  THEN
   BEGIN
    ...  (* then part 1 *)
   END
  ELSE
   BEGIN
    ...  (* else part 1 *)
   END;

IF ((x<>10) AND (y>20))
  THEN
   BEGIN
    ...  (* then part 2 *)
   END;
```

C++:

```
if (x == 10) {
   ...    // then part 1
}
else {
   ...    // else part 1
}

if ((x!=10) && (y>20)) {
   ...    // then part 2
}
```

Assembly:

```
    LOAD R1, x    ; load the variable x into R1
    SET R2, 10    ; set R2 to immediate value 10
    CMP R1, R2
    JMP NEQ, ELSE1  ; if R1 <> R2, then jump to the else part,
    otherwise do the then part
    ...    ; then part 1
    JUMP END1     ; jump over the else part
    ELSE1:
    ...    ; else part 1
    END1:
    LOAD R1, x    ; load the variable x into R1
    SET R2, 10    ; set R2 to immediate value 10
    CMP R1, R2
    JMP NEQ, TEST2  ; if x <> 10 go on to next test
    JUMP END2     ; otherwise skip past then part 2
TEST2:
    LOAD R1, y    ; load the variable y into R1
    SET R2, 20    ; set R2 to immediate value 20
    CMP R1, R2
    JMP GT, THEN2   ; if y > 20 go on to then part 2
    JUMP END2     ; otherwise skip past
THEN2:
     ...    ; then part 2
END2:
```

The Looping statement, FOR

Pascal:

```
FOR i := 10 DOWNTO 1 DO
 BEGIN
   ...  (* loop1 body *)
 END;
WHILE (x <> 20) DO
```

```
BEGIN
  ...  (* loop2 body *)
END;
```

C++:

```
for (i=10; i > 0; i--) {
  ...    // loop1 body
}
while (x != 20) {
  ...    // loop2 body
}
```

Assembly:

```
    SET R0, 0        ; R0 will take value of 0
    SET R1, 10       ; R1 will take the place of i
    SET R2, 1        ; R2 will hold the value to subtract each time
LOOP1TOP:
    ...      ; loop1 body
    SUB R1, R1, R2   ; subtract one from R1
     CMP R1, R0
     JMP NEQ, LOOP1TOP ; keep going until R1 gets to zero
     SET R2, 20       ; R2 will hold our end condition
LOOP2TOP:
     LOAD R1, x       ; load the x variable
     CMP R1, R2
     JMP EQ, LOOP2END  ; if we're done, skip to end  of loop
    ...      ; loop2 body
    LOOP2END:
```

2.3 Source Language/Target Language

For the assembly language program, as well as the translating language programs, it is necessary for the **assembler** or **compiler** to convert these programs to machine code before they can be processed. The compiler or assembler will read these programs, statement by statement, and convert directly to ML or to a language more closely to ML. As an important part of this translation process, the compiler reports to its user the presence of errors in the process. The two basic types of errors are **translation errors** and **execution errors**. The translating errors are normally identified when the programmer did not obey the rules of the source language. In this case the source language would be the Pascal, C++ or assembly language. In the assembly language, a translation error should be detected by the statement AD A where AD was used when the programmer meant to use ADD A. In a translating language, a translation error should be detected for the statement C = = A + B; and the assignment operator should be = and not = =. A simple error to detect during execution is a divide by 0.

Assembly language programming was the main programming tool used from mid-1940s to late 1950s. Programmers soon wanted a faster, easier, and more universal way to talk to the computer. John Backus, working with IBM and a team of programmers in 1959, developed the translating language FORTRAN and wrote a compiler for this language. This task was enormous and took years to complete.

Chapter 2 Exercises

Exercise 1. Use the illustration presented in the text to write a machine language program that will add the contents of memory positions 0000 through 0100 and store the results in memory 0101. Give the contents of the ALU, IAR and LC at the completion of the program and discuss any problems that may be encountered.

Exercise 2. Use the assembly pseudo-code presented in the text to translate the C++ statement — **if**(a > b) z = a + b;

Exercise 3. Give the distinctions between an interpretative language and a compiled language.

Exercise 4. Write a paragraph describing the differences between assembly language and machine language.

Exercise 5. Contrast assembly languages and translating languages.

Exercise 6. Using the assembly language pseudo-code given in the text, write an assembly program to add the numbers 15 and 31, then output 15 if the sum of the two is greater than three times the first number.

Exercise 7. Show the assembly code for the C++ statement — **while**(A <=B) A = A + 2.;

Exercise 8. Write a short paper, at least 1 page, that describes the assembly languages, pre-1960. Tell about their uniqueness and names that were given to various assembly languages.

Exercise 9. Give your view as to why a course in assembly language is no longer a requirement for a computer science degree in many colleges.

Exercise 10. Write a program in the C++ language to input 3 integers, sum the integers, then find and output the sum of the digits of the sum. Ex. If the input is 12 23 67, then the found sum is 102 and the sum of the digits for the sum 102 is 3. Output 3.

Exercise 11. Machine language will let you pick the address or memory location to store a number. See if you can determine how to pick the actual address to store a number in either assembly language or a translating language.

Exercise 12. Using the examples presented in the text, write the assembly code for the basic **go to** statement as defined for FORTRAN.

Exercise 13. Using the examples presented in the text, write the assembly code for the **do/while** statement as defined in C++.

Exercise 14. Use the big C notation to illustrate the various compilers that could have been used to translate the C++ code to machine code.

CHAPTER 3

Programming Languages—Translating

INTRODUCTION

As the use of computers has grown enormously over the years, the concepts behind the varieties of programming languages have also grown. As programmers, we have moved from the sole use of binary coding to complex languages which maintain a surface of simplicity in their instructions and allow us to concentrate less on how the program works and more on the abstracts of what programming can do for us.

In 1974, N. Wirth (creator of Pascal language) said:

We must recognize the strong and undeniable influence that our language exerts on our way of thinking, and in fact, defines and delimits the abstract space in which we can formulate—give form to—our thoughts.

In a sense, computer programming languages have done just that. The differences among and within these languages have served a variety of purposes. They have opened new horizons of abstract thought in computing. As more and more programming languages are developed, it is difficult to comprehend the different types that might be developed in the future. As compilers become better understood and easier to develop, we can expect future languages to become friendlier and more developed perhaps to the point of understanding the spoken word.

As of today, the machine language is the only language the computer understands. It was a great improvement over hard-wired boards of earlier days as a means to communicate with the computer. As the automobile replaced the horse and buggy as a faster and better way to travel, so new and faster ways were found to communicate with the computer. Assembly languages were developed in the 1940s. Translating languages were developed in the 1950s. Today, many well developed languages exist that allow us to communicate with the computer. In the future, the spoken word may be the preferred way to communicate with the computer.

3.1 Translating Languages

A **translating language** is often spoken of as a **high-level language** or English Oriented Language in contrast to a machine oriented or machine language. The development of translating languages began in the early 1950s with the emphasis on solving scientific or military related problems. In fact, during the 1950s and early 1960s these languages were thought of primarily as formula translators rather than as general programming languages. The first fully-developed translating language was **FORTRAN** completed in 1959. This language was developed at **Harvard** by **John Backus** working with **IBM**. Since the language was developed for scientific use and designed mainly for formula translation, its name is an acronym that stands for FORmula TRANslation. This language was the major computer language for scientific programming through the 1960s and into the 1970s. It is still widely used in engineering and scientific communities. The early versions of FORTRAN were difficult to apply to business problems. In the early 1960s, a language (**COBOL**) was developed to be used mainly for business programming. This language's major developer was **Grace Hopper** while working for the Department of the Navy. The language was developed with the business person in mind, realizing that a person with a good business understanding and little computer knowledge would be able to read the programming code even if not able to code the programs. Hence, the name COBOL is derived from COmmon Business Oriented Language. This language is still in use today in the business world. Numerous payrolls, accounting, and other business application programs have been written in COBOL and many are still in use. It is possible that there are more existing lines of programming code in COBOL than in any other programming language. COBOL was an effort to make a programming language that was like natural English: easier to write and easier to read the code after it was written. The earliest versions of the language, COBOL-60 and -61, evolved to the COBOL-85 standard, sponsored by the Conference on Data Systems Languages (CODASYL).

Since the year 2000 (Y2K problem), programmers with COBOL skills have been in demand by major corporations and contractors. A number of companies have since updated COBOL and now sell development tools that combine COBOL programming with relational databases for Internet use. While the language has been updated over the years, it is now generally perceived as out-of-date.

In the late 1950s and early 1960s, the computer was making inroads into the mathematics and science programs of colleges and universities. Computers at this time required users to develop the algorithm for a problem, code the algorithm, place the coded algorithm on some input media and then feed the coded algorithm (usually punched cards) to the computer. Hopefully, all phases of this task would be correct and the computer output would be the desired problem solution. If the algorithm was not correct or the programming code had a **syntax** error (i.e., an error in the spelling and or **grammar** of the programming language), the program would not execute. The expected form of the language is called the syntax of the language. Each computer language defines its own syntactical rules that control which words the computer understands, which combinations of words are meaningful, and what punctuation is necessary. If a syntax error or an input data error were found, the programmer was required to make corrections and re-initiate the process. This process could take hours if not days.

John Kemeny and **Kenneth Kurtz**, mathematicians at **Dartmouth College**, wanted to teach their students numerical problem solving using the computer, and needed to streamline the process to make the total computer problem solving process easier. The two standard languages available at that time were FORTRAN and COBOL. COBOL was not a suitable language for mathematical work and FORTRAN was difficult to learn in a short time. To solve their dilemma, Kemeny and Kurtz initiated a two-prong task: (1) develop a language that students could understand quickly and (2) develop a method that would allow more than one student to interact with the computer at one time. Their efforts were successful and the language BASIC was born and **teleprocessing** or **multiprocessing** became a standard way of computing. The language BASIC, Beginners All purpose Symbolic Instruction Code, consisted of a group of statements that were a subset of FORTRAN, with input and output statements much easier to understand. The language was interactive and allowed for several students or programmers to interact with the computer at one time. BASIC was the language that many students in colleges and universities used during the 1960s. However, as new languages were developed and older languages became interactive, BASIC almost disappeared from the college scene. With the appearance of the personal computer (PC) in the early 1970s the language BASIC was revisited, since a small language was needed for the small memory (1000 bytes) available for the PC.

In the early 1960s, IBM's idea of modular hardware components for the 360 series computer revolutionized the way computer hardware was developed. As this new series of computers (IBM 360s) were being developed, a new language was also being developed by IBM. The translating languages available at that time for the 360 computer were FORTRAN, a scientific language, and COBOL a business oriented language. IBM's objective in developing the new language was to have one language that could be used for both scientific and business problem solving. The language began as a modification of FORTRAN, or possibly a new version of FORTRAN. In the end, the new language looked rather different from FORTRAN and was given the name Programming Language One (PL/I). The language **PL/I** was extensive and required a large program (compiler) to understand the language. Since the compiler required a computer with a large memory in order to process a program, the language was used mainly on IBM's larger computers and was never fully adapted by other computer vendors.

The languages FORTRAN, COBOL, BASIC and PL/I were all good languages in their own right. However, as programming became extensive through the late 1960s and as old programs were being modified or changed; it became apparent that something was missing.

Programs necessary to solve sophisticated problems often have many loops, or segments of programs that are repeated several times. Many programmers were using GO TO and IF statements to form loops and it was often difficult for the programmer to take a program he/she had written and to understand how to make modifications. The difficulty in modifying a program that was not his own was so intolerable that it was often easier to start over. Recognizing this problem in 1968, **Nicklaus Wirth** began developing a new **structured programming** language—Pascal. This language made an attempt to formalize the logic and structure of programs with the objective of making programs:

—Easier to read
—Easier to debug
—Easier to understand
—Easier to maintain
—To allow programmers to work as a team
—To reduce testing time
—To increase programming productivity
—To increase clarity by reducing the program's complexity
—To decrease maintenance and effort

Later, in 1971, a language similar to BASIC, but using modular and structured programming concepts for the first time tried to fill these requirements. The language **Pascal** was developed. Though it was a great breakthrough in the thoughts behind the utilization of programming, the language itself wasn't useful enough as a developmental tool and thus was used mainly as a teaching tool.

The Pascal language was named after the mathematician, Blaise Pascal, who invented the Pascal calculator in 1642. This language was developed to make loops easier and more structured, and it contained statements such as WHILE and REPEAT. These statements were then used to replace the older statements of GO TO and IF. The Pascal compiler was small in comparison to PL/I and could easily be adapted to large, as well as small computers. Pascal was an easier language to learn and use than FORTRAN or PL/I. It became the teaching language used by many colleges and universities from the early 1970s through the late 1980s. Today, all programming languages, from the oldest to the most recent, have structured type statements.

As the translating languages, such as Pascal, became more human oriented, they drifted further from the assembly language of the computer. It became apparent that a language was needed with the power of FORTRAN, and with the structured statements that were available in Pascal and operators that would let the programmer emulate some of the operations of an assembly language. In 1969, Ken Thompson at Bell Labs developed the operating system **UNIX** – an interactive multi-user operating system. Thompson had been using both assembly and a language named B to produce initial versions of UNIX. Dennis Ritchie, also of Bell Laboratories, in 1972, developed a general purpose programming language to overcome some of the limitations encountered by Thompson. The language **C** and its later version **C++** were developed and have since been used extensively as true general purpose programming languages. Their capabilities range from those of simple, interactive computing to complex engineering and scientific calculations. **C** is truly a structured language, having a set method of writing programs and a myriad of ways to further develop those programs. C provides multiple pre-programmed functions and allows the programmer to add his/her functions as desired.

One may ask "**why C?**" when we had several other "good" programming languages. The language C is a small language; it is a good development language for the personal computer; it is portable; it is modular and it is appealing because of its powerful operators.

Programmers became intrigued by "**object oriented programming**" in the early 1980s and the language C++, a close cousin to C, was developed by Bjarne Stroustroup. C and C++ are possibly the languages most used today by development programmers. As the World Wide Web (WWW) became an everyday buzz-word, the language **Java**, a pure object-oriented language, was developed to do web programming. Java is a small language; it provides for good graphical user interface (GUI), multimedia (sound, image and animation) facilities, and "write-once, run-anywhere" feature.

3.2 Genealogy of Translating Languages

A genealogy of programming languages is given below:

Year	Language	Use	Description
1956	FORTRAN (Formula Translator)	Numerical scientific	First language to be widely used and remains in wide use.
1960	Cobol (Common Business-Oriented Language)	Business data processing	English-like in style, developed and maintained by committee of users and manufacturers under Codasyl. One of the most widely used languages.
1960	LISP (List Processing)	List processing	Sophisticated and theoretically oriented with several dialects. Used for much artificial intelligence research.
1964	BASIC (Beginner's All Purpose Symbolic Instruction Code)	Numerical scientific	Very simple language but with some advanced features. Available in many micro- and personal computers for uses beyond just numerical scientific.
1964	PL/I	Multipurpose	First of the very large, powerful languages, combining many features and concepts from Algol, Cobol, FORTRAN, and other languages.
1971	Pascal	Multipurpose	Small but elegant language with many significant features. Used heavily for teaching programming. Many Pascal compilers are written in Pascal.
1971	Prolog	Multipurpose	For use in logic programming, which can itself be applied to many scientific applications. Has a major use in artificial intelligence.

1975	C	Systems Programming	Use to write the Unix operating system and most of its application software.
1979	Ada	Multipurpose	Sponsored by the U. S. Department of Defense, but designed by French language team. Used primarily in embedded computer systems (e.g. military, FAA, NASA), but also in numerous commercial applications.
1982	C++	Multipurpose	An extension of C with facilities for object-oriented programming.
1995	Java	Web Programming	Derives much of its syntax from C and C++ but has a simpler object model and fewer low-level facilities. Incorporated into many web browsers.

3.3 Types of Statements and Examples

All translating languages have six (or five if Input/Output is grouped together) basic types of statements: **Input** – a statement used to enter data into the program; **Output** – a statement to take information from the program and display to the programmer; **Assignment** – a statement used to assign a memory position a value; **Control** – a statement to alter the sequence in which statements are executed (without control statements, the statements in a program are executed sequentially); **Specification** – a statement used to tell the computer about data (integer, real, character, Boolean, etc.); and **Subprogram** – a special purpose program. If a group of statements is used several times within a program or a particular function such as the **absolute value** function is used in different programs, then it is possible to make a program (subprogram) for this function and include it as needed. These six statements provide the necessary tools to carry out the basic operations of any algorithm.

The differences found within languages, and the evolution to a simpler, easier to understand language is apparent in the differences among their various instruction statements. The following list contrasts the basic statements for each language.

Input Statements in Different Languages

Input:

Read(9,1)	FORTRAN
Accept	COBOL
Input	BASIC
Read	PL/I
Readln	Pascal
scanf	C
cin	C++
System.in.readln	Java

Output Statements in Different Languages

Output:

Write(6,2)	FORTRAN
Display	COBOL
Print	BASIC
Put	PL/I
WriteIn	Pascal
printf	C
cout	C++
System.out.println	Java

Assignment Statements in Different Languages

Assignment:

C = a + b	FORTRAN
Add(a,b,c)	COBOL
C = a + b	BASIC
C = a + b;	PL/I
C:=a+b;	Pascal
C = a+b;	C
C = a+b;	C++
C = a+b;	Java

Control Statements in Different Languages

Control:

If(a.gt.b) go to	FORTRAN
If/else	COBOL
If(a > b) then	BASIC
If/else	PL/I
If(a > b) then	Pascal
If(a > b)	C
If(a>b)	C++
If(a>b)	Java

Specification Statements in Different Languages

Specification:

Integer a	FORTRAN
Integer a	COBOL
Int(a)	BASIC
Integer a	PL/I
a:int;	Pascal
int a;	C
int a;	C++
int a;	Java

Subprogram Statements in Different Languages

Subprogram:

Sqrt(a)	FORTRAN
Sqrt(a)	COBOL
Sqrt(a)	BASIC
Sqrt(a)	PL/I
Sqrt(a)	Pascal
Sqrt(a)	C
Sqrt(a)	C++
Sqrt(a)	Java

3.4 Phases of a Compiler

The two basic phases of each translating language compiler is the **translation phase** and the **execution phase**.

The first task in programming is algorithm development. The programmer must understand the problem to be programmed, and be able to solve the problem independent of the computer, even if it may take several hours. Once the method of solution, or algorithm, has been developed, then the language must be selected and the algorithm coded in the preferred language. In the 1960s, the language FORTRAN was selected if the algorithm was scientific in nature and COBOL was selected if business oriented. Today, most translating languages can be used for both business and scientific problems. The coded algorithm is spoken of as the **source program**. Initially, a programmer writes a program in a particular programming language. This form of the program is called the source program, or more generically, source code. The coded algorithm will then be entered into the computer through the key-board or other input device. The operating system will assist the programmer and select the specified compiler to convert the source program to **object program**. The object program is a machine language program and is in binary. The object program is normally the output from the **translation phase**–the phase of compilation that converts the source program to object program. During this phase, the compiler will check to see that the programmer has obeyed all rules (syntactic rules) of the language and produce helpful error messages if all rules have not been obeyed. If there are errors, the programmer will continually correct and resubmit until the translation phase is error free. If the translation phase is successful, the compiler will produce an **object program** – a program the computer can understand. The programmer can then perform the second phase of running a program, the **execution phase**. The object program together with data, if needed, will be submitted to the execution phase and the coded algorithm will be carried out, step by step. If a proper algorithm has been developed and the data is correct, then the desired results will be produced. If either the algorithm or data is incorrect, the programmer must correct and re-initiate the total process.

During the **execution phase,** a segment of the compiler inputs the object program and carries out the instructions of the object program – data is read if needed and output is generated.

Before actually coding the algorithm, the programmer must know and follow the specified **shell, or basic structure**, of that language. The programmer can create a template for the shell, through an editor normally provided with the compiler, and then insert the program statements in the appropriate places of the shell. The shell for the described languages is given in section 3.5.

3.5 Programming Shell for Translating Languages

FORTRAN

Variable declaration – which is optional

Body

Stop
End

BASIC

Body

Stop
End

Pascal

Program name (input, output);
Begin
Variable declaration
Body
End

C

```
void main (void)
{
variable declaration
body
}
```

C++

```
void main (void)
{
variable declaration
body
}
```

Java

```
public static void main (String [ ] args)
{
variable declaration
body
}
```

As stated earlier, assembly languages and translating languages allow the programmer to give names to memory positions rather than use the binary address as must be done in machine language programming. The naming convention accepted by most translating languages is to start the name with a character 'a' ... 'z', at most 8 characters in length, and any character, other than the first, being a ... z or 0 ... 9. Names assigned memory positions normally relate to the data to be stored in a given position, such as, RATE, HOUR, PAY for rate of pay, hours worked and pay due. Numeric data, data involving numbers and not characters, such as 15, 33.44, -6789 are classified as integer data or real or float data. The **mode** of the data refers to its type – integer, float or character. **Integer data** are numbers without decimals and float or **real data** are data with decimals. Some languages, such as the early versions of BASIC, considered all numeric data as float data. **Character data** is non-numeric data such as the symbols used to write this book. Today, most translating languages force the programmer to specify the mode of the data, through a **specification statement** as either **integer, float, character,** etc. The language FORTRAN allows the programmer to use either a specification statement or the datum name to specify its mode. If the data name in FORTRAN is not specified explicitly and the name starts with "i,j,k,l,m,n" then it is considered as integer data and otherwise as float data. Unless specified with a **specification** statement, character data in FORTRAN is specified by the format of input.

3.6 Data Specification Statements

The mode specification or **data specification** for the various languages is given by:

BASIC: All numeric data to be considered as real

FORTRAN: Explicit statements

```
real a, b, c
integer i, j, k
character x,y,z
```

Pascal: Explicit statements

```
a, b, c: float;
i, j, k: int;
x,y,z: char;
```

C: Explicit statements

```
float a, b, c;
int i,j,k;
char x,y,z;
```

C++: Explicit statements

```
float a, b, c;
int i,j,k;
char x,y,z;
```

Java: Explicit statements
float a,b,c;
int i,j;
char x,y,z;

Once the data has been specified, an input statement is needed if data are to be imported from outside the actual program code. The programmer must be careful to input the data, with proper mode, requested by the input statement, as well as know how to code the data on the line of input. Assignment statements are used to act on the data and operations such as multiply, subtract, divide and add can be performed on the data. Control statements allow the programmer to specify the order that program statements are to be executed. Output statements will print information to paper or to the monitor (Cathode Ray Tube-CRT or screen) or other output devices. To illustrate how all statements work together, to perform a given task, an algorithm to input two integers and then find and print the larger of the two is given below. The algorithm is then coded in each of the languages FORTRAN, BASIC, PASCAL, C, C++ and Java.

3.7 Programming Examples

The following algorithm will accept two integers as input and then finds and prints the larger of the two.
Steps:

1. Define the two integers, call one N and one M
2. Check to see if M is larger than N, IF (M > N) Then N ← M (define N to be M)
3. Output N
4. Stop

The above algorithm is coded in each of the languages:
FORTRAN BASIC Pascal C C++ Java

FORTRAN:

```
    INTEGER N, M
    READ(9, 1)N, M
1 FORMAT(I5,I4)
    IF(M.GT.N) N=M
    WRITE(6,2)N
2  FORMAT(1X,'THE LARGER OF THE TWO IS:, I5)
    STOP
    END
```

Input line follows:

```
    12   15
```

The input must obey the format specification #1 – the two elements are on one line and the first occupies the first 5 columns, right justified and the second occupies the next 4 columns, right justified.

BASIC:

```
10 INPUT N, M
20 IF (N>M) THEN 40
30 N=M
40 PRINT N
50 STOP
60 END
```

Input line follows:

```
12,15
```

The input must be separated by a comma.

PASCAL:

```
PROGRAM LARGER(INPUT,OUTPUT);
VAR
  N,M:INTEGER;
```

```
BEGIN
  READLN(N, M);
  IF(M>N) THEN
    N=M;
  WRITELN(N);
END.
```

Input line follows:
12 15

The input must be separated by at least one blank space.

C:

```
void main(void)
{
  int n,m;
  scanf("%d,%d",&n,&m);
  if(m>n)
    n=m;
  printf("The larger number is: %d", n);
}
```

Input line follows:
12 15

The input must be separated by at least one blank space.

C++:

```
void main(void)
{
  int n,m;
  cin>>n>>m;
  if(m>n)
    n=m;
```

```
  cout<<n<<endl;
}
```

Input line follows:
12 15

The input must be separated by at least one blank space.

Java:

```
public static void main(String args [ ])
{
  int n,m;
  n = new Int(Keyboard.readLine()).intValue();
  m = new Int(Keyboard.readLine()).intValue();

  if(m>n)
    n=m;
  System.out.print(n);
}
```

Input follows:
12
15

The following examples will demonstrate how the statements of C++ can be used to code basic algorithms and solve problems:

Example 1 – Devise an algorithm and write a C++ program to input three numbers, all on one line of input, then output the largest of the three numbers.

Algorithm:
1. Name numbers a,b,c and let la hold the largest
2. Input a,b,c
3. Let la = a
4. Compare b with la if greater than, let la = b

5. Compare c with la if greater than, let la = c
6. Output la
7. Stop

Program – to input 3 numbers

```
#include <iostream> // pre-processor directory
int main(void) // the main function will start execution
{ // braces encloses the body of a program
int a,b,c,la; // specify what variable(s) to be used and mode
cin >> a >> b >> c; // the three numbers must be integers
la = a;
if (b > la) la = b;
if (c > la) la = c;
cout << "The largest of the three is" << la;
}
```

Example 2 – Devise an algorithm and write a C++ program to input 10 numbers, one per line, then find and output the largest of the ten.

Algorithm:

1. Name the number x as it enters and let la hold the largest
2. Let k be a count for the number of numbers entered k = 0
3. Input the first number and call it la
4. Add one to k
5. Check k and if 10 output la and stop
6. Input a number and call it x
7. Compare x with la and if larger make la equal to x
8. Go to statement 4)

Program – using a WHILE loop

```
#include <iostream>

int main(void)
{
  int k,x,la;
  k = 0;
```

```
  cin >> la;
  k = k + 1;

  while ( k < 10)
  {
    cin >> x;
    if( x > la)
      la = x;
    k = k + 1;
  }
  cout << "The largest of the ten numbers is" << la;
}
```

Program – using a DO/WHILE loop

```
#include <iostream>

int main(void)
{
  int k,x,la(0); // assuming the numbers are zero or positive
  k = 0;
  do
  {
    cin >> x;
    k = k + 1;
    if( x > la)
      la = x;
  }
  while (k < 10);

  cout << "The largest of the ten numbers is" << la;
}
```

Program – using a FOR loop

```
#include <iostream>

int main(void)
{

  int k,x,la;
  cin>> la;

  for ( k = 2; k<=10; ++k)
  {
    cin >> x;
    if( x > la)
      la = x;
  }
  cout << "The largest of the ten numbers is" << la;
}
```

Example 3 – Devise an algorithm and write a C++ program to input 100 real numbers, one per line, then find and output the sum.

Algorithm:

1. Let sum represent the sum of the numbers and x represent each number as entered. Use k to count the numbers as entered.
2. Make sum zero – sum = 0 , make k zero – k = 0
3. Input a number called x
4. add x to sum
5. add 1 to k
6. check k to see if 100 and if less return to 3
7. check k and if k is 100 then print sum
8. stop

Program – to input 100 numbers

```
// use a FOR loop
#include <iostream>

int main(void)
{
  int k;
  float x, sum = 0;

  for ( k = 1; k <= 100; ++k)
  {
    cin >> x;
    sum = sum + x;
  }
  cout << "The sum is" << sum;
}
```

Example 4 – Devise an algorithm and write a C++ program to input x real numbers (number of input values not known), then find and output the average. To solve this problem it will be necessary to make some assumptions on the data. Let us assume that the numbers are all positive and use a negative input to trip from the loop.

Algorithm:

1. Let x represent each number as entered, let sum represent the sum of the numbers, k represent the count and av the average.
2. Make sum zero – sum = 0 and k equal zero – k = 0
3. Input a number and call x
4. Check x to see if negative and if yes go to 8
5. Add x to sum
6. Add one to count called k
7. Return to 3
8. Calculate average as av = sum/k
9. Output av
10. Stop

Program – to input x real numbers then find and output the average

```
#include <iostream>

int main(void)
{
  int k;
  float x, sum, av;
  sum = 0.; k = 0;
  cin >> x;
  while ( x != 0)
  {
    sum = sum + x;
    k = k + 1;
    cin >> x;
  }
  av = sum / k;
  cout << av;
}
```

Example 5 – Devise an algorithm and write a C++ program to input n real numbers, then find and output the sum. In this case we will make the problem more general. The program will accept n as the number of numbers to input.

Algorithm:

1. Let sum hold the sum, k hold the count, n hold the number of numbers to input and x hold the real numbers before adding to sum
2. Make sum zero – sum = 0 and make k zero – k = 0
3. Input n
4. Input x
5. Add x to sum, sum < – sum + x
6. Add 1 to k, k = k + 1
7. Check k and if not n then return to 4
8. If k is n then output sum
9. Stop

Program – to input n real numbers then find and output the sum

```
#include <iostream>

int main(void)
{
  int k, n;
  float x, sum(0);

  cout << "Input the number of numbers to sum:";
  cin >> n;

  for ( k = 0; k<n; ++k )
  {
     cin >> x;
     sum = sum + x;
  }

  cout << "\n The sum of" << k << "numbers is" << sum;
}
```

Example 6 – Devise an algorithm and then code in BASIC, FORTRAN, Pascal, C, C++ and Java to form the sum of the integers 1 ... 100. Do not use an input statement.

Algorithm:

1. Let s represent the sum and let n take on the values 1..100
2. Make s zero and start n with 1
3. Add n to s
4. Add 1 to n
5. Check n and if less than or equal to 100 then return to 3
6. If n is greater than 100 then output s
7. Stop

REM BASIC

```
  s = 0
  for n = 1 to 100 step 1
  s = s + n
  next n
  print "The sum of the integers 1 ... 100 is", s
  stop
  end
```

C FORTRAN

```
  s = 0
  do 7 n = 1, 100, 1
7   s = s + n
  write(6,2) s
2 format("The sum of the integers 1 ... 100 is", i10)
  stop
  end
```

// **Program Pascal**

```
int main(void)
begin
  int s,n;
  s = 0;
  for n = 1 to 100
     begin
        s:= s + n;
     end;
  writeln( "The sum of the integers 1 ... 100 is", s);
end
```

```
// Program  C

#include <stdio.h>

int main(void)
{
  int s,n;
  s = 0;
  for ( n = 1; n<= 100; ++n)
     s = s + n;
  printf( "The sum of the integers 1 ... 100 is %d", s);
}

// Program  C++

#include <iostream>

int main(void)

{
  int s,n;
  s = 0;
  for ( n = 1; n<= 100; ++n)
     s = s + n;
  cout << "The sum of the integers 1 ... 100 is" << s;
}

// Program Java

public static void main (String args [ ])
{
   int s,n;
   s = 0;
   for ( n = 1; n<= 100; ++n)
      s = s + n;
  System.out.print("The sum of the integers 1 ... 100 is ",s);
}
```

3.8 A Beginner's Language

For the beginner in algorithm development and programming, the language **LADYBUG** or **LOGO** is an ideal language to begin the journey. This language allows the programmer to demonstrate one of the techniques of good programming – module programming. Through **module programming**, a lengthy or difficult algorithm can be subdivided into smaller, simpler tasks. An interesting use of the LOGO language that demonstrates the use of module programming is the construction of a square with an inscribed circle, and continuing this process several times. The structure in translating languages that facilitates module programming is called subprograms. Subprograms are built through functions, procedures, subroutines, etc.

The LOGO language has some basic commands that will allow the programmer to draw on the terminal screen with ease. The turtle (the position of the cursor) will move around the screen and trace out a line as directed by the programmer. Some of the commands are listed below:

FORWARD L (move the turtle forward L units)
BACK L (move the turtle back L units)
RIGHT D (turn the turtle right D degrees)
LEFT D (turn the turtle left D degrees)
CLEARSCREEN (clear the screen)
PENUP (pick up drawing pen)
PENDOWN (place drawing pen in drawing mode)
HOME (move the turtle to home position – center of screen)
CLEARWS (clear workspace – careful)

Once the program is loaded into memory, you can draw directly on the screen by typing a proper command and pressing enter. The commands listed below will draw a square on the screen.

FORWARD 50
RIGHT 90
FORWARD 50 (after each command press the enter key)
RIGHT 90 (this set of instructions will trace out a square)

```
FORWARD 50
RIGHT 90
FORWARD 50
```

The language allows the programmer to build subprograms (special purpose programs) and then use as needed. As stated above this language is quite useful for the novice programmer as a means to learn how modular programming is developed.

3.9 Interpreted, Compiled and Object Oriented Languages

The translation of high-level languages to machine languages can occur in two ways: (1) **interpreted**, where the instructions are individually translated and immediately executed (the method primarily used for BASIC) or (2) **compiled**, where instructions are translated and executed as a whole (as is found for most versions of C, C++, Pascal, and Fortran). The types of output one can get from high-level languages can have an orientation toward procedures or objects. Procedure-oriented languages have the capabilities of using specific, "pre-packaged" groups of instructions which are transferred to execute certain procedures and output results (like functional equations in mathematics). **Object-oriented languages** are derived from greater abstract usage of programming and can be used to produce graphics as well as "window" applications. When using object-oriented languages, characteristics of objects must be defined and constructed of units to pass to the objects and produce results. All of these languages with their different methods of translation and orientations are used to write either application programs, which serve the purpose of immediate use for the programmer or system software, which is available for entire computer system operations. Though all programming languages serve basically the same function, each language has its own types of input data, each makes its own types of calculations, and each reports its output based on the requirements of the application.

Chapter 3 Exercises

Exercise 1. For each of the languages FORTRAN, COBOL, BASIC, PL/I, C, C++ and Java
(a) provide the person or organization instrumental in its development
(b) provide the approximate date of development
(c) describe what led up to its development
(d) describe how it differed from languages that preceded it
(e) describe the main use of each language and its longevity

Exercise 2. For the translating languages given in exercise 1, identify the five basic types of statements for each and give the purpose of each statement.

Exercise 3. For the language C++, describe in detail the input statement and the output statement – include formatting, line control, etc.

Exercise 4. Contrast the basic control statement (IF) for the language C and the language Pascal.

Exercise 5. Pick three of the languages given in exercise 1 and write the complete program to input 4 float numbers then find and output the range (high – low + 1) for the four numbers.

Exercise 6. Pick three of the languages given in exercise 1 and write the complete program to input N float number (N<=100), then sort and output from high number to low number.

Exercise 7. Give the distinction between source language and object language.

Exercise 8. (a) Who or what writes the source program?
(b) Who or what writes the object program?

Exercise 9. Use the big C notation to illustrate how the Java compiler could have been developed.

Exercise 10. Describe the translation phase and execution phase of a compiler.

Exercise 11. Try your skills at example 6 from the text but input a stopping point for your sum. Your stopping points could be 400 but could also be 750.

Exercise 12. Try your skills. A prime number is a number that has no divisors other than 1 and itself. Examples are 2, 3, 5, 7,11, 13, and 17, ... Devise an algorithm, and code in the language C++ that will find and output all prime numbers less than 10,000.

Exercise 13. Try your skills. A perfect number is a number that is equal to the sum of its divisors, not including itself. Example of a perfect number is 28 = 1 + 2 + 4 + 7 + 14. Devise an algorithm, and code in the language C++, a program that will find and output all perfect numbers less than 30,000.

Exercise 14. Write a program in BASIC, FORTRAN, Pascal, C, C++ and Java that will input a set of 10 numbers, then will find and output the unique numbers and the number of times that each appears in the list. It will only be necessary for you to compile and execute the code of the language that you will use for your compiler.

CHAPTER 4

The Transy_Source Language

INTRODUCTION

One of the most important features of the modern computer is the ability to program the machine to solve a wide variety of problems. Early computers were mainly large calculators and the operator was responsible for entering the information step by step and the "computer" would immediately perform the calculation and then wait for another instruction or data. Although, they were fantastic "**super-calculators**" and the best computing devices for that day, it was soon realized that a total new world of computing would open if just an easier way to communicate to the machine could be found. Hence, the success of the computer industry is in large part due to the ability of individuals with imagination able to devise easier and better ways to enter instructions and data into the expensive mechanical device. These individuals, eventually known as programmers, were able to develop software that made the computer available to the individual with just basic training. The cornerstones of this **software revolution** are the programming languages used to create versatile and efficient software. Our objective in this chapter is to define a new language that we will call Transy_source. We will then write a program (compiler) in future chapters to tell the computer how to understand our language.

4.1 The Transy_Source Language – General Characteristics

The Transy_source language is a complete translating language and patterned after early translating languages, BASIC, FORTRAN and Pascal. The language characteristics are developed in this chapter and students may choose to take the language as developed. However, it is general enough that a student can add new statements or modify the existing statements as they choose. The language has 20 basic statements, ranging from the specification statement DIM used to tell the computer that a variable is an array to a looping statement, LOOP I = N1, N2, N3. The programmer familiar with the older languages will note that DIM is a statement found in BASIC, and LOOP is very similar to the DO statement found in FORTRAN. The statements are purposely made similar to statements found in other languages, hoping that the compiler writer will not have to devote an enormous amount of time understanding the language. However, it is imperative that the writer understand the language, in complete detail, as he/she will be writing a program to tell the computer how to translate the language to object code. The DIM is the only specification statement as this language is presently defined. It would be relatively easy to use a specification statement to declare all variables before they are used as C, C++ and Pascal currently do. Neither BASIC nor FORTRAN requires declaration of variables before they are used. This can be an asset in developing a quick program which requires little planning before implementing. However, the compiler writer may find it easier to declare all variables at the outset of the program and build the **symbol table** immediately. As presented here, the symbol table is built as variables and constants are found. The language has statements **CDUMP** and **LISTO** that are not found in other languages. CDUMP allows the programmer to view information stored in positions of core, and LISTO will list the object program.

As presented here all output is to the screen. It would be an easy modification to list the output to a file. There are two types of data – numbers (**float**) and literal (**character data**). Integers can be used as input and output, however, all numbers are stored as float and all operations are performed in float arithmetic. Operations will not be performed on literal data as it will be used strictly for informational messages to the operator and to assist in interpreting the output.

4.2 Transy_Source Specifics

The Transy_source language will include the following features:

(1) The **alphabet** will be any characters on the keypad, alpha, numeric or special. (i.e., all characters such as 0,1,2,3,4...9, a,b,c,...z,A,B,C... Z, #,$,%,^,...] are legal). To assist with de-bugging, it is highly recommended that the compiler writer adopt either upper case or lower case for all variable names and key-words.

(2) **Statement input** will be free format. The statements

```
READ A,B,C
R E A D  A,  B,  C
R   E   A   D   A,   B,   C
```

will all be interpreted as the same statement.
One of the first passes of our compiler will remove all excessive blanks and will make the statements above appear as:

```
READA,B,C
```

(3) **Statement labels** will be allowed. The order of statement labels will not be important and numbers or labels can be any string of five digits or less. As this compiler is written, it is assumed that the labels will be numbers. The labels are strictly for cross referencing and are necessary only for the GO TO, the IF/THEN and the IFA( ) statements.

(4) Only **numeric and literal data** will be required. Literal data are a string of characters, and numeric data are float numbers. Integers as well as numbers with decimals can be entered, however all numbers will be stored as float.

Numeric data may take on any of the standard types:

(15.6, 22, 19.3, -.145002, -350)

Literal data will be void of spaces and will have the form:
"This_is_literal_data"

(5) **Variable names** can be any string of characters or digits or combination of characters and digits. The length of the variables is only determined by the language the compiler is written in. However, it is recommended that the variable name be no longer than 8 characters in length. Array names must be declared before using and other variable names can be defined through an explicit statement such as

```
VARS A,B,C
LIT  AA,BB,CC
```

or placed in the symbol table as found. As discussed here, variable names other than array names will be placed in the symbol table as found. The symbol table does not distinguish between float variables and literal variables so it will be important for the programmer to note this. If the compiler writer chooses to distinguish between array variables, float variables and literal variables, it would be a simple task to do this in the symbol table.

Proper variable names:

rate_pay   hourly_r   days_w   a123$#

Improper variable names:

rate pay   hr rate   these would be treated as ratepay and hrrate.

(6) **Comments** will be allowed. The comment line will appear as: C* THEN COMMENT. The C* must be the first nonblank character of a statement.

Examples:

```
C* This_is_a_comment.
C* Input_three_real_numbers
```

(7) The basic **core** will consist of a float array. The float array in this text has been made of size 1001. However, its size is declared by the compiler writer and can be made much larger. A file will be used to store the core as it is passed from the translation phase to the execution phase.

(8) The **Transy_source file** can be created through any **text editor**. The computer language to build the compiler demonstrated here is C++. The C++ editor was also used to build the Transy_source files.

(9) A **literal file** will be used to store the literal strings. Literal variables stored in the symbol table will have a pointer to a position in this file.

(10) **Error diagnostics** will be generated for both the translation and execution phase.

Some possible errors:

a. Variable not assigned before using
b. Branch to a label not assigned
c. A loop with no loop end
d. Statement not identified (no keyword or assignment operator)
e. Operation symbols improperly formed
f. Operation not allowed in IFA statement

Upon finding an error condition, compilation will continue until all Transy_source statements are read and checked. A signal must be passed to the execution phase to tell if the translation was successful or not successful. The signal used in this compiler is to place a 0 in position 1000 of core if no translation errors and a 1 in position 1000 if an error(s) is found.

4.3 Arithmetic Operators

(11) The **arithmetic operators** will be the standard: +, –, *, /, ^ . The raising to a power can be a function operation POW(A,B) similar to what C and C++ utilize or the symbol ^ that BASIC uses.

There are three ways to assign data to memory positions; through a replacement or assignment statement or through a READ or an AREAD statement. In any case, each number may begin with a negative sign or no sign (implied positive); a '+' sign before a positive constant will not be accepted. If data is read by either a 'READ' or 'AREAD' statement, it may be entered on any number of lines. Numbers on data input must be separated by commas, and no imbedded blanks are permitted, as the occurrence of a blank will result in reading another line. A maximum of ten numbers can be read from one READ data line. A decimal point may occur anywhere or not at all in a DATUM.

4.4 Relational Operators

The **relational operators** are the standard found in BASIC or PASCAL <, >, <=, >=, =, <>. For simplicity in constructing the compiler, the relational operator symbols chosen here are those found in FORTRAN .LT.(<), .GT.(>), .LE.(<=), .GE.(>=), .EQ.(=), .NE.(<>). These symbols are only used in the construction of the logical expression for the logical IF statement such as IF(A.GT.B) then 20. Again, to assist in the actual coding of the compiler the periods before and after the relational operator have been replaced with the symbol | (i.e., .LT. becomes |LT|).

4.5 Transy_Source Statements

The basic **Transy_source statements** are given below

(a) DIM
(b) READ
(c) WRITE
(d) STOP

(e) END
(f) CDUMP
(g) LISTO
(h) NOP
(i) GO TO
(j) IFA
(k) AREAD
(l) AWRITE
(m) SUBP
(n) LOOP
(o) LOOP-END
(p) LREAD
(q) LWRITE
(r) IF THEN
(s) CLS
(t) ASSIGNMENT

All statements are coded in **free format,** one per line. A 'C*' starting in column one of a line causes the compiler to ignore translating that line; however, the line will be listed in the source output. This line will be called a **comment line.**

All **executable statements** are assigned numbers by the compiler (**transparent numbers**) based on the order of entry. These numbers will be used to locate a statement when it is referred to or referenced by a control statement. Comment lines are **non-executable** (no object code generated), and hence not assigned numbers and not counted by the compiler. Only executable lines will be translated and added to the object file.

4.6 Transy_Source Statements Syntax

DIM AA[S1],AB[S2]...

AA,AB....Array names.

S1,S2....The size of the array associated with this parameter and must be constants. The sum of all subscripted variables must be less than or equal to 500 or at least be careful not to exceed core. Only the line length of the statement string itself determines the number of arrays that can be defined on one line. A program can have more than one DIM statement and the statement(s) do not have to appear at the beginning of the program. However, all array variables must have been defined through a DIM statement before they are referenced in other statements.

The DIM statement will reserve the proper space in '**core**' for the designated array(s). As presented in this text, the DIM is translated to object and assigned the token statement number of 0. However, the statement is non-executable and it is not necessary to create an object line for this statement. The examples presented in this text will show the DIM statement as the first statement. However, as stated above, this is not necessary.

Example:
DIM A[100], B[50]

A and B will be stored in the symbol table with A having memory address 0 assigned as its starting address and B having memory address 100 as it starting address. The compiler as presented does not check the right hand boundary for array limits.

The compiler writer can also specify in the symbol table that the variables A and B are of type array. If this is not done, it will be impossible to distinguish between an array variable and a single value variable.

The compiler writer is given the option of using a specification statement for all variables or of assigning variables location in memory as found.

Example:
DIM A[10]
VARS B,C,D,E
Here A starts at address 0, B will be assigned address 10, C address 11, D address 12 and E address 13.
Or
DIM A[10]
READ B,C,D,E
Addresses will be assigned as above.

READ <LIST>

List – A series of 10 or less non-subscripted variable names, separated by commas

This statement, when executed, causes a data line to be read and numbers to be stored in memory locations specified by the symbol table.

Example:

READ A,B,C,D,E

When this statement is executed, 5 numbers will be read and stored in memory at the addresses assigned to A,B,C,D,E by the symbol table. The data values on the input line(s) will be separated by a comma. If 5 numbers are not on the first input line, then other lines will be read until 5 values are input. The numbers can be of float or integer mode but will be stored as float.

READ A,B,C

Data line:

15,22.3,12

The number 15 will be assigned to the variable A, 22.3 to B and 12 to C.

The data input could also consist of two or three lines.

15,22.3

12

Or

15

22.3

12

The values assigned to A,B,C would be the same as if all came from one line. The data values could also be of exponential form

.15e+02,.223e+02,.12e+02

WRITE <LIST>

List – A series of 10 or less non-subscripted variable names separated by commas

This statement, when executed, causes the numbers stored in memory locations specified in the list to be displayed five to a line.

Example:
WRITE A,B,C,D

The values stored in memory addresses assigned to A,B,C,D will be displayed on the standard output device – the screen. However, output to a file could be easily arranged. The standard output is 5 elements per line. If A,B,C,D,E,F are assigned the values 10,20,30,40,50,60 then

WRITE A,B,C,D,E,F

will produce the output
10 20 30 40 50
60

STOP

This statement, when executed, terminates execution when control is passed to it. A program can contain many STOP statements.

END

This statement terminates the translation phase and is not translated to object code.

CDUMP <START, STOP>

START, STOP - Positive integers or variable names

This statement, when executed, prints five numbers per line, the contents of memory with absolute address from START to STOP.

Example:
CDUMP 0, 10
The numbers stored in memory at addresses 0 through 10 will be displayed on output 5 per line.

Or

CDUMP A,B

The compiler will check memory addresses assigned to A and B and get the numbers (N(A), N(B)) stored in these positions and then display on output the values in core from position N(A) to position N(B). An error message should be generated if N(A) or N(B) are out of core range.

LISTO

This statement, when executed, prints the object code.

Example:

LISTO

The statement has no arguments and will simply print to output the object file. The statement can be useful in debugging a program.

NOP

This statement is referred to as a do-nothing statement and, is used strictly as a place holder.

Example:

NOP

The statement has no arguments and is used mainly for the purpose of assigning a label to the statement and then branch to the statement if needed.

GO TO <N1>

This is an unconditional GO TO

N1 - a branch label.

This statement, when executed, causes control to be transferred to the statement with label N1.

Example:

GO TO 22

The label should be an integer constant and assigned to a statement in the source program. If the label has not been assigned then an error message should be generated.

IFA(<NAME>) <N1,N2,N3>

This statement is referred to as the Arithmetic IF statement.
NAME – the name of a non-subscripted variable
N1,N2,N3 – labels of other statements in the program

This statement, when executed, causes a transfer of control to label–
N1 if N(NAME) is negative
N2 if N(NAME) is zero
N3 if N(NAME) is positive
N(NAME) is the number stored at address NAME.

Example:

IFA(Z) 22, 33, 44

The labels should be integers and the float variable Z should be defined and if not then an error message should be generated.

AREAD <NAME, START, STOP>

NAME – The name of a previously dimensioned and operative array
START, STOP – Variable names or integer constants

This statement, when executed, will read and store data in the memory locations specified by NAME, START and STOP. N(NAME) will determine the start location in core of the array and N(START) and N(STOP) will specify integer numbers. These integer numbers will determine the number of values to read and where to store the read values in core.

Example:

AREAD AA,12,15

The AA should be a defined array name and the 12 and 15 can be either integer constants or variable names. If not, an error message should be generated.

AWRITE <NAME, START, STOP>

NAME – The name of a previously dimensioned and operative array

This statement, when executed, will take from memory positions specified by NAME, START and STOP and list 5 elements per line to output.

Example:
AWRITE AA,0,20
The AA should be a defined array name and the 0 and 20 can be either integer constants or variable names. If not, an error message should be generated.

SUBP < >

This statement, when executed, is used to call pre-defined subprograms. Examples of pre-defined subprograms are:
SIN, COS, EXP, ABS, ALG, ACG, SQR.
SIN, COS, EXP, and ABS have their standard meaning, ALG is for the natural logarithm, ACG is for common logarithm and SQR is the square root function.

The calling sequence is:

SUBP SIN(X,Y)

where Y is the argument passed and X the value to return after the operation is performed (X = SIN(Y)). The second argument can be either a constant or variable name, and the first must be a variable name.

Example:

SUBP ABS(A,-22)

The first argument must be a variable name; If not, an error message should be generated. The second value can be either a number or variable name.

LOOP <N1> = <N2,N3,N4>

This statement, when executed, is used to build a loop. N1 is the runner, N2 is the initial value, N3 is the terminal value, N4 is the increment. N1 must be a variable name and N2, N3 and N4 can be constants or variable names. Loops can be nested.

Example:

LOOP N1= N2,N3,N4

N2,N3,N4 can be specified as numbers or variable names. Again, if they are specified as variable names and the memory position assigned to these names has not been defined, then an error should be generated. The compiler presented here will assume that N4 has a positive value. Again, it will be an easy task for the compiler writer to allow for either positive or negative N4. It would then be either an up-to or down-to loop as some compilers allow. The loop is a post-test loop and will be executed at least one time regardless of N1,N2,N3 and N4.

LOOP-END

This statement, when executed, is used to signal the end of a loop. It will be used only if loops exist. When this statement is reached in the execution phase, it will transfer control to its corresponding LOOP statement.

LREAD <LA>

This statement, when executed, will allow literal data (a string of characters) to be read.

LREAD LA

The message LA will be at most 60 characters in length.

Example:
LREAD LA
The variable LA must have an address assigned by the symbol table and the address will be a location in the "literal" file.

LWRITE <   >

This statement, when executed, makes it possible to write literal information.

LWRITE "message_message_message"
or
LWRITE LA

Example:
LWRITE LA   OR   LWRITE "THIS_IS_MY_OUTPUT"
The message "THIS_IS_MY_ OUTPUT" will be placed in the literal file at translation and the address or location that the string was stored will be assigned to LWRITE. The underscores are used since one of the first passes of the compiler removes blanks and the underscores help to make the string more readable.

IF <   > **THEN** <   >

This statement is referred to as the **Logical IF** statement.

IF(A#B) THEN SN

where # can take on any one of the relational operators
< less than
> greater than
= equal
<= less than or equal
>= greater than or equal
<> not equal
and SN a statement label.

When executed, if the logical statement is true, then control is passed to the statement with label SN. As stated earlier, the compiler writer is also allowed to use the FORTRAN convention for the relational operators: < .LT., > .GT., = .EQ., <= .LE., >= .GE., <> .NE. Also as stated, the bar | can be used on each side of the relational expression rather than the period (.)

Example:
IF(A|GT|B)THEN 22
A and B must be variables or constants and the 22 a defined label and if not true an error message should be generated. The relational expression A.GT.B will be evaluated and if true then the statement with label 22 will be executed next and if false the statement immediately following the IF will be executed next.

CLS

This statement, when executed, clears the terminal screen.

ASSIGNMENT STATEMENT

N1=N2 + N3 / N4 – N5 * ...

This statement causes the specified operation(s) between the variables to take place and the results to be stored in N1. N1 must be strictly a variable name and the variables in the right member must be defined and if not an error message should be generated. The compiler writer will make a functional transducer – a tool that takes a complicated mathematical expression and places it in a form that is easier for the computer to understand.

The mathematical operations that are available in the Transy language and their symbols are given below:

OPERATION	SYMBOL	EXAMPLE
addition	+	**A + B**
subtraction	-	**C - B**

multiplication	*	**A * B**
division	/	**A / B**
raise to power	^	**A ^ B**

4.7 Programming in the Transy_Source Language

4.7a Getting Started

A first program in our new language is no more than a greeting program.

```
lwrite "Hello_World"
stop
end
```

The first statement is called a literal write statement and just prints the characters contained inside the quotes. The underscore will make the output more readable in case your compiler first makes a pass to remove blanks.

The stop statement is needed for all programs and tells the computer to stop executing the object program. The end statement is also needed for all programs and tells the compiler to stop translating the source code to object code. However, in some languages there may be a statement that can check for end of file and this could be used when writing one's compiler and then the end statement can be omitted.

Most common programming languages perform their calculations by manipulating items called **variables.** In the Transy language, a variable is written as a string of characters and digits. Some sample names for variables are:

X Y Z SUM N1 N2 SALLY rate distance Time

Variables in the Transy language can hold either numbers or literal data. For now we will confine our attention to variables that hold only numbers. It is not necessary to declare variables before they can be used in the body of a program. However, the compiler writer may choose to declare all variables at the beginning and this may facilitate the building of a symbol table. All variables that store numbers will be of float type.

Example:

```
lwrite "Input_two_numbers"
read a,b
c = a + b
stop
end
```

When the program is executed, it will print the line:

```
Input_two_numbers
```

The next statement is used to read two numbers and the compiler will wait until the operator enters the number. The numbers can appear on a single line or on two lines. The numbers will be separated with a comma if on a single line:

```
33.4, 55.6
```

Or

```
33.4
55.6
```

The next statement c = a + b is an assignment statement.

The symbol = is the **assignment operator**. There can be spaces in the statement as the language is a free format language, i.e., the statement could appear as c = a + b.

Data Types

A **data type** is a description of a category of data. Each variable can hold only one type of data and as previously mentioned the only data types available in the Transy language are numbers and character strings. In our sample program, the variables a, b and c were of type float. That means that their values will be stored with a decimal. It is not necessary to include the decimal with an integer when a number is read or when contained in an assignment statement. The number 15 could be read with the following statement or the number 15. would also be proper.

```
read a
15
```

Literal data or a character string is the second type of data that can be considered in the Transy language. The same convention used for naming float data is used for literal data. It is perfectly acceptable to have variables of both types in the same program.

The following program will input a string and then print the string:

```
lread la
read a,b
lwrite la
write a,b
stop
end
```

INPUT:
The_two_numbers_read_are
15,22
OUTPUT:
The_two_numbers_read_are
15 22

Programming Examples in the Transy Language

PROBLEM: What is the output produced by the following four lines (when correctly embedded in a complete program)?

```
x = 2
y = 3
y = x * 7
write x , y
```

ANSWER:

PROGRAM #1: Write a Transy program that will print your name on one line and your home town on the next line.

The following example is a program to print the letter L in magnified form:

```
C* The following will print the letter L
   lwrite "    **     "
   lwrite "    **     "
   lwrite "    **     "
```

```
lwrite "    ******  "
lwrite "    ******  "
stop
end
```

PROGRAM #2: Write a Transy program that will print your initials in magnified form.

PROGRAM #3: Write a Transy program that will read in two integers and will then output their sum, difference, and product. Use print statements to label the output properly.

PROGRAM #4: Write a Transy program to convert hours and minutes to minutes only. Ask the user for the number of hours and the number of minutes. Then print the answer. Label the output.

4.7B LOOPS

In order to convert temperature from degrees Centigrade to degrees Fahrenheit, we multiply the Centigrade temperatures by 9/5 and then add 32. The following is an example of a simple program that converts 100 degrees Centigrade to degrees Fahrenheit.

```
c = 100
C* formula for Fahrenheit
f= (c*9)/5. + 32.
write c , f
stop
end
```

Notice that this program only converts one value, 100, from Centigrade to Fahrenheit. It would be more useful and interesting to calculate the Fahrenheit temperature for lots of different values for Centigrade; for example 100, 110, 120, ... etc. This is accomplished by using a loop. The loop structure in the Transy language is similar to the For Loop in C or C++ and is illustrated below:

```
loop i = 1, 10 , 1
lwrite "Input_C"
read c
C* formula for Fahrenheit
```

```
f= (c*9)/5 + 32
write c,f
loop_end
stop
end
```

The above program will input 10 values of c, calculate and output f for each c. The loop begins with the loop statement and ends with the end_loop statement. The i is called the runner and the initial value of i is 1, the terminal value is 10 and the increment is 1. The increment can be any positive number but must be included in the statement, even if it is just 1. Loops can be nested. The limit on nested loops is left to the compiler writer but the compiler demonstrated in this text limits nested loops to 10.

The loop statement is a post-test statement. When the loop statement is reached the runner i will take on the initial value 1 and control is transferred to the statement immediately following the loop statement. When the loop_end statement is reached, it will immediately send control to the top of the loop – the loop statement. The variable i (the runner), is incremented by the increment value and then i is tested against the terminal value and if i is less than or equal to the terminal value, then control is transferred to the statement following the loop statement. If i is greater than the terminal value, then control is transferred to the statement immediately following the loop_end statement.

4.7c DECISION STATEMENTS

The basic relational operators that are needed for control statements are as follows:

= equal	.eq.	or	|eq|
< less than	.lt.	or	|lt|
> greater than	.gt.	or	|gt|
<> not equal	.ne.	or	|ne|
<= less than or equal	.le.	or	|le|
>= greater than or equal	.ge.	or	|ge|

The Transy language has two IF statements. One is spoken of as a Logical IF and the second an Arithmetic IF.

The Logical IF is possibly the most used **control statement** in the Transy language and has form IF/THEN. In its simplest form, it evaluates an expression and then proceeds on the basis of the result of that comparison. For example, the following program reads in a set of scores and counts the number of students that made an A. An A is considered to be 90 or above. A **sentinel** value of 0 is used. This signals that no more data will follow and normally this is not a good data value – here we would not expect 0 to be one of the scores.

```
C* A program to count the number of A's
count = 0.
loop i = 1, 100, 1
read score
if (score |eq| 0) then 30
if (score |lt| 90) then 20
count = count + 1
20 loop_end
30 lwrite "The_count_for_number_of_A's_is"
write count
stop
end
```

The input could be as follows:

```
75
80
90
95
84
 0
```

Note that the input of 0 transfers out of the loop and it is assumed that the number of data values will be less than 100. Even though we can transfer out of a LOOP statement, it will not be proper to transfer into a LOOP statement.

The program above could also be solved using the Arithmetic IF.

```
C* A program to count the number of A's
count = 0.
```

```
Loop i = 1, 100, 1
read score
ifa (score)10, 30, 10
10 temp = score – 90
ifa (temp) 20,15, 15
15  count = count + 1
20  loop_end
30 lwrite "The_count_for_number_of_A's_is"
write count
stop
end
```

The input could be as follows:

```
75
80
90
95
84
 0
```

Example:

Here is a short program that asks the user to guess the digit the computer is thinking of. If the digit agrees with the one the program is trying to match (which is 6 in our case), the program prints "Right. Good job." If the digit is not 6, the program prints "Sorry, wrong number."

```
Lwrite "I_am_thinking_of_a_digit.__What_is_it?"
read x
if (x |ne| 6) then 20
lwrite "Right._Good_job"
stop
20 lwrite "Sorry,_wrong_number."
stop
end
```

PROGRAM #5: Put the above Transy program in a loop so that it will continue to play the game until the person guesses the digit. Have it count the number of guesses it takes. It should print a message to the user telling how many guesses it took him/her to get the correct digit.

In the following program, a company pays every employee $7.25 per hour. This program asks for name and number of hours worked. It then calculates and prints the total wages for the week.

```
lwrite "Enter your name: "
lread name
lwrite "hours worked:"
read hours
paydue = hours * 7.25
lwrite name
write paydue
stop
end
```

PROGRAM #6: Write a Transy program that pays an employee $7.25 per hour for all hours less than or equal to 40 and pays twice that amount for all hours over 40. For example, if you worked for this company last week for 52 hours, you would receive $7.25 per hour for 40 hours (290 dollars) plus $14.50 per hour for 12 hours (174 dollars) for a total of 464 dollars.

PROGRAM #7: Write a Transy program to determine how much fine you should pay for a speeding ticket. Assume the fine is computed as follows:

Amount over limit (miles/hour)	**Fine**
1 - 10	**$10**
11 - 20	**$20**
21 - 30	**$25**
31 - 40	**$40**
41 or more	**$60**

The input will be the person's name and miles over speed limit.

PROGRAM #8 Write a Transy program to find and print the sum of the odd integers 1 through 99. (Form the sum 1 + 3 + 5 +...+99)

4.7D ARRAYS

Suppose we wish to process grades for several classes of students. The number of students in each class will vary, but we wish to write a program that will calculate the average grade and then find the number of grades less than the average grade in the class. We cannot calculate the average until all the grades for the class have been entered. So, we must save the grades and count the ones below average after the average is calculated.

Should we save each grade in a variable of different name? This would lead to a long repetitious program. Fortunately, the Transy language lets us solve the problem in a very nice way using **arrays**. An array is a data structure used for storing a collection of data items that are all the same type. First, we must describe the structure of an array in an **array type declaration**. The array GRADE of 20 elements is declared as

DIM grade[20]

Transy reserves 20 memory cells for the GRADEs; these memory cells will be adjacent to each other in memory. Each cell of GRADE may contain a single student's grade. We can use each one, just as we did variables, by calling it by its name. In the case of an array, it will be like this: GRADE[1] means the grade of the first student in the class.

To read the score of each student into the array GRADE, we would do the following:

```
dim grade[20]
 loop i=1, 20, 1
lwrite " Please enter your score:"
read score
grade[i] = score
loop_end
```

To find the average of the class, we would change the main part of the program to this:

```
dim grade[20]
sum = 0
loop i=1, 20, 1
```

```
lwrite "Please enter your score:"
read score
grade[i] = score
sum = sum + grade[i] ;
loop_end
average = sum / 20.0;
lwrite "The_average_is :"
write average
stop
end
```

PROGRAM #9: Change the above program so that it finds the average grade for a class of 10 students; then it prints each grade and whether it is "below average," "average," or "above average."

The Transy language also has statements for reading arrays and writing arrays. The statement **aread** will read an array of elements and **awrite** will write elements from an array.

To read the 20 scores for the programs presented above, the following program segment could be used:

```
dim grade[20]
aread grade, 1,20
C* The following will write the 20 elements
awrite grade, 1,20
stop
end
```

PROGRAM #10: Write a Transy program to print the smallest element in a list of 20 numbers and its position within the list. (Be careful with this one, test all possible cases.)

FUNCTIONS

The Transy language has some built-in functions that come in quite useful. For example, in the program below the function SQR finds the square root of the numbers 2, 4, 6, ... through 20 and prints the number and its square root.

```
loop i = 2, 20 , 2
subp sqr(x,i)
write i, x
```

```
loop_end
stop
end
```

This would result in the following being printed:

```
2     1.414
4     2.0
6     2.449
8     2.828
10    3.162
12    3.464
...
```

Note that in the function call sqr(x,i) the right variable i is passed and must be a variable name or constant. The left variable x is a place-holder for the result return and must be a variable name. Other functions, the standard as found in most languages, are also available.

The Transy language, as implemented, does not allow the programmer to develop functions. However, the compiler writer looking for an additional challenge may want to consider what is necessary to allow the programmer the facility of writing user-defined functions.

PROGRAM #11: Write a Transy program that finds the cube of a number. For example, the cube of 5 is 125 (5*5*5) and the cube of 2 is 8 (2*2*2). Test your program by making a table of the number 1 through 10 with their cubes. It should look something like this:

NUMBER	**CUBE**
1	1
2	8
3	27
.	.
.	.

4.7e Special Type Statements

The Transy language has the special purpose statement **cdump, listo** and **cls**. The cdump will let the programmer view what is in core, the listo will list the object code and cls will clear the output screen.

The statements are illustrated in the program below:

```
cls
listo
cdump 1,10
stop
end
```

This program segment will first clear the output screen and then list the object code for the program. The cdump statement will print the values in core positions 1 through 10.

4.7F Executed Programs with Output

SAMPLE PROGRAMS WITH OUTPUT

Original Source

```
 45 Read AA,A4
    Z1=AA+A4
    IFA(AA+A4)1,1,4
    GO TO 12
    Z1=AA[1]
    Z1+Z2=Z3
 22 WRITE Z7
    STOP
    END
```

Output from Compiler

```
0 45 Read AA,A4
1    Z1=AA+A4
2    IFA(AA+A4)1,1,4
3    GO TO 12
4    Z1=AA[1]
5    Z1+Z2=Z3
```

```
6  22 WRITE Z7
7      STOP
8      END
```

Statement label 2 operation not allowed in IFA
Statement label 3 statement label 12 does not exist
Statement label 4 has invalid variable name
Statement label 5 has invalid assignment name
Statement label 6 has undefined variable

Original Source

```
DIM AA[100], AB[50]
LOOP A1 = 1, 10, 2
AA[A1] =A1
LOOP-END
B1=0.0
LOOP A2 = 1, 10 , 2
ZZ = AA[A2]
B1=B1+ZZ
LOOP-END
WRITE B1
STOP
END
```

Output from Compiler

```
0  DIM AA[100], AB[50]
1  LOOP A1 = 1, 10, 2
2  AA[A1] =A1
3  LOOP-END
4  B1=0.0
5  LOOP A2 = 1, 10 , 2
6  ZZ = AA[A2]
7  B1=B1+ZZ
8  LOOP-END
```

```
9  WRITE B1
10  STOP
11  END
```

THE OUTPUT IS: 25

4.8 More Programs in Transy_Source Language

Below are some **source programs** that will give you a better understanding of the Transy_source language. The **core** memory to store numeric data will consist of a float array of size 1001. The core will be initialized as .12345e+50. Statements are free format, as observed in the examples below.

```
C*                         Compiler Test 1
C* THIS IS A TEST OF THE  READ,WRITE,STOP AND END
C* STATEMENT.
C* THIS TEST SHOULD NOT GIVE ERRORS.
C* WITH THE SUPPLIED DATA WHAT IS THE OUTPUT?
C*
10   READ A,B,C
20   READ E,F,H,R,K,M
30   READ G
     WRITE A,E,F,H,R,K,M
     WRITE B
40   WRITE C
50   STOP
     END
C* data
C* 33.33, 44.44, -55.55
C* 1,2,3,4,5,6
C* 0.1234E+04
```

```
C*                         Compiler Test 2
C*  THIS PROGRAM WILL GIVE SOME ERRORS.
C*  FIND AS MANY ERRORS AS YOU CAN?
C*
```

```
C*
C*  READ A,B,C,D
     WRITE A
   WRITE AA,A1
    cdump aa
     go to la
       nop 4
         dim aa(4)
40       READ C1,B1,
       READ 1A,B1
        WRITE A1,,A2
         READ A,B,C,D,F,H,G,R,I,K,L,S
50        STOP
60  WRITE A,B
70    HALT
      END

C*                   Compiler Test 3
C*   THIS PROGRAM SHOULD COMPILE
C*
C*  THIS WILL DO SOME TESTING OF YOUR
C*  DIMENSION STATEMENT
C*  DETERMINE THE OUTPUT
    DIM AA[10],AB[50],AC[100]
C*
  L=1
  LOOP I=1, 20, 2
   AA[L]=I
  L=L+1
  LOOP-END
C*
  L=1
  LOOP I=1, 150, 3
    AB[L]=I
    L=L+1
  LOOP-END
C*
```

```
 LOOP I=1, 10, 1
  AC[I]=AA[I]+AB[I]
  AWRITE AC, I,I
 LOOP-END
C*
   CDUMP 501, 550
  STOP
  END

C*                    Compiler Test 4
C*
C*      THIS PROGRAM WILL GIVE ERROR MESSAGES
C*      HOW MANY ERRORS CAN YOU FIND?
30  READ A1,AA
   WRITE A6, A7, D$
    GO TO A
     GO FOR IT
  20   WHY NOP
     NOPP
    CUMP 1,4
   CDUMP 4,A9
 10  INPUT  A1,
   PRINT A2
   LISTE
C* DID YOUR COMPILER DETECT MORE THAN 10
C* ERRORS?
   S T O P
   E N D

C*                    Compiler Test 5
C*
C*  THIS PROGRAM SHOULD TRANSLATE WITHOUT
C*  ERRORS
C*  WITH THE DATA GIVEN BELOW, DETERMINE THE
C*  OUTPUT
LISTO
READ A,B,Z
```

```
  WRITE A,B,Z
 nop
  IF(A)3,5,7
3 WRITE A
  GO TO 12
5 WRITE B
  GO TO 12
7 WRITE Z
12 nop
  LOOP I=1, 10, 1
   nop
    LOOP J=2,2,1
     WRITE I,J
    LOOP-END
  LOOP-END
  WRITE I
STOP
END

/DATA
33.45,-15.2,.76E+02

C*         Compiler Test 6
C*
C*    THIS PROGRAM WILL GIVE ERROR MESSAGES, OR
C*    WILL IT?
C*    HOW MANY ERRORS CAN YOU FIND?

    DIM AA[50],AB[100],A4[50],AC[50],AD[M]
1   READ A1,A2,AA
    AREAD BA,4,10
5   AWRITE AA,50,60
    CDUMP
    LREAD AA
    AB[4]=A1+A2
    AB[A3]=AA[4]+A2
    LWRITE LA
```

```
   IFA(A2),9,11
   DO 77 I1=N1,N2,N3
   L1=A1B1
   WRITE A9
   GO TO 7
   B9=AA[51]+AB[80]
   GO TO B9
   LISTO 5,9
C*
C** IS THE ABOVE STATEMENT AN ERROR IN YOUR
C*  COMPILER?
C*
8  STOP
   END
```

```
C*          Compiler Test 7
C*
C* THIS PROGRAM SHOULD EXECUTE AND TEST LOOPS
C*  WITH THE SUPPLIED DATA WHAT IS THE OUTPUT?
LISTO
READ A ,B ,Z
  D =A +B
   WRITE A ,B ,Z ,D
 RA=0.0
   IFA(RA)3,5,7
3 WRITE A
  GO TO 12
5 WRITE B
  GO TO 12
7 WRITE Z
12 S=0
  LOOP IA=1, 10, 1
    S =S +IA
     LOOP IB=2,2,1
      WRITE IA,IB
     LOOP-END
  LOOP-END
```

```
  WRITE IA,S
STOP
END

/data
3, -5.0, 12

C*                 Compiler Test 8
C*  THIS WILL CHECK YOUR ASSIGNMENT STATEMENT
C*   WHAT IS THE OUTPUT?
A = 15.6
B = 12.4
C =  9
D = A + B/C * (A + B)
E = (D + A) / (B + A) * C
WRITE A,B,C,D,E
STOP
END

C*                 Compiler Test 9
C* HOPEFULLY THIS PROGRAM WILL TEST MOST
C*  STATEMENTS.
C*  WHAT IS THE OUTPUT?
   DIM AA[10],AB[20],AC[10]
C*
    LOOP I =1,10,1
     AA[I ]=I
     AB[I ]=11-AA[I ]
    LOOP-END
C*
    K =1
4    AC[K ]=AA[K ]+AB[K ]
     AWRITE AC,K ,K
      K =K +1
      Kb=11-K
      IFA(Kb)6,6,5
5       GO TO 4
```

```
6    READ A ,B
     WRITE B ,A
C*
    SUBP EXP(C,2)
     WRITEC
    AREAD AA,1,2
    AWRITE AA,1,2
     STOP
     END

/data
15,22
44,66,93

C*                       Compiler Test 10
C*
     DIM AA[50]
C* WOULD YOU LIKE TO TEST YOUR COMPILER WITH
C* SOME SORTING? SURE!
C* WHAT IS THE OUTPUT?
     AREAD AA,1  ,50
3     IA=0
       LOOP KA=1,49,  1
          KB=KA+1
            XA=AA[KB]-AA[KA]
             IFA(XA)7,7,6
6           XB=AA[KA]
          AA[KA]=AA[KB]
            AA[KB]=XB
          IA=1
7      LOOP-END
       IFA(IA)3,13,3
13          LOOP  IA=1,48,3
          XA=AA[IA]
           IB=IA+1
        XB=AA[IB]
           IC=IB+1
```

```
        XC=AA[IC]
         WRITE XA,XB,XC
16          LOOP-END
      XA=AA[49]
        XB=AA[50]
       WRITE XA,XB
        LISTO
        CDUMP 261,300
C* I HOPE YOUR COMPILER DIDN'T DETECT ANY ERRORS.
     STOP
      END
```

DATA:
50,1,49,2,48,3,47,4,---[50 NUMBERS-NUMBER PER LINE IS UP TO YOU.]

```
C*                    Compiler Test 11
C*
C*  THIS PROGRAM WILL CHECK SUBPROGRAMS AND
C*  OTHER THINGS
C*  WHAT IS THE OUTPUT?
    DIM AA[50], AC[50], AZ[50]
    CDUMP 1,20
    READ A,B,Z1,Z2,P,R,F
    AREAD AA,1,50
    B = 1
    A = 1
    F = 50
  2 AC[A] = A
    A = A + B
    K = F – A
    IFA(K) 3,2,2
  3 AWRITE AC,1,50
    A0 = 1
  4 Z1 = AA[A]
    Z2 = AC[A]
    Z = ( Z1 + Z2)/ (Z1 + Z2) * Z1
```

```
   AZ[A] = Z
   A = A + B
   K = F – A
   IFA( K ) 10 , 8, 8
 8  GO TO 4
 10 AWRITE AZ 1,50
   SUBP SIN(Z,B)
   SUBP COS(Y,Z)
   SUBP EXP(P,Z)
   SUBP ALG(Q,P)
   SUBP ABS(R,S)
   X = Z
   WRITE X,Y,P,Q,R
   STOP
   END

/DATA
1.,2.,-2.,5,.55
18.3,9.,11.2,19.6
1,2,3,4,5,6,7,8,9,10
11,12,13,14,15,16,17,18,19,20
21,22,23,24,25,26,27,28,29,30
31,32,33,34,35,36,37,38,39,40
41,42,43,44,45,46,47,48,49,50

C*                    Compiler Test 12
C*
C* THIS PROGRAM WILL TEST YOUR COMPILER SKILLS
C*  THIS PROGRAM WILL EXECUTE
C* WHAT IS THE OUTPUT AND ALSO CHECK CORE
C* AFTER EXECUTION
10   READ A,B,D
 20 R E A D ZA, ZB, ZC, AA
 30     RE AD  CA
      WRITE A,b,d
    25  W R I T E  CA
C* BE CAREFUL TO CHECK YOUR CORE FILE AFTER
```

```
C* COMPILATION
C* TO SEE THAT CONSTANTS HAVE BEEN ASSIGNED
C* THE PROPER
C* MEMORY LOCATIONS.
      35 GO TO 12
        12  LISTO
            CDUMP 1,90
      120 G O T O  A
    150  R E AD BA
     ad = 160
   180 C DUMP  A,AD
             200  C D U M P 261,280
      240 STOP
   E N D

/DATA
150,120,-22.3,1876
222
33,567.7,888.888
34.4,22
1,1,1,2,3,4,5,6,7
```

Chapter 4 Exercises

Exercise 1. Define each of the following:
(a) source language
(b) alphabet of a language
(c) executable statements
(d) non-executable statements
(e) symbol table

Exercise 2. Define and describe the two basic phases of a compiler.

Exercise 3. Give meaning to the term "executing a program."

Exercise 4. Show the big C notation for a compiler written in C++ that takes the Transy_source language to the Transy_object language.

Exercise 5. Give an example of a compile time error and an example of a run time error.

Exercise 6. For the statement C = A / B + C – D / 12; identify tokens, type of token and how treated.

Exercise 7. (a) Give the purpose of labels in a translating language
(b) Illustrate how labels are used in the Transy_source language
(c) Illustrate how labels are use in the language C++

Exercise 8. Contrast the comment statement in the Transy_source language with the comments(s) in C++.

Exercise 9. Give the data types and the alphabet for the Transy_source language.

Exercise 10. Describe the CDUMP and the LISTO statements in the Transy_source language.

Exercise 11. (a)What does it mean to say that a statement is executable?

(b) In the Transy_source language identify executable and non-executable statements.

Exercise 12. Describe the control statements in the Transy_source language and give examples of each.

Exercise 13. Write a program segment in the Transy_source language that sums the integers 1 through 100.

Exercise 14. Write a program segment in the Transy_source language that finds and prints the square root of the numbers 2 through 100.

Exercise 15. Write a program in the Transy_source language that inputs N float numbers, then find and output (a) the largest, (b) the average, (c) the count of those greater than 50. Use proper prompts for input and output.

Exercise 16. Describe the 5 basic types of statement for the Transy_source language.

Exercise 17. Write a program in the Transy_source language to perform the selection sort for a set of N numbers.

Exercise 18. Write a program in the Transy_source language to read N numbers (make general), then find and output the average of the positive numbers. Assume that N will be less than 200.

Chapter 5

The Transy_Object Language

Introduction

An object language is a low-level language consisting of numeric symbols. Just like a translating source language, the object language is a well defined language. It is possible to learn this language and write programs essentially without a compiler. The **Transy_object** language presented here consists of numbers (integers) which make it easy for the computer to understand. It is similar to the languages used to program computers in the 1950s. Our objective in this chapter is to learn this language and write programs independent of knowing other languages. Since the Transy_object language is not a true binary or machine language, it will be necessary for us to write a segment of the compiler that will translate this language into a binary language. Because it consists of just numbers, it will be an easy programming task to execute this language. The program needed to execute this code is developed in chapter 8 – **The Execution Phase of the Transy Compiler.**

If we use the big C notation, then symbolically the process for compiling this language looks as follows:

Transy_object → assembly code	assembly code → machine code
C	C
C++	machine code

Since the syntax of this language does not resemble the syntax of the translating languages of the previous chapters, the task of learning to write programs in this language will be no different than when the programmer learned his/her first programming language. We have seen in previous languages that mnemonics and actual meaningful names could be used for operators and addresses. Here it will be necessary for the programmer to give the actual address, in number form, as to where a number is to be stored. One must also remember the op-code numbers for operators. An op-code of 0010 in machine language, or an op-code of ADD in assembly language, or an op-code of + in a translation language, means add. In the Transy_object language to distinguish op-codes from addresses, we will use negative numbers for op-codes. The op-code for add will be -1.

5.1 System Characteristics for the Transy Language

The **system characteristics** for the computer and Transy_object language are as follows:

1. The computer will have 1001 memory cells of 4 bytes each for storing float numbers. The addresses for these float numbers will be 0 through 1000. The core will be written into a file at the end of the translation phase in order to have available for the execution phase.
2. The position 1000 of core will be used as a flag position to indicate error(s) in the translation phase or no errors in translation. A 1 in position 1000 will signify errors and a 0 will signify no errors in translation.
3. A file, independent of memory, will be used to store the object code generated in the translation phase.
4. A file will also be used to store the literal data.

The "hand-shake" between the translation phase and the execution phase:

The translation phase and the execution phase can be developed as disjoint projects with the translation phase consuming approximately 80% of the total time to construct the compiler and the execution phase only 20%.

The information common to both the translation phase and the execution phase will be:

1. A file of 1001 float numbers – memory.
2. A file containing the object code generated by the translation phase.
3. A file containing the literal data created by the translation phase.

5.2 THE EXECUTION PROCESS

The flow of the compiler will be:

Translation Phase

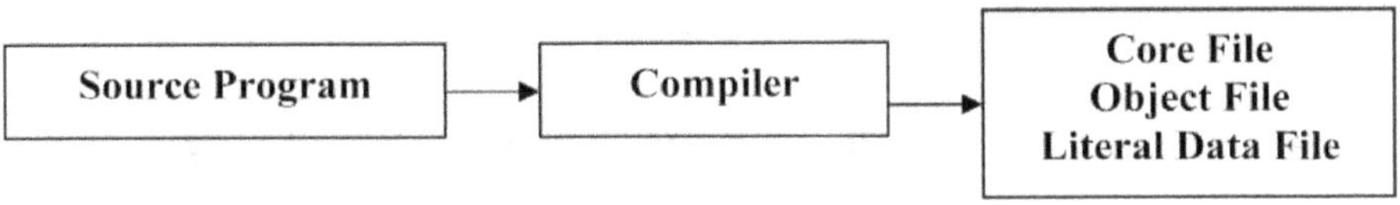

Execution Phase

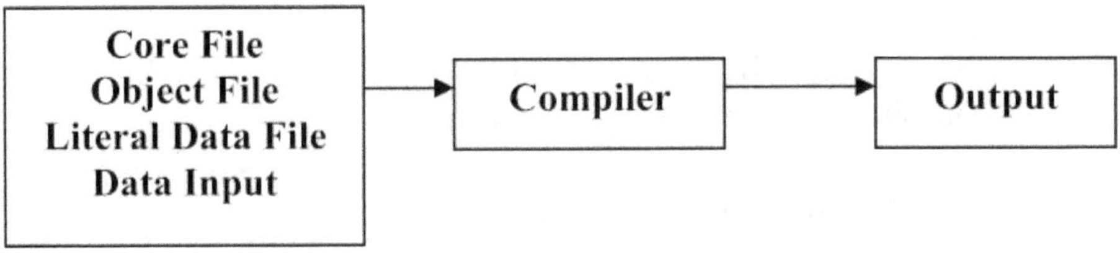

The output from the translation phase will be the three files specified above and the source program. The source program will be printed to the screen and if syntax errors are encountered, they will be listed under the source with some indication as to what created or caused these errors. Also, if errors were found, a 1 will be stored in position 1000 of the core before it is written to the file to pass to the execution phase. If constants are found during translation, they will also be stored in memory at the position assigned by the **symbol table**. The actual process of translation from source file to object file and the function of the symbol table will be given in later chapters.

5.3 Transy_Object Code for Corresponding Transy_Source Code

Below, each Transy_source line is given along with the object code generated by the translation phase:

For each executable line of the source file found without syntax errors, an object line will be generated and written to the object file.

Statement: DIM (to declare a variable as an array)

SOURCE: DIM AA[10], AB[20]
Object code: 000 nn1 nn2

000 – The op-code for the statement

nn1,nn2 – The starting addresses in memory for the arrays

Statement: READ (to input numbers and store in specified memory cells)

SOURCE: READ A1,B1,C1
Object code: 001 nn1 nn2 nn3 nn4

001 – The op-code for the statement

nn1 – The number of variables in the list

nn2 ... nn4 – The addresses in memory to store the input

Statement: WRITE (list to the screen contents of specified memory cells)

SOURCE: WRITE A1,B1,C1
Object code: 002 nn1 nn2 nn3 nn4

002 – The op-code for the statement

nn1 – The number of variables in the list to be written
nn2...nn4 – The core addresses of the variables to be written

Statement: STOP (to terminate execution of the object code)

SOURCE: STOP
Object code: 003

003 – The op-code for the statement

Statement: CDUMP (to list contents of specified core memory to screen)

SOURCE: CDUMP A1,B1
Object code: 005 nn1 nn2

005 – The op-code for the statement

nn1 – The address of the first core position to list

nn2 – The address of the last core address to list

Statement: LISTO (to list object program to screen)

SOURCE: LISTO
Object code: 006

006 – The op-code for the statement

Statement: NOP (label holder statement)

SOURCE: NOP
Object code: 007

007 – The op-code for the statement

Statement: GO TO (unconditional go to statement)

SOURCE: GO TO N1
Object code: 008 nn1

008 – The op-code for the statement

nn1 – The address of the object line to which this statement will branch

Statement: IFA (arithmetic if statement)

SOURCE: IFA(A1)3,5,7
Object code: 010 nn1 nn2 nn3 nn4

010 – The op-code for the statement

nn1 – The address of the value being tested

nn2 – The location of the object line to branch to if the value is negative

nn3 – The location of the object line to branch to if the value is zero

nn4 – The location of the object line to branch to if the value is positive

Statement: AREAD (to read an array of values)

SOURCE: AREAD AA, N1, 7
Object code: 011 nn1 nn2 nn3

011 – The op-code of the statement

nn1 – The starting core address of the array

nn2 – The core address of the value which augments the first position in the array to store input

nn3 – The core address of the value which augments the first position in the array to determine the last address to store input

Statement: AWRITE (to output to screen an array of values)

SOURCE: AWRITE AA,7,11
Object code: 012 nn1 nn2 nn3

012 – The op-code of the statement

nn1 – The starting core address of the array

nn2 – The core address of the value which augments the first position in the array to determine first output

nn3 – The core address of the value which is used to determine the last value to write

Statement: SUBP (subprogram call statement)

SOURCE: SUBP SIN(A1,A2)
Object code: 013 nn1 nn2 nn3

013 – The op-code for the statement

nn1 – The op-code for subroutine type

001 – SIN function

002 – COS function

003 – EXP function

004 – ALG function(natural logarithm)

005 – ACG function(common logarithm)

006 – ABS function

007 – SQR function(square root routine)

nn2 – address of the value returned

nn3 – address of the value passed

Statement: LOOP (the beginning of a loop)

SOURCE: LOOP A1=1,5,N1
Object code: 014 nn1 nn2 nn3 nn4

014 – The op-code of the statement

nn1 – The address of the counter variable

nn2 – The address of the initial value

nn3 – The address of the limit value

nn4 – The address of the increment

Statement: LOOP-END (end of a loop)

SOURCE: LOOP-END
Object code: 015 nn1

015 – The op-code of the statement

nn1 – The location of the object line at the top of the loop

Statement: LREAD (reads literal data)

SOURCE: LREAD LA
Object code: 016 nn1

016 – The op-code of the statement

nn1 – The location in file to store the line read

Statement: LWRITE (writes a literal line or string)

SOURCE: LWRITE LA or LWRITE "This String"
Object code: 017 nn1

017 – The op-code of the statement

nn1 – The location in literal file of line to output to screen

Statement: IF THEN (logical if statement)

SOURCE: IF(A|GT|B) THEN ST #
Object code: 018 nn1 nn2 nn3 nn4

018 – The op-code of the statement

nn1 – relational operator code
nn1: 1 < (|LT|), 2 > (|GT|), 3 = (|EQ|),
4 <= (|LE|), 5 >= (|GE|), 6 <> (|NE|)

nn2, nn3 – addresses of A and B

nn4 – location of object statement to branch if true

Statement: CLS (clear screen)

SOURCE: CLS
Object code: 019

019 – The op-code of the statement

Statement: END (used to signify end of source input – non executable)

SOURCE: END
Object code: none generated

Statement: ASSIGNMENT (to perform the indicated operation and store results)

SOURCE: Z = A * B / C ...
Object code: 020 nn1 nn2 nn3 ...

A transducer will be used to take this infix expression and make it into a postfix expression. Variable names will be replaced with numeric addresses and operators will be replaced with negative integers. The total number of variables and operators on one line should not exceed 24. This limit can be determined by the compiler writer, however, here we allowed an integer array of 25 elements to store the op-code, addresses and operators.

The selection of op-code numbers for the statements has evolved over the past 25 years. Their selection was made partially in the order that the statements evolved and were translated. As the compiler is presented in this text, the op-code numbers 4 and 9 are missing. At one time they were used for statements that have since been removed from the Transy_source language. Rather than reordering the op-codes 0 through 18 the numbers 4 and 9 have remained with the thought of giving the compiler writer an opportunity to add two additional statements of choice.

5.4 Transy_Source and Transy_Object Code Synopsis

Commands, Op-Codes and Arguments:

Command	Op-Code	Arguments
DIM	0	nn1, nn2, ... starting position of each array
READ	1	nn1, nn2, ... nn10 nn1 the number of arguments nn2 up to nn10 addresses
WRITE	2	nn1, nn2, ... nn10 nn1 the number of arguments nn2 up to nn10 addresses
STOP	3	No arguments passed
END	NONE	No object code is generated
CDUMP	5	nn1, nn2 nn1 – starting point to dump core nn2 – ending point to dump core both arguments can be either variables or integers
LISTO	6	No arguments are passed
NOP	7	No arguments are passed

GOTO	8	nn1 nn1 is the location in the object file to branch
IFA (variable)	10	nn1, nn2, nn3, nn4 nn1 – address of the condition variable nn2-nn4, statement numbers to branch to. Can only be numbers
AREAD	11	nn1, nn2, nn3 nn1 – starting memory location for the specified array nn2 – core address of starting position relative to the array nn3 – core address of ending position relative to the array
AWRITE	12	nn1, nn2, nn3 nn1 – starting memory location for the array nn2 – core address of starting position relative to the array. nn3 – core address of ending position relative to the array
SUBP	13	nn1, nn2, nn3 nn1 – token for the seven different subprograms statements – Sin, Cos, Exp, Alg, Acg, Abs, Sqr nn2 – address of the value returned nn3 – address of the value passed

LOOP	14	nn1, nn2, nn3, nn4 nn1 – address of runner must be a variable nn2 – address of initial value nn3 – address of maximum value nn4 – address of increment value nn2 – nn4 can be variables as well as constants
LOOP-END	15	nn1 – the location of the object line of LOOP which is dedicated to this LOOP-END statement
LREAD	16	nn1 – The line in the literal file to store literal data
LWRITE	17	nn1 – The line in the literal file to get literal data to output
IF (var op var) THEN	18	nn1, nn2, nn3, nn4 nn1 – token for the relational operator defined as: <, >, = ... nn2 & nn3 – addresses for the two values to compare nn4 – statement number to branch to if statement is true
CLS	19	No arguments
ASSIGNMENT	20	nn1, nn2, ... nn(n) nn1 – nn(n) are either variable locations or operator numbers (nn(n) <= 24)

5.5 Programming in the Transy_Object Language

—The Transy **read** statement has form

1 2 0 1

This statement will cause 2 numbers to be read from the input (keyboard) and will store the numbers in address 0 and address 1 of core.

—The Transy **write** statement has form

2 2 0 1

This statement will take two numbers from core positions 0 and 1 and will display to the output screen.

—The Transy **stop** statement has form

3

This statement will stop executing the object program.

Example 1. Write a program in the Transy_object language that will input three numbers, then output the three numbers in reverse order of input.

Object Program:

```
13012
23210
3
```

Source Program:

```
C* program to input 3 numbers, then output in reverse order
C*  of input.
    read a,b,c
    write c,b,a
    stop
    end
```

The data input and output could look as follows:

I: 12,22,33

O: 33 22 12

```
I:  12,22
    33
O:  33  22  12

I:  12
    22
    33
O:  33  22  12
```

Example 2. Write a program in the Transy_object language that will input four numbers, then output the first and last to be read.

Object Program:

```
1 4 0 1 2 3
2 2 0 3
3
```

Source Program:

```
C* program to input 4 numbers, then output the first and last
C*  to be read.
    read a,b,c,d
    write a,d
    stop
    end
```

—The Transy **cdump** statement has form

5 0 3

This statement will cause the numbers stored in memory or core at positions N(0) through N(3) to be printed to the output screen. (N(i) – the number stored at memory position i).

Example 3. Write a program in the Transy_object language that will input 3 numbers, then output the three numbers and also output what is found in core at positions 0 through 2. Assume 0 is stored in memory position 4 and 2 is stored in memory position 5.

Object Program:

```
1 3 0 1 2
2 3 0 1 2
5 4 5
3
```

Source Program:

```
C* program to input 4 numbers, then output the first and last
C* also output what is in core positions 0 through 2.
   read a,b,c,d
   write a,d
   x = 0
   y = 2
   cdump x,y
   stop
   end
```

The data input and output could look as follows:

I: 12,22,33,44

O: 12 44

O: 12 22 33

Example 4. Write a program in the Transy_object language that will input 5 numbers, one per line, then output the first and last.

Object Program:

```
1 1 0
14 1 2 3 4
1 1 5
15 1
2 2 0 5
3
```

Source Program:

```
C* program to input 5 numbers, one per line, then output the
C*  first and last.
      read x
      loop i = 2, 5, 1
         read  y
      loop-end
      write x, y
      stop
      end
```

Example 5. Write a program in the Transy_object language to input 20 numbers, one per line, then output the count for the number of negatives, the count for the number of zeros and the count for the number of positives.

Object Program:

```
20 0 1 -1
20 2 1 -1
20 3 1 -1
14 4 5 6 5
1 1 7
10 7 6 8 10
20 0 0 5 -6 -1
8 11
20 2 2 5 -6 -1
8 11
20 3 3 5 -6 -1
15 3
2 3 0 2 3
3
```

Source Program:

```
C* a program to input 20 numbers, one per line, then output the
C* number of negative, the number of zeros and the number of
C* positive.
```

```
C*
      cn = 0
      cz = 0
      cp = 0
      loop i = 1,20,1
        read x
        ifa(x) 10, 20, 30
10        cn = cn + 1
          go to 40
20        cz = cz + 1
          go to 40
30        cp = cp + 1
40    loop-end
        write cn, cz, cp
        stop
        end
```

Example 6. Write a program in the Transy_object language to input 3 numbers, then output the sum of the 3 numbers.

Object Program:

```
1 3 0 1 2
20 3 0 1 -6 2 -6 -1
2 1 3
3
```

Source Program:

```
C*  Program to input 3 numbers, then output the sum
    read a,b,c
    s = a + b + c
    write s
    stop
    end
```

Example 7. Write a program in the Transy_object language to input 2 numbers, then output the larger of the two numbers.

Object Program:

```
1 2 0 1
18 2 1 0 4
2 1 0
3
2 1 1
3
```

Source Program:

```
C*  Program to input 2 numbers, then output the larger
C*  of the two numbers.
    read a,b
    if(b|gt|a)then 20
    write a
    stop
 20 write b
    stop
    end
```

Example 8. Write a program in the Transy_object language to input 10 numbers, one per line, then output the largest of the 10 numbers.

Object Program:

```
1 1 0
14 1 2 3 2
1 1 4
18 1 4 0 5
20 0 4 -1
15 1
2 1 0
3
```

Source Program:

```
C*  Program to input 10 numbers, then output the largest
C*  of the 10
    read largest
    loop i = 1, 9, 1
    read x
    if(x|lt|largest)then 10
   largest = x
10 loop-end
    write largest
    stop
     end
```

Example 9. Write a program in the Transy_object language to input a value for a,b,c,d,f, then output the value of the expression a + b / c – d * f.

Object Program:

```
1 5 0 1 2 3 4
20 5 0 1 2 -5 3 4 -4 -7 -6 -1
2 1 5
3
```

Source Program:

```
C* Program to input 5 numbers, then output the value of the
C* expression  a + b / c – d * f
  read a,b,c,d,f
  x = a + b / c – d * f
  write x
  stop
  end
```

Example 10. Write a program in the Transy_object language to test the IF statements and the subprograms.

Object Program:

```
20 0 1 -1
20 2 3 -1
10 0 3 5 7
17
3
17 1
3
17 2
13 1 4 2
2 2 2 4
13 3 4
2 2 0 4
18 2 0 2 15
17 3
3
17 4
3
```

Source Program:

```
C*  Program to test the IF statements and the subprograms.
    a = 1.
    b = 3.14159
    ifa(a) 3,5,7
3    lwrite "A_IS_NEGATIVE"
    stop
5   lwrite "A_IS_ZERO"
    stop
7   write "A_IS_POSITIVE"
    subp sin(c,b)
    write b,c
    subp exp(c,a)
    write a,c
```

```
    if(a | GT | b ) then 20
    lwrite "A_IS_NOT_GREATER_THAN_ B"
20  lwrite "A_IS_GREATER_THAN_B"
    stop
    end
```

CORE Generated:

```
0 1.2345e+24
1 1
2 1.2345e+24
3 3.14159
4 1.2345e+24
5 1.2345e+24
6 1.2345e+24
7 1.2345e+24
8 1.2345e+24
9 1.2345e+24
10 1.2345e+24

1000 0
```

LITERAL FILE Generated:

```
A_IS_NEGATIVE
A_IS_ZERO
A_IS_POSITIVE
A_IS_NOT_GREATER_THAN_B
A_IS_GREATER_THAN_B
```

Chapter 5 Exercises

Exercise 1. Write a Transy_source and a Transy_object program to input 3 numbers, then find and output the range (high number minus low number + 1).

Exercise 2. Write a Transy_source and a Transy_object program to input 10 numbers, then find and output the largest.

Exercise 3. Write a Transy_source and a Transy_object program to generate the following output:

X	sin(X)	cos(X)	exp(X)
0	...	...	...
.1	...	...	...
.2	...	...	...
1.	...	...	...

Exercise 4. Write a Transy_source and a Transy_object program to input a numeric grade and output the letter grade.

Numeric grade	Letter grade
60 – 69	D
70 – 79	C
80 – 89	B
90 – 100	A

Exercise 5. Write a Transy_source and a Transy_object program to input a set of 20 numbers, then output the average of the positive numbers and the average of the negative numbers.

Exercise 6. Write a program in the Transy_object language to find and output the sum of the integers 1 through 100. (1 + 2 + ... 100)

Exercise 7. Write a program in the Transy_object language to input 10 numbers, then output one of the following for each number: "the number is positive" or "the number is negative." If zero is encountered then terminate execution.

Exercise 8. Write a program in the Transy_object language to store the numbers 10 and 15 in core, and then use the CDUMP command to output these two numbers.

Exercise 9. Write a program in the Transy_object language to print the object code for the program created for exercise 6.

Exercise 10. Write a program in the Transy_object language that uses the IF/THEN statement to output all numbers greater than 25 from a set of 10 numbers.

Chapter 6

Compiler Theory

Introduction

A **compiler** is a **computer program** that transforms **source code** written in a computer language (the **source language**) into another computer language (the **target language**, often having a binary form known as **object code**). The main purpose of a compiler is to take a language that a programmer understands and from this create a language that the computer understands. The language the programmer understands is called a high-level language. The language the computer understands is called a low-level language. In converting the high-level language to a low-level language, the compiler process will include the following: **lexical analysis, syntax analysis, symbol tables, transducers, parsing**, and **code generation.** Often the topics of **set theory, automata theory, finite-state machines** and some **theory of programming languages** are studied to better understand these processes.

6.1 Language Characteristics

The software for a computer consists of the instruction set and the necessary logic that tells the computer how to understand the original algorithm of the problem. To program computers before 1944, it was necessary to communicate with the computer in **binary code** (0s,1s). Today, we have programs called compilers which make it possible to relate to the computer in a **formal** or well defined language. Simply stated, a **language** is a set of rules and conventions to relay information. A computer language, like the English language, has its **alphabet** (set of legal characters) as well as rules and conventions in order to relay information. Each computer language is comprised of a set of strings that satisfy a specified set of rules and conventions. The languages FORTRAN, COBOL, BASIC, PL/I, C, C++ and Java all have their particular alphabet, rules and conventions. In all languages, a character or group of characters form what is called **keywords** of the language. The process of determining if a set of characters is a keyword is called **lexical analysis**. Once it has been determined that a string contains a keyword of the language, then a process known as **syntax analysis** is used to determine if all rules of the language have been obeyed within a particular string. An example of a keyword for the language BASIC is INPUT and for the language C is SCANF.

At first glance, the variety of compilers may appear overwhelming. There are many source languages, ranging from traditional programming languages of C and C++ to specialized languages that have arisen in virtually every area of computer application. Target languages are equally as varied. A **target language** may be another programming language, or the machine language of any computer between a microprocessor and a supercomputer. Compilers are classified as **single-pass** – the source code is translated in a single pass, **multi-pass** – two are more passes are necessary to translate the source code; an example would be to allow for control statements, **load-and-go** – compiles the source directly into memory and immediately runs the code, **debugging compiler** – has built-in routines that can be activated to assist in locating bugs in the code or **optimizing compiler** – routines that assist in generating efficient code, depending on how they have been constructed or on what function they are supposed to perform. Despite this apparent complexity, the basic tasks that any compiler must perform are essentially the same. By understanding these tasks, we can construct compilers for a wide variety of source languages and target machines using the same basic techniques. Our knowledge about how to organize and write compilers has vastly increased since the first compilers appeared in the early 1950s. It is difficult to give an exact date for the first compiler because initially a great deal of experimentation and implementation was done independently by several arithmetic formula conversions. Throughout the 1950s, compilers were considered notoriously difficult programs to write. This was due to hardware constraints as well as software constraints. Today, both hardware and software are abundant and available, thus making compiler writing much easier.

The compiler developed in this course will consist of two phases. One phase will be called the **translation phase** and one the **execution phase**. The translation phase will take the high-level language and convert it to a low-level language. The execution phase will take the low-level language (code) and execute (perform) the tasks of the original code. The two steps of translation and execution necessary for high-level languages is called **executing a program**. The source program is translated to the target (object language) then the resulting object program is loaded into memory and executed. In the beginning, compilers were considered to be impossible programs to write. The first and possibly the most important compiler ever written was FORTRAN and required the equivalent of one person working 10 years to implement. The hardware at this time was expensive and much less sophisticated than today. Hence, the machine requirement for speed of program execution and efficiency of storage was a major priority. Today, having essentially unlimited memory space as well as a high speed computing machine, the writing of compilers now requires less time for code optimization. Also, systematic techniques for handling many of the important tasks that occur during compilation have been discovered. Good implementation languages, programming environments, and software tools have also been developed. With these advances, a substantial compiler can be implemented, even in a one-semester compiler-design course.

Programming languages can be classified from the viewpoint of readability. Languages whose readability is close to that of machine languages are called **low-level languages**, i.e., assembly languages or assembly-like languages. Those whose readability is close to that of human languages are known as **high-level languages**. C and Pascal are examples of high-level languages. Programs written in low-level languages usually can be executed faster and require less memory space in a computer than those written in high-level languages. In high-level languages it is necessary for the compiler to convert the language to a low-level language. The compiler may not be as efficient in conversion as the programmer can be by writing the program initially in assembly or a low-level language. In fact, during the 1950s and 1960s programmers were reluctant to write in a high-level language as they thought, and possibly with reason, that they were better coders and able to make more efficient use of the hardware resources than the compiler could.

Programming languages are further classified according to their main applications or the manner of solving problems. FORTRAN and ALGOL are classified as programming languages for scientific or engineering applications, while COBOL and RPG are suited for business problems. Some languages, such as PL/I, BASIC, C, C++, Java and Pascal, are considered **general-purpose languages** – scientific/engineering programs as well as business programs can be written in these languages.

Instructions are program steps written in a computer language and command the computer to perform a particular task. Each step of a high-level language is called a statement. The instruction specifies an operation of the **Arithmetic Logic Unit** (ALU), **Memory**, or other hardware. Each statement, however, specifies a computational task, which may not be directly related to hardware operations and which generally corresponds to more than one instruction when translated into assembly or machine language.

Computer programs are made to do many different things and range in size from a simple two-line program in BASIC to a program in a language such as C++ that contains thousands of lines of code. In fact, the compiler that you write for this course may contain as many as 1000 lines of code.

Programming statements are entered into a compiler as **character strings**. The compiler must be smart enough to determine the type of string – Input, Output, Assignment, Control, Specification or Subprogram. The string is then dissected into **tokens**, a character or group of characters with a specific meaning, such as + (a numeric operator) or RATE (a variable name). Once the statement type, variable names, operators, constants, etc. have been determined, a **symbol table** is used to assign variable names addresses in memory.

The compiler process, as presented here, will be developed using two phases: the **lexical analysis** phase and the **syntax analysis** phase. The lexical analysis phase will be used to determine the type of statement and the syntax analysis phase will be used to get tokens from the statement. Tokens will then be assigned addresses and operator numbers if the rules of the language for the given statement have been obeyed.

The compiler must be smart enough to know that multiplication takes place before addition. The compiler must also check to see that the expression is correctly formed, i.e., has proper syntax. High-level languages have many advantages, the most important being the ease of coding algorithms. High-level languages also have disadvantages such as the programmer's lack of complete control of the hardware and the need for an extensive compiler.

6.2 Interpreters/Compilers

Interpreters function very much like a single-pass compiler with the exception of generating object code. The interpreted statements are executed as read and program output is immediately produced, assuming the program is error free. Again, assuming the program is error free the output of a compiler will be a lower-level computer code.

Consider the example presented earlier that stores two numbers in memory and then calculates and outputs the product of the two numbers

Compiler:	Interpreter:
A = 2; B = 3;	A = 2;
Print (A * B);	B = 3;
-----------------	Print(A * B)
MOVE A, 2	-----------------
MOVE B, 3	6
LOD R1, A	
MUL R1, B	
STO R1, Temp	
OUTP Temp	

For a compiler to produce the output 6, it is necessary to take the assembly code to object code and then execute the object code. The big C notation to take the BASIC code to machine code is given by:

S → O
C
I

BASIC → Assembly
C
C++
Assembly → Object
C
C++

The **source language** (S) is the input to a compiler; the **object language** (O) is the output of the compiler; and the **implementation language** (I) is the language used to write the compiler.

Today, the computers and compilers are sufficiently fast and thus make it easy for the student to confuse the compiler and the interpreter. The student will often click the **compile/run** rather than the **compile** button and will not observe that an actual object code of the program was generated. If a second run of the program is necessary, the compile/run button will be clicked again and thus not using the compiled version of the program that already exists.

6.3 Lexical Analysis

The **Lexical Analysis** phase takes the input string and determines the type of statement, whether **READ, WRITE, ASSIGNMENT**, or other. The **Syntax Analysis** phase checks for proper syntax, outputs atoms or tokens, variable names, operators, and constants, and builds the symbol table. The syntax analysis will use a **transducer** (syntax tree), presented later in this chapter, to convert a source statement to object.

A statement will be parsed into tokens with identification as to token type (identifier, constant, operator, etc.).

Given the statement:

S := Sum + Unit * 1.2E-12; the tokens and token types are:

Tokens	Type	How treated
S	Identifier (variable name)	Place in symbol table and give address
:=	Assignment Operator	Assign an operator #
Sum	Identifier	Place
+	Operator	Assign
Unit	Identifier	Place
*	Operator	Assign
1.2E-12	Constant	Assign, Place, store

Consider the statement

A := B + C * D;

To get the compiler to understand this statement, we must first use a transducer to place the statement in a form easier for the computer to understand. Normally, a reverse Polish notation is used.

With the token legend:

:= is -1
+ is -6
– is -7
* is -4
/ is -5

and assigned addresses:

addressA	op	addressB	op	addressC	op	addressD
0	-1	1	-6	2	-4	3

The statement:

A := B + C * D;

in reverse Polish notation has this form:

A B C D * + :=

When addresses and operator numbers replace the token, the statement has this form:

0 1 2 3 -4 -6 -1

6.4 Optimizing Compilers

To develop the most efficient compiler, two methods of **optimization** are considered: **global optimization** and **local optimization**. Some compilers of today make an effort to consider optimization. Regardless of the type of compiler being used, the programmer should make efforts to write efficient code. The compiler we will write will depend on the programmer for efficient code. Each type of optimization is considered below:

Global Optimization

Non – optimized	**optimized**
Read A, B	Read A,B
Go To 30	30 Write A,B
Write A – Remove	
Write B – Remove	
30 Write A,B	

The following code prints the square root of x 10 times:

Non – optimized

```
x = 18.0
for (i = 0; i < 10; ++i)
{
   z = sqrt(x);
   cout << i << ' ' << z << endl;
}
```

optimized

```
x = 18.0;
z = sqrt(x);
for(i=0; i<10; ++i)
   cout<<i<<' '<<z<<endl;
```

Local Optimization

Translating language code:
C = A + B

In Assembly code:

Non – optimized	**optimized**
CL R1	
LOD R1, A	LOD R1,A
ADD R1, B	ADD R1,B
STO R1, Temp	STO R1,C
LOD R1, Temp	
STO R1, C	

In global optimization, redundant code is eliminated. In local optimization, efficient methods are sought that reduce the number of statements to perform a given task.

In many cases it will be necessary for the compiler to make **multiple passes** through the source code. One example that requires more than one pass is when the source code contains labels. In the first pass, the label locations will be identified for jump purposes.

Example: Program with labels,

```
10  read a,b
    c = a + b
    if (c > 0) then 20
    d = a  + b + c
    write d
    stop
20  write a, b, c
    stop
```

The read statement and assignment statement can be executed as found, however, the control statement **if(c>0) then 20** will need to look ahead to find the label 20. Hence, a first pass is made to locate the labels and their locations in the source file. A table will be made of the labels and locations and the labels will be removed from the source. As the source is translated and a jump to a label is found, then the table of labels and locations will be searched to find the proper statement to transfer control.

6.5 Language Theory

The theory presented below will check each string to see if it is a member of the Transy language. If the statement is a member of the Transy language it will then be further checked for type, then broken into atoms or tokens and eventually converted to object code.

Once the Lexical Analysis phase determines that a string contains a keyword, the string will then be passed to a segment of the compiler called the **syntax analysis phase** which checks for language syntax and converts the input string to object code.

Before looking at the compiler code that actually performs the lexical and syntax analysis phase, a theory of formal languages will be considered. A **language** is simply a way to convey information. The information can be conveyed by sign language (smoke and hand signals) can be spoken (English, German Spanish, etc.) or the language can be a method (set of rules, etc.) to tell the computer how to understand the message. The two basic types of languages are **formal language** and **natural language**. A **formal language** is a set of **words**, i.e., finite strings of letters, or symbols. The inventory from which these letters are taken is called the **alphabet** over which the language is defined. A formal language is often defined by means of a **formal grammar** – a grammar that can be specified precisely and can be understood by a computer. A **natural language** is one spoken by people. Some basic concepts necessary for understanding formal languages are given below.

6.5A Sets

1) **Set** – a collection of objects. The objects could be chairs, people, characters of the alphabet or planets of the solar system. Each member of a set is spoken of as an element. In listing the elements of a set each

element is listed only once and the elements can appear in the set in any order. Also we use the symbolism { } to delineate the elements. A set consisting of the planets, Earth, Mars and Jupiter would formally be denoted as: { Earth, Mars, Jupiter }. This set is the same as the set { Mars, Jupiter, Earth } but different than the set { earth, mars, Jupiter }. Sets are sensitive to the case (upper or lower) of the elements of the set.

The elements of a set are listed only one time within the set. The set {aa, bb, cc} is the same set as {bb, aa, cc, bb}. Upper case letters are used to denote sets, A = { a, b, c }. We use the equality operator to denote that two sets are the same. The symbol ϵ is used to denote that a particular element is a member of a set, i.e., x ϵ { x,y,z}. The set {a,b,c,d,e,f,..z,0,1,2,..9,#,^,&,...+} of all elements found on a normal keypad is often the **alphabet** used in defining a formal language.

A set can be **infinite** (one that cannot be placed into a 1–1 correspondence with the set {1,2,3,4,5,..N} where N is some specified integer); or it can be **finite** (one that can be placed into a 1-1 correspondence with the set {1,2,3..N} where N is some specified integer), or it can be a set with no elements (**empty or null set**), denoted as { } or Ǿ.

There are three basic **set operations**: **intersection**, **union**, and **complementation**. The intersection of two sets is the set containing the elements common to the two sets and is denoted by the symbol ∩. The **union** of two sets is the set containing all elements belonging to either one of the sets or to both, denoted by the symbol U. Thus, if C={1, 2, 3, 4} and *D*={3, 4, 5}, then *C*∩*D*={3, 4} and C U D={1, 2, 3, 4, 5}. Each operation, intersection and union, obey the **associative law**. The associative law holds true if when any given operation combining three quantities, two at a time, the initial pairing is arbitrary. For example, using the operation of addition, the numbers 2, 3, and 4 may be combined (2+3)+4=5+4=9 or 2+(3+4)=2+7=9. For any three numbers *a, b,* and *c* the associative law for addition is expressed as $(a+b)+c=a+(b+c)$. Multiplication of numbers is also associative, i.e., $(a\times b)\times c=a\times(b\times c)$. **The commutative law** holds true if for a given binary operation (combining two quantities) the order of the quantities is arbitrary; e.g., in addition, the numbers 2 and 5 can be combined as 2+5=7 or as 5+2=7. In general, the commutative law holds true if for any two numbers a and b $a+b=b+a$. Multiplication of numbers is also commutative, i.e., $a \times b = b \times a$. These two laws work together to form the distributive law. The **distributive law** holds true if for any two operations, symbolized by * and ° and elements a, b and c, then $a*(b°c)=(a*b)°(a*c)$ for all possible choices of a, b, and c. If this is true then we say the operation * is distributive over the second operation °. Multiplication, ×, is distributive over addition, +, since for any numbers a, b, and c, $a \times (b+c)=(a \times b)+(a \times c)$.

The set of all things currently under discussion is called the **universal set** (or sometimes, simply the universe). It is denoted by U. The universal set doesn't contain everything in the whole universe. On the contrary, it restricts us to just those things that are relevant at a particular time. For example, if in a given situation we're talking about numeric values – quantities, sizes, times, weights, or whatever – the universal set will be a suitable set of numbers. In another context, the universal set may be {alphabetic characters} or {all living people}, etc. If the universal set is U={1, 2, 3, 4, 5} and A={1, 2, 3}, then the complement of A (written A') is the set of all elements in the universal set that are not in A, or A'={4, 5}. The intersection of a set and its complement is the **empty set** (denoted by Ø), or $A \cap A' = \emptyset$; the union of a set and its complement is the universal set, or $A \cup A' = U$.

The **roster method** is used to denote a set by listing the elements – A = {1,2,3,4}. The **rule method** for denoting a set uses a rule to specify the elements of the set – A = {x | x is an integer > 0 and less than 5}.

As stated a null or empty set is denoted by a pair of empty braces { }, or by the symbol Ø. It may seem odd to define a set that contains no elements. However, one may be looking for solutions to a problem where it isn't clear at the outset whether or not such solutions even exist. If it turns out that there isn't a solution, then the set of solutions is empty.

For example:
If U = {words in the English language}, then {words with more than 100 letters} = Ø
If U = {whole numbers}, then $\{x \mid x^2 = 15\} = \emptyset$

Several sets are used so often, they are given special symbols.

The natural numbers

The 'counting' numbers (or whole numbers) starting at 1 are called the natural numbers. This set is sometimes denoted by **N**. So N = {1, 2, 3, ...}

Integers

All whole numbers, positive, negative and zero form the set of integers and is denoted by **Z**. So Z = {..., -3, -2, -1, 0, 1, 2, 3, ...}

Real numbers

If we expand the set of integers to include all decimal numbers, we form the set of **real numbers**. The set of real numbers is denoted by **R**.

A real number may have a finite number of digits after the decimal point (e.g. 3.14), or an infinite number of decimal digits. In the case of an infinite number of digits, these digits may:

— repeat; e.g. 3.14141414...
— or they may not repeat; e.g. 3.141592653...

Rational numbers

Those real numbers whose decimal digits are finite (.25) in number, or which repeat (.333...), are called **rational numbers**. The set of rational numbers is denoted by the letter **Q.**

A rational number can always be written as an exact fraction p/q, where p and q are whole numbers.

— For example: 0.5, -17, 2/17, 82.01, 3.282828... are all rational numbers.

Irrational numbers

If a number can not be represented exactly by a fraction p/q, it is said to be irrational.

— Examples include: $\sqrt{2}$, $\sqrt{3}$, π.

Equality of sets

Two sets A and B are said to be **equal** if, and only if, they have exactly the same elements. In this case, we simply write: A = B

Note two further facts about equal sets:
— The order in which elements are listed does not matter.
— Any repeat occurrences are ignored, if an element is listed more than once.

For example, the following sets are all equal:

— {1, 2, 3} = {3, 2, 1} = {1, 1, 2, 3, 2, 2}

Why would one ever come to write a set like {1, 1, 2, 3, 2, 2}? Recall that when we defined the empty set, we noted that there may be no solutions to a particular problem – thus the need for an empty set. Here we may be trying several different approaches to solving a problem, some of which lead us to the same solution. When we come to consider the distinct solutions, however, any such repetitions would be ignored.

6.5B Subsets

If all the elements of a set A are also elements of a set B, then we say that A is a **subset** of B, and we write:

A ⊂= B

For example:
— If T = {2, 4, 6, 8, 10} and E = {even integers}, then T ⊂= E
— If A ={alphanumeric characters} and P = {printable characters}, then A ⊂ P
— If Q = {quadrilaterals} and F = {plane figures bounded by four straight lines},
then Q ⊂= F

Notice that A ⊂ B does not imply that B must necessarily contain extra elements that are not in *A*; the two sets could be equal – as indeed *Q* and *F* are. However, if in addition *B* does contain at least one element that isn't in *A*, then we say that *A* is a **proper subset** of *B*. In such a case we would write:

$A \subset B$

In the examples above:

E contains 12, 14, ... , so $T \subset E$

P contains $, ;, &, ..., so $A \subset P$

But *Q* and *F* are different ways of saying the same thing, so $Q = F$.

The use of ⊂ and ⊂= is clearly analogous to the use of < and ≤ when comparing two numbers.

Notice also that every set is a subset of its **universal set**, and the **empty set** Ø is a subset of every set.

How can the empty set be a subset of anything, when it doesn't contain any elements? The point here is that for every set *A*, the empty set does not contain any elements that are not in *A*. So $\emptyset \subset A$ for all sets *A*.

Finally, note that if $A \subset B$ and $B \subset A$ then *A* and *B* must contain exactly the same elements and are therefore equal. In other words:

If *A* ⊂= *B* and *B* ⊂= *A* then $A = B$

Two sets are said to be **disjoint** if they have no elements in common. For example:

If $A = \{\text{even numbers}\}$ and $B = \{1, 3, 5, 11, 19\}$, then *A* and *B* are disjoint.

If A and B are disjoint then $A \cap B = \emptyset$.

6.5c Venn Diagrams

A **Venn diagram** can be a useful way of illustrating relationships between sets. It is a pictorial representation of a set. Normally, the universal set is represented by a rectangle. Points inside the rectangle represent elements that are in the universal set; points outside represent things not in the universal set. Sets contained in the universal sets are represented by circles or loops, drawn inside the rectangle. Points inside a given loop represent elements in the set and points outside represent things not in the set.

Venn diagrams: Fig. 1

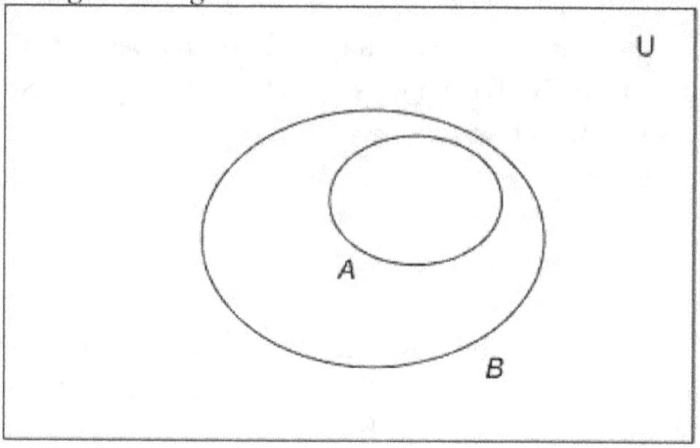

$A \subset B$

The set *A* is a subset of *B*, because the loop representing set *A* is entirely enclosed by loop *B*.

Venn diagrams: Fig. 2

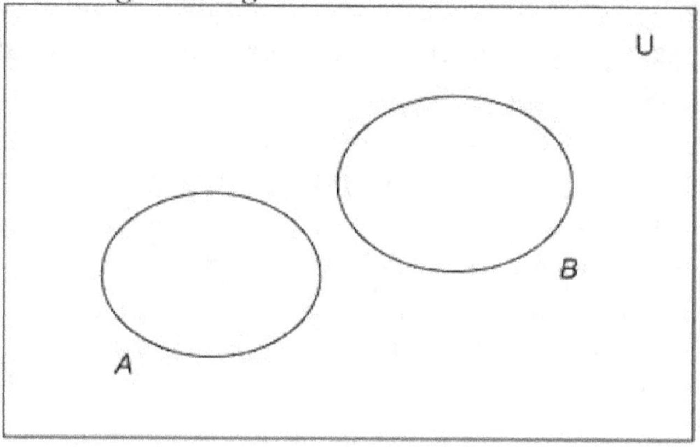

A and *B* are *disjoint*

Sets *A* and *B* are **disjoint**, because the loops don't overlap. $A \cap B = \emptyset$

Venn diagrams: Fig. 3

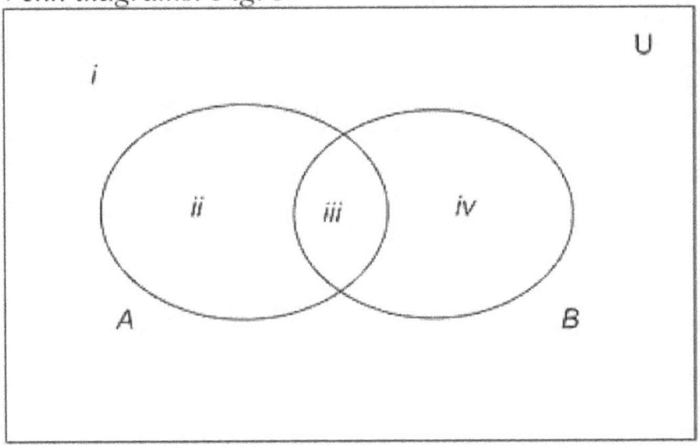

Example 1

Fig. 3 represents a Venn diagram showing two sets *A* and *B* in the general case where nothing is known about any relationships between the sets.

Note that the rectangle representing the universal set is divided into four regions, labeled *i, ii, iii* and *iv*.

What can be said about the sets *A* and *B* if it turns out that:

(a) region *ii* is empty?

(b) region *iii* is empty?

(a) If region *ii* is empty, then *A* contains no elements that are not in *B*. So, *A* is a subset of *B*, and the diagram should be re-drawn like *Fig* 1.

(b) If region *iii* is empty, then *A* and *B* have no elements in common and are therefore disjoint. The diagram should then be re-drawn like *Fig* 2.

Example 2

(a) Draw a Venn diagram to represent three sets *A, B* and *C,* in the general case where nothing is known about possible relationships between the sets.

(b) Into how many regions is the rectangle representing U divided now?

(c) Discuss the relationships between the sets *A, B* and *C,* when various combinations of these regions are empty.

Venn diagrams: Fig. 4

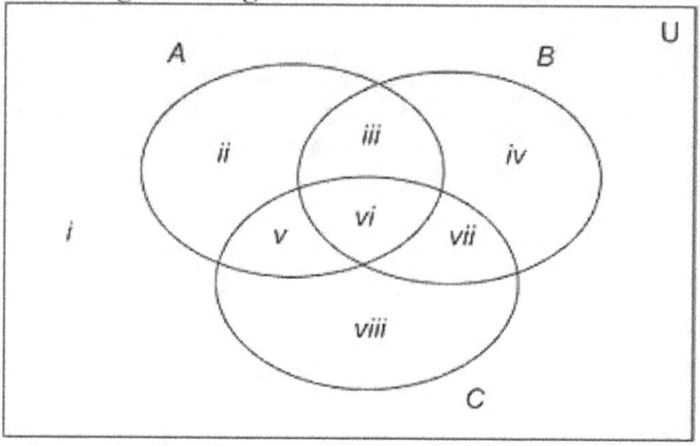

(a) The diagram in *Fig. 4* shows the general case of three sets where nothing is known about any possible relationships between them.

(b) The rectangle representing U is now divided into 8 regions, indicated by the Roman numerals *i* to *viii*.

(c) Various combinations of empty regions are possible. In each case, the Venn diagram can be re-drawn so that empty regions are no longer included. For example:

If region *ii* is empty, the loop representing *A* should be made smaller and moved inside *B* and *C* to eliminate region *ii*.

If regions *ii*, *iii* and *iv* are empty, make *A* and *B* smaller and move them so that they are both inside *C* (thus eliminating all three of these regions), but do so in such a way that they still overlap each other (thus retaining region *vi*).

If regions *iii* and *vi* are empty, 'pull apart' loops *A* and *B* to eliminate these regions but keep each loop overlapping loop *C*.

Example 3

The following sets are defined:

U = {1, 2, 3, …, 10}

A = {2, 3, 7, 8, 9}

B = {2, 8}

C = {4, 6, 7, 10}

Use the Venn diagram to represent these sets, marking all the elements in the appropriate regions. See Fig. 5 below.

Venn diagrams: Fig. 5

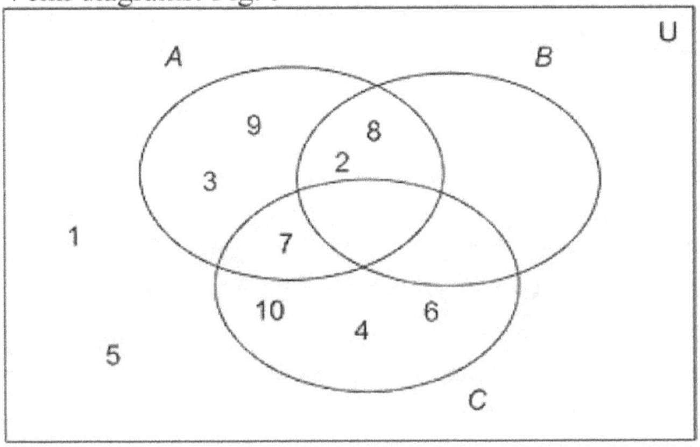

6.5d Strings

A list of characters from a given alphabet (legal characters) is called a **string**. The elements of a string do not need to be unique but the order in which they are listed is important: "abc" and "cba" are different strings. The string with no characters is still a string and is called a **null string** denoted by έ

Basically, a **string** is an ordered sequence of symbols. These symbols are chosen from a predetermined set or alphabet. Also, in programming, a string is generally understood as a data type storing a sequence of data values, usually bytes, in which elements stand for characters differentiating it from the more general **array data type**. A variable declared to have a string data type causes storage to be allocated in memory that is capable of holding some predetermined number of symbols. When a string appears literally in source code, it is known as a **string literal** and has a representation that denotes it as such.

String operations

A number of additional operations on strings commonly occur in the formal theory of strings. Operations that we often use in computer programming are **string compare** (check to see if one string is the same as another) and **string length** (determine the number of characters in a string).

String datatypes

A **string datatype** is a datatype modeled on the idea of a formal string. Strings are such an important and useful datatype that they are implemented in nearly every programming language. In some languages they are available as primitive type (**string my_string**) and in others as composite type (**char my_string**[**30**]). The syntax of most high-level programming languages allows for a string to be defined in one or both of these ways.

String length

The most basic example of a string function is the **length(string)** function. This function returns the length of a string literal, e.g., **length("hello world")** would return 11. For many languages, the length function is usually represented as **len(string)**. Although formal strings can have an arbitrary (but finite) length, the length of strings in real languages is often constrained to an artificial maximum. In general, there are two types of string datatypes: **fixed length strings** having a fixed maximum length and using the same amount of memory whether this maximum is reached or not; and **variable length strings** whose length is not arbitrarily fixed and use varying amounts of memory depending on their actual size. Most strings in modern programming languages are variable length strings. Despite the name, even variable length strings are limited in length; although, generally, the limit depends only on the amount of memory available.

Character encoding

Historically, string datatypes allocated one byte (8 bits) per character, and although the exact character set may vary, character encodings were similar enough that programmers could generally ignore this. These character sets are typically based on **ASCII** (American Standard Code for Information Interchange), **EBCDIC** (Extended Binary Coded Decimal Interchange Code) or **UNICODE**. Unicode provides a unique number for every character regardless of platform, program or language. The Unicode Standard has been adopted by such industry leaders as Apple, HP, IBM, Microsoft, Oracle, SAP, Sun, Sybase and Unisys. Unicode is required by modern standards such as XML, Java, and ECMAScript (JavaScript).

Implementation

The length of a string can be stored implicitly by using a special terminating character. This is the **null character** having value zero, a convention used and perpetuated by the popular C programming language. This representation is commonly referred to as C string. The length of a string can also be stored explicitly, for example, by prefixing the string with the length as a byte value.

String processing algorithms

There are many **algorithms** for processing strings, each with various trade-offs. Some categories of algorithms include string searching algorithms for finding a given substring or pattern within a larger string or text. In practice, how the string is encoded can affect the feasible string search algorithms. In particular, if a variable width encoding (codes of different lengths used to encode characters) is in use, then it is slow (time proportional to N) to find the Nth character. This will significantly slow down many of the more advanced search algorithms. A possible solution is to search for the sequence of code units instead, but doing so may produce false matches unless the encoding is specifically designed to avoid it.

String functions are used in computer programming languages to manipulate a string or query information about a string (some do both). Most computer programming languages that have a string datatype will have some string functions. It should be noted, however, that there may be other low-level ways within each language to handle strings directly. In object oriented languages, string functions are implemented as properties and methods of string objects. In Prolog a string is represented as a list (of character codes), therefore, all list-manipulation procedures are applicable.

6.5E Sorting Algorithms

In computer science and mathematics, a **sorting algorithm** is an algorithm that puts elements of a list in a certain order. The most used orders are **numerical order** and **lexicographical order**. Efficient sorting is important to optimizing the use of other algorithms (such as search and merge algorithms) that require sorted lists to work correctly; it is also often useful for **canonicalizing** data and for producing human-readable output. More formally, the output must satisfy two conditions:

1. The output is in non-decreasing order (each element is no smaller than the previous element according to the desired total order);
2. The output is a permutation, or reordering, of the input.

Since the dawn of computing, the sorting problem has attracted a great deal of research, perhaps due to the complexity of solving it efficiently despite its simple, familiar statement. For example, the **bubble sort** was analyzed as early as 1956. Although many consider it a solved problem, useful new sorting algorithms are still being invented (the **library sort** was first published in 2004). Sorting algorithms are prevalent in introductory computer science classes, where the abundance of algorithms for the problem provides a gentle introduction to a variety of core algorithm concepts, such as **big O notation**, **divide and conquer algorithms**, **data structures**, **randomized algorithms**, **best worst and average case** analysis, **time-space tradeoffs**, and **lower bounds**. For more information on these topics see any recent book on Discrete Computer Math.

6.5f Regular Expressions

Regular expressions provide a convenient means for identifying strings of text of interest, such as particular characters, words, or patterns of characters. **Regular expressions** are used in a formal language since machines can be designed to interpret such expressions.

The following examples illustrate a few specifications that can be expressed in a regular expression:

- — the sequence of characters "car" in any context, such as "car" "cartoon", or "bicarbonate"
- — the word "car" when it appears as an isolated word
- — the word "car" when preceded by the word "blue" or "red"
- — a dollar sign immediately followed by one or more digits, and then optionally a period and exactly two more digits

Regular expressions can be much more complex than these examples. Regular expressions are used by many text editors, utilities, and **programming languages** to search and manipulate text based on patterns. For example, Perl has a powerful regular expression engine built directly into its syntax. Many modern computing systems provide **wildcard** characters in matching filenames from a file system. This is a core capability of many command-line shells and is also known as 'globbing.' Wildcards differ from regular expressions in that they generally only express very limited forms of alternatives.

Parsing a string

In computer science and linguistics, **parsing**, or, more formally, **syntactic analysis**, is the process of analyzing a sequence of tokens to determine their grammatical structure with respect to a given (more or less) formal grammar. Parsing is also a term used for the diagramming of sentences of natural languages.

6.5G Formal Language

A **formal language** is a set of strings (sometimes called sentences) made up by concatenating symbols (characters or words) drawn from a finite alphabet or vocabulary. If a language has only a finite number of sentences, then a complete characterization of the set can be given simply by presenting a finite list of all the sentences. But, if the language contains an infinite number of sentences, then some sort of recursive or iterative description must be provided to characterize the sentences. This description is sometimes given in the form of a **grammar**, a set of pattern-matching rules that can be applied either to produce the sentences in the language one after another or else to recognize whether a given string belongs to the language. The description may also be provided by specifying an automaton, a mechanistic device that also operates to either produce or recognize the sentences of the language.

Languages have been categorized according to the complexity of the patterns that their sentences must satisfy. The basic classifications are presented in all the standard textbooks on formal language theory. The sentences of a **regular language** (a set of symbols from a finite alphabet that can be determined by some rule), for example, have this property; what appears at one position in a string can depend only on a bounded amount of information about the symbols at earlier positions. Consider the language over the alphabet a, b, c whose sentences end with a 'c' and contain an 'a' at a given position only if there is an earlier 'b'. The strings cccc and bac belong to this language but abc does not. This is a regular language since it only requires a single bit to record whether or not a 'b' has previously appeared. On the other hand, the language whose sentences consist of some number of a's followed by exactly the same number of b's is not a regular language since there is no upper bound on the number of a's that the allowable number of b's depends on. This set of strings belongs instead to the mathematically and computationally more complex class of **context-free languages**.

6.5h Finite-State Machine

A **regular language** can be described by **grammars** in various notations that are known to be equivalent in their expressive power. The most common way of specifying a regular language is by means of a **regular expression**, a formula that indicates the order in which symbols can be concatenated, whether there are alternative possibilities at each position, and whether substrings can be arbitrarily repeated. **Regular languages** are those languages that can be accepted by a particular kind of **automaton**, a **finite-state machine**. A finite-state machine (fsm) consists of a finite number of states and a function that determines transitions from one state to another as symbols are read from input. The machine starts at a defined **initial state** and passes from state to state as new input is defined. The transitions continue until coming to the end of the string. At that point, if the machine is in one of a designated set of **final states**, we say that the machine has **accepted** the string or that the string belongs to the language that the machine characterizes. An fsm is often depicted in a **state-transition diagram** where circles representing the states are connected by arcs that denote the transitions. An arrow points to the initial state, and final states are marked with a double circle. A fsm is illustrated by a **finite-state diagram** – Figure 6 below:

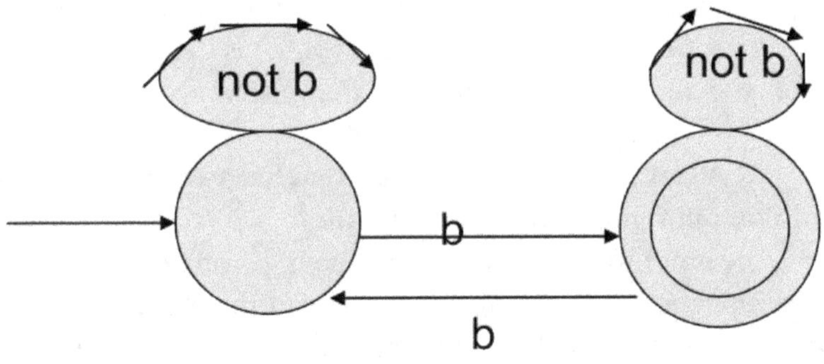

Figure 6 Finite-state machine diagram. (accepts strings with an odd number of b's)

Because of their mathematical and computational simplicity, regular languages and finite-state machines have been applied in many information-processing tasks. Regular expressions are often used to specify global search patterns in word-processors and in operating-system utilities. The **lexical analysis** component of most modern programming language compilers is defined as a **finite-state machine** that recognizes identifier classes, punctuation, numbers, etc.

As previously defined, a **formal language** is a **set of strings** from a given alphabet satisfying a specified rule. Given the alphabet $\{0,1\}$, the following are examples of languages from the alphabet:

1){ 0, 10, 10110}
2){ }
3){ 0, 00, 000, 0000, 1010101 }
4)The set of all strings of zeros and ones having an even # of 1s.
Here 1), 2) and 3) are finite and 4) is infinite.

A **finite-state machine** is used to specify the strings in an infinite or very large language. The study of finite-state machines is called **Automata Theory**.

More specifically, a finite-state machine consists of:

1) **A finite set of states**, one of which is designated the **starting state**, and zero or more which are designated **accepting states**. The starting state may be an accepting state.

2) **A state transition function that has two arguments** – a state and an input symbol and returns a state.

The input to a finite-state machine is a string of symbols from the given alphabet. The machine is initially in the starting state. As each symbol is read from the input string, the machine proceeds to a new state as indicated by the transition function, which is a function of the input symbol and the current state of the machine. When the entire input string has been read, the machine is either in an accepting state or in a non-accepting state. If it is in an accepting state, then we say the input string has been accepted. Otherwise, the input string has not been accepted. The set of all accepted strings form a language.

Finite-state machines can be represented with a **state diagram** as shown in Figure 6 or as a **state table** as shown in Figure 7. Each state of the machine is represented by a circle, and the transition function is represented by arcs labeled by input symbols leading from one state to another. Accepting states are double circles, and the starting state is indicated by an arc with no state at its source or tail end.

A finite-state table assigns names to the states (A,B,C,...) and these label the rows of the table. The columns are labeled by the input symbols. Each entry in the table shows the next state of the machine for a given input and current state and an * is used to show an accepting state.

	0	1
A	D	B
B	C	B
* C	C	B
D	D	D

Figure 7 Finite-state machine table

As shown above with an alphabet of $\{0,1\}$, if the machine was in state B and the input was a 0, the machine enters state C. If the machine is in state B and the input is a 1, the machine remains in state B. State A is the starting state, and state C is the only accepting state. This machine accepts any string of zeroes and ones which begins with a one and ends with a zero, because these strings (and only these strings) will cause the machine to be in an accepting state when the entire input string has been read.

More examples of finite-state machines (the alphabet in each case is $\{0,1\}$):

1) Strings containing an odd number of zeros

	0	1
A	B	A
*B	A	B

2) Strings containing three consecutive ones

	0	1
A	A	B
B	A	C
C	A	D
*D	D	D

3) Strings containing exactly three zeros

	0	1
A	B	A
B	C	B
C	D	C
*D	E	D
E	E	E

4) Strings containing an odd number of zeros and an even number of ones

	0	1
A	B	C
*B	A	D
C	D	A
D	C	B

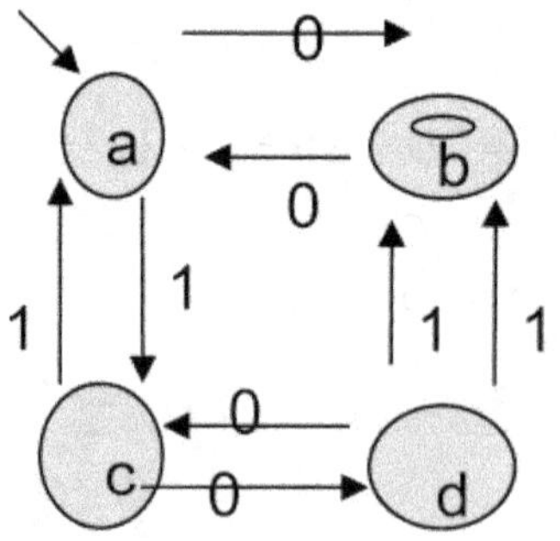

Figure 8.

A Finite-state diagram and table showing a finite-state machine that accepts an odd number of zeros and an even number of ones.

	0	1
A	B	C
*B	A	D
C	D	A
D	C	B

The first phase of a compiler is called the **Lexical Analysis** phase. This phase identifies a group of characters that have a special meaning. We will refer to this special group as a **lexical token** or **keyword**. Some of the tokens for the Transy_source language are READ, WRITE, STOP, IFA, IF, GOTO, LOOP, etc. Only one of these keywords will be found in each proper input string.

A C++ function to determine the keyword or tokens of our language is given below:

```
int gettoken(char stng[])
 {
 char *tokens[20] = {"dim", "read", "write", "stop", "xxx", "cdump",
             "listo","nop", "goto", "xxx", "ifa", "aread",
             "awrite", "subp", "loop", "loop-end", "lread",
             "lwrite", "if", "cls"};
 int tl,i,j, vtr = 20;
 int found;
 for(i=0; i<=19; ++i)
  {
  tl = strlen(tokens[i]);
  found = 1;
  for(j=0; j<tl; ++j)
   if(stng[j] != tokens[i][j])
    found = 0;
  if( (found) && (stng[4] == '-'))
   i = 15;
  if(found)
   {
    vtr = i;
    break;
   }
  }
 return(vtr);
 }
```

A character string, a statement in the Transy language, is passed to the function gettoken(), then the function checks to see if a keyword or token is found and returns the token number that identifies the token found. If no keyword is found, the token number 20 is returned signifying that the string might be an assignment statement. Later the syntax analysis phase will check to verify that each statement so labeled from this function does obey the rules for given statement.

Once the keyword or token has been identified, the string will be parsed into identifiers, operators, numeric constants, etc. At this time the statement will be analyzed to see that it obeys the rules of the language and a **symbol table** will be constructed to assign each variable and constant an address in memory. Each **constant** will also be stored in core at the assigned address. **Operators** will be assigned negative integer values. This portion of the compiler will be spoken of as the **syntax analysis phase**.

Consider the following input string which is an accepting string for Transy compiler:

```
R E A D  A1,  A2,  A3
```

The keyword READ will be parsed by the lexical scan. This string will then be sent to the syntax analysis phase and further checked to see if the rules of the language have been obeyed. Identifiers or variable names, A1, A2 and A3 will be placed in the symbol table and addresses assigned. The object language for the given source statement will appear as follows:

Source	Object
READ A1,A2,A3	1 3 0 1 2

The leading 1 in the object line identifies the statement as an input statement, the 3 implies that three numbers will be entered and the 0, 1 and 2 will be the addresses assigned to A1, A2 and A3.

All numeric data for the Transy language will be of type float so it will not be necessary to identify numeric data type in the symbol table. Also, to speed compilation time we will assume that our language is not case sensitive. Immediately after reading a string of the source language, a function will translate all alphabetic characters to either upper or lower case, depending on the compiler writer's preference.

The following will be some valid statements in our Transy_source language:

```
READ A1,B1
WRITE A1,B1
C = A1 + B1
GO TO 20
LOOP I = 1, 10, 2
IF(A1 |GT| B1) THEN 30
```

Exercises:

1. Study all the statements in the Transy_source language and determine what will be used as the alphabet for the language.
2. Determine the lexical tokens for the Transy_source language.
3. What special characters will be used as delimiters (characters with special meaning, such as: *,-,=, etc.) for the Transy_source language?

What translation errors will be generated from the following code?

```
READ A1,B1,
WRITE A1 + B1
C = +A1 – B1
GO TO A1
DO 7 I = 10 TO 1
IF(A1 |GT| 17.63) GO TO 40
```

A **finite-state machine** can be used to determine the keywords of the language. However, some programming languages make this scan a trivial task. The computer code (illustrated previously – gettoken) to implement the lexical analysis phase places each key-word into an array of strings. The subset of each input string that contains the key-word, if it exists, will be checked against the array of strings containing the key-words; if a match is found then the subset is a lexical token or key-word of the language. The key-words are placed in the tokens string in the order of their token number.

Figure 9 illustrates the translation process with tokens identified by a finite-state machine as implemented here by the gettoken function:

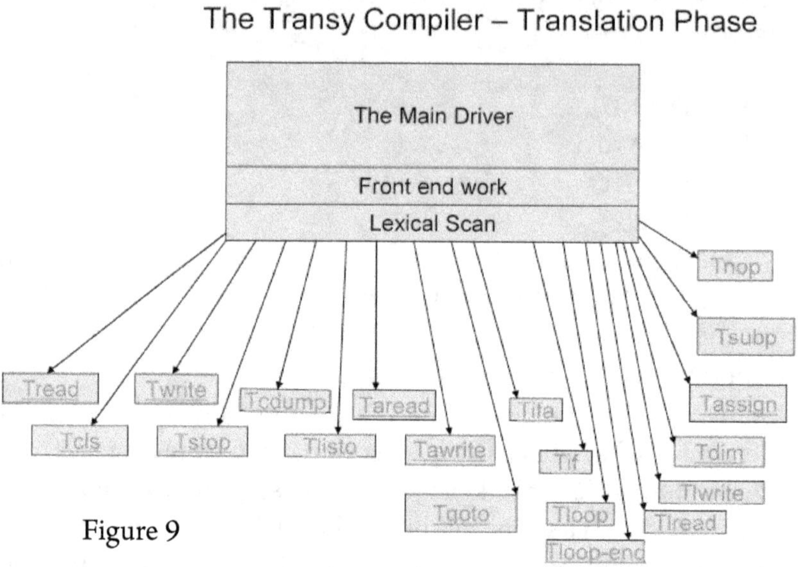

Figure 9

Finite-state machines can also be used to help take the next step. As key-words have been identified the string is passed to a function that determines **identifiers** (variable names, operators, delimiters, etc) and places variable names into a symbol table and assigns addresses and treats other identifiers such as operators (+, –, *, /, [, etc) appropriately. Numerical constants will also be placed in the symbol table and given an address. The constant, which comes in as a string, must also be determined before placing in core at the assigned memory address.

Finite-state machines can be used to convert a string containing a constant into a number, either integer or float. The following program demonstrates how to convert strings containing numeric data into a number:

```
#include <iostream>
#include <string>
#include <cstdlib>

// Takes strings of form 123.45 or 123.45e5
// and give the number as output
```

```
using namespace std;
double places;
double n;
double expp,sign;
void p1(int);
void p2(int);
void p3(int);
void p4();
void p5(int);
int dig(char);

int main(void)
{
int i = 0, j = 0, d, decp = 0,exppf = 0;
char stng[20];
char digc[11] = “0123456789”;
double result;
cout << “Enter the number to convert:”;
cin >> stng;

for(i=0;i<strlen(stng);i++)
{
   d = dig(stng[i]);
   if(stng[i] == ‘e’ )
   exppf = 1;
  if(stng[i] == ‘.’)
  decp = 1;
  if(i == 0)
   p1(d);
  else
   if( (isdigit(stng[i])) && (decp == 0) )
  p2(d);

 if( ((decp == 1)&& (isdigit(stng[i]))) && !exppf )
  p3(d);
 if(stng[i] == ‘ – ’)
```

```
 p4();
if(exppf == 1 )
 p5(d);
} // end of for
result = n * pow(10.0, (sign*expp – places));
cout<<"The output is:" << result <<endl;
system("PAUSE");
return 0;
}

int dig(char c)
{
char ch[11] = "0123456789";
int i;
for( i = 0; i<10; ++i)
if(c == ch[i])
return(i);
return(0);
}

void p1(int d)
{
places = 0;
n = d;
expp = 0;
sign = 1;
}

void p2(int d)
{
n = n * 10.0 + d;
}

void p3(int d)
{
n = n * 10.0 + d;
```

```
places = places + 1;
}

void p4()
{
sign = -1;
}
void p5(int d)
{
expp = expp * 10.0 + d;
}
```

The second step or phase of the compiler is called the **syntax analysis phase**. The input to this phase will consist of a string with key-word defined. This string is checked for proper syntax, to make sure the statements and expressions are correctly formed. Below are some syntax errors for the language Pascal:

```
x := (2+3) * 9)              {mismatched parentheses}
if (x>y) x := 2              {missing 'then'}
for i := 1 to 10 by 3 do     {invalid increment by 3}
```

When the compiler encounters such an error, it should output an informative message for the user. At this point, it is not necessary for the compiler to generate an object line for the given source line. A compiler is not expected to guess the intended purpose of a program or to give some correction to the syntax errors. A good compiler, however, will continue scanning statements for additional syntax errors.

The output of the syntax analysis phase (if there are no syntax errors) will be a stream of **atoms** or syntax trees. An **atom** is a primitive operation which is found in most computer architectures, and which can be implemented using only a few machine language instructions. Each atom also includes operands, which are ultimately converted to memory addresses on the target machine. A syntax tree is a data structure in which the interior nodes represent operations, and the leaves represent operands. The parser can be used not only to check for proper syntax but to produce output as well. This process is called syntax directed translation.

Just as we used formal methods to specify and construct the lexical scanner, the same can be done for syntax analysis. In this case, however, the formal methods are far more sophisticated. Here some theory is presented, and for the actual implementation a more simplified and direct method is used. Most of the early work in the theory of compiler design focused on syntax analysis. We will introduce the concept of a **formal grammar** as a means of not only specifying the programming language, but also as a means of implementing the syntax analysis phase of the compiler.

6.51 Grammars and Languages

Some basic concepts of formal language theory are presented here. These concepts can play a vital role in the design of the compiler. They are also important for the understanding of programming language design and programming in general.

Grammars

Recall our definition of a language as a set of strings. We have already seen a way of formally specifying a language – finite-state machines. We will now define another way of specifying languages, i.e., by using a grammar. **A grammar** is a list of rules which can be used to produce or generate all the strings of a language, and which does not generate any strings which are not in the language. More formally, a grammar consists of:

1. A finite set of characters, called the input alphabet, the input symbols, or terminal symbols
2. A finite set of symbols, distinct from the terminal symbols, called non-terminal symbols, only one of which is designated the starting non-terminal
3. A finite list of rewriting rules, also called productions, which define how strings in the language may be generated. Each of these rewriting rules is of the form α – »β where α and β are arbitrary strings of terminals and non-terminals, and α is not null

The **grammar** specifies a language by beginning with the starting non-terminal. Any of the rewriting rules are applied repeatedly to produce a sentential form which may contain a mix of terminals and non-terminals. If at any point the sentential form contains no non-terminal symbols, then it is in the language of this grammar. The language specified by a grammar is denoted as L(G).

A **derivation** is a sequence of rewriting rules applied to the starting non-terminal and ending with a string of terminals. A derivation thus serves to demonstrate that a particular string is a member of the language.

Assuming that the starting **non-terminal** is S, we will write derivations in the following form:

$$S \Rightarrow \alpha \Rightarrow \beta \Rightarrow \gamma \Rightarrow \ldots \quad x$$

where α, β, γ are strings of **terminals** and/or non-terminals, and x is a string of terminals. In the following examples, we observe the convention that all lower case letters and numbers are terminal symbols, and all upper case letters (or words which begin with an upper case letter) are non-terminal symbols. The starting non-terminal is always S unless otherwise specified. Each of the grammars represented here will be numbered (G1, G2, G3,...) for reference purposes. The first example is grammar G1, which consists of four rules, the terminal symbols {0,1}, and the starting non-terminal, S.

G1:

1. S –» 0S0
2. S –> 1S1
3. S –> 0
4. S –» 1

An example of a derivation using this grammar is:

S=>0S0=>00S00=>001S100=>0010100

Thus, 0010100 is in L(G1): it is one of the strings in the language of grammar G1. The student should find other derivations using G1, and verify that G1 specifies the language of palindromes of odd length over the alphabet {0,1}. A **palindrome** is a string which reads the same from left to right as it does from right to left.

L(G1)= {0, 1, 000, 010, 101, 111, 00000, ... }

In the next example, the terminal symbols are {a, b} (e represents the null string and is not a terminal symbol):

G2:

1. S –» ASB
2. S –» e
3. A –» a
4. B –» b

S=>ASB=>AASBB=>AaSBB=>AaBB=>AaBb=>Aabb=>aabb

Thus, aabb is in L(G2). G2 specifies the set of all strings of a's and b's which contain the same number of a's as b's, and in which all the a's precede all the b's. Note that the null string is permitted in a rewriting (or replacement) rule.

L(G2) ={ e, ab, aabb, aaabbb, aaaabbbb, aaaaabbbbb, ...}
= $\{a^n b^n\}$ such that n>0

This language is the set of all strings of a's and b's which consist of zero or more a's followed by exactly the same number of b's.

Two grammars, G1 and G2 are said to be **equivalent grammars** if L(G1) = L(G2) (they specify the same language). In this example (grammar G2) there can be several different derivations for a particular string, i.e., the rewriting rules could have been applied in a different sequence to arrive at the same result.

Show three different derivations using the grammar shown below: (terminal symbols {a,b})

1. S –> a S A
2. S –» B A
3. A –» a b
4. B –» b A

Solution

S=> a S A => a B A A => a B a b A => a B a b a b
=> a b A a b a b => a b a b a b a b S = > a S A = > a S a b =>
a B A a b => a b A A a b
= > a b a b A a b = > a b a b a b a b S = > B A = > b A A
=> b a b A => b a b a b

Note that in the solution to this problem we have shown that it is possible to have more than one derivation for the same string: abababab.

6.5J Symbol Table and Transducer

Two key components of the Transy compiler are the **symbol table** and a **transducer**.

The symbol table will be used to assign variable names and constants' addresses in core. The transducer will be used to place expressions from the assignment statement in a form easier to parse. The symbol table for the Transy compiler can be constructed by using two arrays. One will be an array of strings and the other an integer array. As previously stated, the core memory will be a float array of 1001 elements. Positions 0 through 999 will be used for storage of data assigned to tokens or variable names.

Position 1000 of core will be used to store a flag to signify errors or no errors in the translation phase of the compiler.

The source statement:

READ ABBY, CABBY, COMPILER

would translate as:

1 3 0 1 2 (the first 1 in the object line is the object token to signify that the source statement is READ; the 3 implies that 3 elements are to be read and the 0, 1 and 2 give the address of the storage location for the 3 values to read)

The **symbol table** would look as follows, assuming this was the first statement in a source program

Symbol table	variable name(token)	address
	ABBY	0
	CABBY	1
	COMPILER	2

Using the language C++, the symbol table could be defined as follows:

```
// symbol table
        string vn[100];
        int v_loc[100];
//
```

The code for the **symbol table** in C++ would look as follows:

```
getvarn(stng,tempv,&fav);  // stng is the source statement and tempv is
          //the name of a variable returned from the function getvarn.
          // fav is a parameter that tells where the next atom
          // is located in the source string, if another exist.
  found = -1;

  for(i = 0; i<nvars; ++i)
        // nvars is the number of variables already found.
  {
   if (strcmp(symbolt[i],tempv) ==0)
        // strcmp is a string compare function in C++.
    found = i;
             // if variable (tempv) is already in symbol table,
             // then found is  the location.
  }

   if (found ==-1)
        // found will be -1 if variable is not already in the string.
    {
    strcpy(symbolt[nvars], tempv);
        // variable is now copied into the string at the proper position.
    found = nvars;
    locvar[nvars] = nvloc;
    nvloc++;
    nvars++;
    }
```

```
tempa[nvf] = locvar[found];
nvf = nvf + 1;
        // nvf is number of variables found in a particular statement.
fav = fav + 1;
        // fav will add one to look for another var, if it exists.
}
```

To translate source statements, such as Z = A + B/C * D – F, from **infix notation** to **post-fix notation**, a **transducer** must be used. The transducer will change an expression from infix (var1 operator var2) to postfix (var1 var2 operator). The computer code necessary to understand the infix notation is difficult and prone to errors. A statement in postfix or **reverse Polish notation** is much easier to translate to object form and less prone to errors in the code.

The transducer used for the Transy compiler is given below:

INPUT SYMBOL

		Identifier	=	+,-	*,/	(	)	[	]	|
	Null	S1	S2	E	E	E	E	E	E	E
TOP OF	=	S1	E	S2	S2	S2	E	S1	U4	U3
S2	+,-	S1	E	U1	S2	S2	U2	S1	U4	U3
	*,/	S1	E	U1	U1	S2	U2	S1	U4	U3
	(	S1	E	S2	S2	S2	U2	S1	U4	U3
	)	S1	E	E	E	E	E	E	E	E
	[	S2	S2	S2	S2	S2	S2	E	E	E
	]	E	E	E	E	E	E	E	E	E

S1 = stack input onto S1
S2 = stack input onto S2
E = error occurred, input not valid
U1 = unstack S2 to S1, stack input onto S2(one element)
U2 = unstack S2 to S1 repeatedly until (is encountered; discard (
U3 = unstack S2 to S1 until S2 is empty
U4 = unstack S2 to S1 repeatedly until [is encountered, place [onto S1, discard]
| = End of Statement

Two stacks are operated by the **transducer**. Stack S1 is a push-down stack which stores the output of the machine, and stack S2 is a temporary 'scratch pad' memory used by the transducer during operation. For simplicity, only operands in the form of identifiers, operators [=,+,–,*,/], and parentheses will be allowed as input. The output set can consist of all of the above except parentheses. The Transy_source statement Z = A + B/C * D – F would be translated to object, using the above transducer, as follows:

Step #1	stack – 1	stack – 2	Z=A+B/C*D-F
	Z	=	
	A	+	
	B	/	
	C		
Step #2	Z	=	
	A	+	
	B	*	
	C		
	/		
	D		
Step #3	Z	=	
	A	+	
	B	–	
	C		
	/		
	D		
	*		
	F		
Step #4	Z		
	A		
	B		
	C		
	/		
	D		
	*		

F
–
+
=

The postfix expression becomes:

Z A B C / D * F – + =

The actual variable names and operators would be replaced with core addresses and negative integers representing the operators.

If this statement was the first source statement in a program, then the addresses assigned to the variables would be as shown below. The operators are assigned negative integers also as shown.

Variable	Address	Operator	Object Token Assigned
Z	0	+	-6
A	1	–	-7
B	2	*	-4
C	3	/	-5
D	4	=	-1
F	5		

The object code for the statement

Z = A + B/C * D – F becomes

20 0 1 2 3 -5 4 -4 5 -7 -6 -1

The leading 20 signifies that the statement is an assignment statement.

Chapter 6 Exercises

Exercise 1. Determine if the operations, intersection and union, obey the commutative and distributive laws for the set of integers.

Exercise 2. The set of real numbers is distributive with respect to normal multiplication, x, and addition, +. Determine if the set of complex numbers is distributive with respect to these operations? A complex number is a number of form a + bi where a and b are real and $i = \sqrt{-1}$.

Exercise 3. Given U = { x| x is a positive integer < 100 }, A = {x | x is an even positive integer < 90}, B = {3,5,7,9,... 99}. Find A', B', AUB, and A∩ B.

Exercise 4. U ={x | x is a compiler } and P = {Pascal compiler}, C = {C compiler}. Determine the following P', (P ∪ C)', P∩C, U∩P and (U∩P)'.

Exercise 5. Given the following sets.

U = {1,2,3,... 10}
A = {2,3,7,8,9}
B = {2,8}
C = {4,6,7,10}

Use Venn diagrams to represent each set, then shade A∩B, U∩C, and (A∩B∩C)' .

Exercise 6. For the following Venn diagram;

a. use the roster method to identify the sets A, B, C and U.

b. find $(A \cap B) \cup (A \cup C)$.

c. find $(A \cup B') \cap C'$.

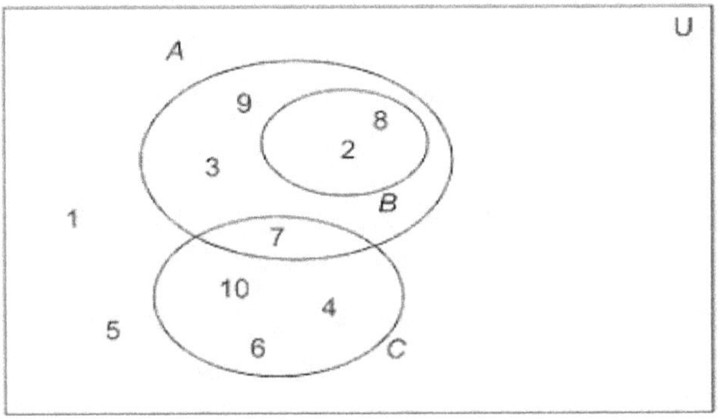

Exercise 7. For the C++ compiler, installed on your computer system (personal or school), determine if the string data type has fixed length or variable length. Are you able to determine the maximum size regardless if fixed or variable?

Exercise 8. Write a program in C++ or the language of your choice to input a string and a sub-string. Search the string to find the sub-string, and print the location where the sub-string starts in the string (first occurrence) or print "sub-string not found".

Exercise 9. Describe, in your own words, the language specified by each of the following finite-state machines, given their finite-state table with alphabet {a,b}.

(a)

	a	b
*A	A	B
*B	C	B
C	C	C

(b)

	a	b
A	B	B
*B	B	B

(c)

	a	b
A	A	B
B	C	B
*C	C	C

(d)

	a	b
A	B	B
*B	B	C
C	B	B

Exercise 10. Show a finite-state machine with input alphabet {0,1} which accepts any string having an even number of 1s and an odd number of 0s. Use both the finite-state table and the finite-state diagram.

Exercise 11. Use the transducer given in the text to translate the source statement Z = A*B + B/C *(D – F) to postfix notation.

Exercise 12. Given the grammar Gl:

1. S → 1S1
2. S → 0S0
3. S → 0
4. S → 1

with terminal symbols {0,1}, find derivations using Gl. Can you determine the language that G1 represents?

Exercise 13. Use the transducer given in the text to translate the infix expression Z = A*B/C + D – F*(A + B) to post-fix notation.

Exercise 14. Repeat exercise 13 for the expression:

Z = A[B] * C – (F[3] + G).

Exercise 15. Give an example of global optimization and an example of local optimization.

CHAPTER 7

The Translation Phase of the Compiler

INTRODUCTION

The translation phase is the heart of the compiler. During this phase of the compiler, **automata theory**, **transducers**, **symbol tables** and other tools are used to take each source statement and convert it to an object statement. The **Lexical Analysis** phase that determines the statement type is developed and will also generate the proper error message if the input string is not a statement of the language. Once the input string has been determined to be a statement of the language, the **Syntax Analysis** phase will generate the atomic parts of the string. Again, if the syntax of the language is not obeyed, then a proper error message will be generated. A transducer is used to take the assignment statement from infix notation to postfix notation – a form less difficult to translate. If the grammar of the language is proper, then each input statement (source statement) is converted to an output stream of numbers (object statement). If the input statement(s) do not obey all the rules of the language, then an error message or messages will be generated. If error(s) are found then at the completion of the translation phase, the source file will be listed to the screen and error message(s) will follow with some indication to the statement causing the error and reason for the error. Also, a flag (1) will be placed in position 1000 of core to indicate errors in translation. If the translation phase was successful (without errors), then an object file, a core file and literal file will be generated. A flag (0) will also be placed in position 1000 of core to indicate a successful translation. The source file will then be listed to the screen with an indication of a successful translation.

7.1 The Translation Process

The process from source to object:

Phases for conversion from source program to object:

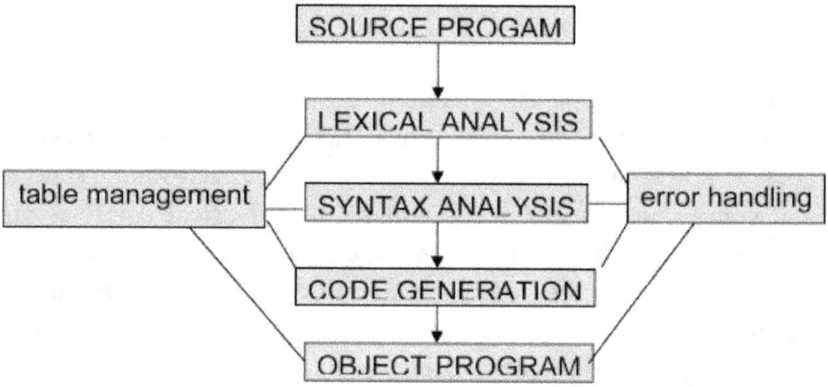

The translation process will consist of the following steps:

a. Input a Transy_source file, line by line, suppress all blanks, convert all input characters to lower case(or upper case) and write output to a second file; do not write any line starting with a C* to the second file (**first pass**).

b. Input the file created in (a), line by line, and remove any leading numbers or labels and place them in numeric form in an integer array and place the line number that the label was found in a second integer array. Write the new lines, without label, to a new file (**second pass**).

c. Input the file created in (b), line by line, and check the first part of each string for keywords (read, write, stop, if, etc) – the Lexical Scan (**third pass**).

d. If a key-word is found in (c) then pass the string to one of 20 functions that will perform the syntax analysis.

7.2 The Transy_Source Statements

Remember, the **key-words** for the Transy_source language are:

(a) DIM
(b) READ
(c) WRITE
(d) STOP
(e) CDUMP
(f) LISTO
(g) NOP
(h) GO TO
(i) IFA
(j) AREAD
(k) AWRITE
(l) SUBP
(m) LOOP
(n) LOOP-END
(o) LREAD
(p) LWRITE
(q) IF THEN
(r) CLS
(s) ASSIGNMENT
(t) END

Comment lines will be allowed. The comment line will appear as: C* COMMENT. The C* must be the first character of a comment line.

Each **Transy_source line**, properly formed, generates a corresponding **object line**. Our task will be to determine the type of source line, using the lexical scan, and then by using the syntax scan determine if the source line has the proper syntax and if so generate the object line. If the source line has errors, then a proper error message must be prepared for the programmer.

For each **executable source line** found without errors, an object line will be generated and written to the object file.

7.3 The Transy_Source with Corresponding Transy_object

A representative form of each source statement is given below with its corresponding object line. For more detail on each source and each object statement, see Chapters 4 and Chapter 5.

Statement: DIM (declare a variable an array)

SOURCE: DIM AA[10], AB[20]
Object code: 000 nn1 nn2

Statement: READ (input numbers and store in specified memory cell)

SOURCE: READ A1,B1,C1
Object code: 001 nn1 nn2 nn3 nn4

Statement: WRITE (list to the screen specified memory cells)

SOURCE: WRITE A1,B1,C1,Z1
Object code: 002 nn1 nn2 nn3 nn4 nn5

Statement: STOP (terminate execution of the object code)

SOURCE: STOP
Object code: 003

Statement: CDUMP (to list specified core memory to screen)

SOURCE: CDUMP A1,B1
Object code: 005 nn1 nn2

Statement: LISTO (list object program to screen)

SOURCE: LISTO
Object code: 006

Statement: NOP (label holder statement)

SOURCE: NOP
Object code: 007

Statement: GO TO (unconditional go to statement)

SOURCE: GO TO N1
Object code: 008 nn1

Statement: IFA (arithmetic if statement)

SOURCE: IFA(A1)3,5,7
Object code: 010 nn1 nn2 nn3 nn4

Statement: AREAD (input an array of numbers)

SOURCE: AREAD AA, N1, 7
Object code: 011 nn1 nn2 nn3

Statement: AWRITE (list an array of numbers to the screen)

SOURCE: AWRITE AA,7,11
Object code: 012 nn1 nn2 nn3

Statement: SUBP (subprogram call statement)

SOURCE: SUBP SIN(A1,A2)
Object code: 013 nn1 nn2 nn3

Statement: LOOP (beginning of a loop)

SOURCE: LOOP A1=1,5,N1
Object code: 014 nn1 nn2 nn3 nn4

Statement: LOOP-END (end of a loop)

SOURCE: LOOP-END
Object code: 015 nn1

Statement: LREAD (input a literal string)

SOURCE: LREAD LA
Object code: 016 nn1

Statement: LWRITE (list a literal string to the screen)

SOURCE: LWRITE LA or LWRITE “This_String”
Object code: 017 nn1

Statement: IF THEN (logical if statement)

SOURCE: IF(A|GT|B) THEN ST #
Object code: 018 nn1 nn2 nn3 nn4

Statement: CLS(clear screen)

SOURCE: CLS
Object code: 019

Statement: END (signifies the end of source input – non executable)

SOURCE: END
Object code: none generated

Statement: ASSIGNMENT (perform the indicated operation and store results)

SOURCE: Z = A * B / C ...
Object code: 020 nn1 nn2 nn3 nn4 ...

The lexical scan will take each source line and determine its keyword or type. Once the type has been determined, it will then pass the statement to a function that will use syntax analysis to determine if the rules of the language have been obeyed. If the rules have not been obeyed, then a proper error message will be generated. If the source line is proper, without errors, the syntax phase will break the statement into tokens (atoms). A symbol table will be used to assign variable names core addresses and to assign operators negative integers. The negative integer will uniquely define the operator.

Before the source program can be converted to object, some basic house keeping (front-end work) must be performed. A first pass is made of the source program that converts all input characters to upper case, suppresses all blanks and removes all comment lines. A pass is then made to strip statement labels and build a table of statement labels and corresponding statement location as to where the statement is found in the new source file. The new source file will then be upper case (or lower case) with comment lines and statement labels missing. This **new source file** (condensed source) will be read statement by statement and used in the lexical scan to get key-words (statement type). Once a **keyword** is found, this statement will be passed to the appropriate function to check for syntax. If the statement is formed properly (with proper syntax), it will be converted to object code. If the syntax was not proper, an appropriate error message will be generated. If no errors were found, the created object code for the statement will be written to the object file. As the statement is parsed, a **symbol table** will be built with **variable names** and corresponding **variable locations** in **core**. **Constants**, as they are found, will be given a location in core and the constant value will be placed in core. For the literal data and strings, however, the location in the symbol table for literal data will be the corresponding location in the literal file assigned to the literal string. Also, literal strings such as:

LWRITE "My_String"

My_String will be written in the file and its location will be stored with the token number 17 that is assigned to LWRITE. If this was the first time the literal file had been referenced, then the object code for this source line would be:

17 0

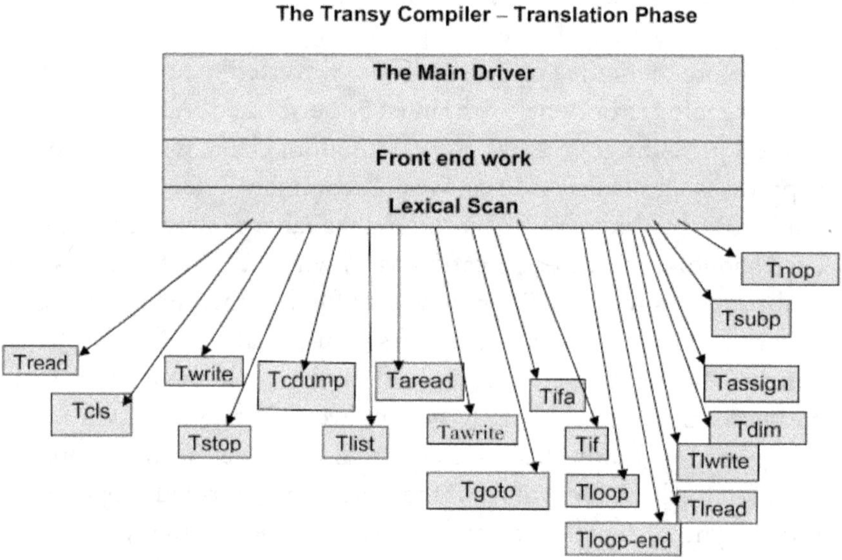

7.4 The Lexical Scan Process Given Pictorially

The main calling program for the translation phase has the following characteristics:

```
int main(int argc, char *argv[])
{
int tn,i;
char stng[74];
```

```
char sourcef[15]; // move argv[1] into this
cout<<"Input file parameters as follows \n";
cout<<" <tlc> <sourcefile> \n";

if (argc!=2) /* if 2 command line parameters haven't been passed */
{
 /* explain command line options */
 cout<<"Usage:\n  <tlc> <sourcefile>  \n";
 exit(1); /* exit with a error signal */
}

for(i=0;i<=strlen(argv[1]); ++i)
 sourcef[i] = argv[1][i];

firstp(sourcef); // suppress blanks, remove comments and place
                 // statement numbers and statement loc into arrays
icore(); // initialize core – global
         // object file obj[ ] [ ]  also global

 sfc.close();
 sfc.open("sourcefc.cpp", ios::in);
 while(!sfc.eof())
  {
  lics = lics +1;  //counts lines for error purposes
  sfc.getline(stng,70);

  tn = gettoken(stng);

  switch(tn)
   {
   case 0:
    tdim(stng);
    break;
   case 1:
    tread(stng);
    break;
   case 2:
```

```
twrite(stng);
break;
case 3:
tstop(stng);
break;
case 4:
terrors(stng);
break;
case 5:
tcdump(stng);
break;
case 6:
tlisto(stng);
break;
case 7:
tnop(stng);
break;
case 8:
tgoto(stng);
break;
case 9:
terrors(stng);
break;
case 10:
tifa(stng);
break;
case 11:
taread(stng);
break;
case 12:
tawrite(stng);
break;
case 13:
tsubp(stng);
break;
case 14:
tloop(stng);
```

```
  break;
 case 15:
  tloopend(stng);
  break;
 case 16:
  tlread(stng);
  break;
 case 17:
  tlwrite(stng);
  break;
 case 18:
  tif(stng);
  break;
 case 19:
  tcls(stng);
  break;
 case 20:
  tassgall(stng);
  break;
};

}
// now to write core to file before closing translation phase
fstream coref;
coref.open("core", ios::out);
core[1000] = ne;
for(i=0;i<1001; ++i)
 coref <<i<<' '<< core[i] <<endl;

// output symbol table and location
//  for(i=0;i<nvars; ++i)
//  cout<<symbolt[i]<<' '<<locvar[i]<<endl;

sf.close();
sf.open(sourcef, ios::in);
clrscr();
```

```
cout<< "The following program was compiled by the Transy
          Compiler"<<endl;
cout<<endl;
cout<< "Statement Number"<<"        "<<"   Statement "<<endl;
cout<<endl;
i = 0;
while(!sf.eof())
{
 sf.getline(stng,70);
 cout<<"   "<<i<<":-----   "<< stng<<endl;
 i = i + 1;
 }
 if(ne == 0)
 {
  cout<<endl<<endl;
  cout<<" No errors in translation"<<endl;
  }
 else
 {
  cout<<endl<<endl;
  cout<<" The following errors were found"<<endl;
  cout<<endl;
  for(i=0; i<ne; ++i)
   cout<<" At about "<<swe[i]<<' '<<errm[i]<<endl;
 }
return 0 ; // return 0 as signal of completion
} // end of main
```

7.5 The Syntax Analysis Given Pictorially

Once the lexical scan has determined the keyword, then the syntax analysis associated with each keyword is given below:

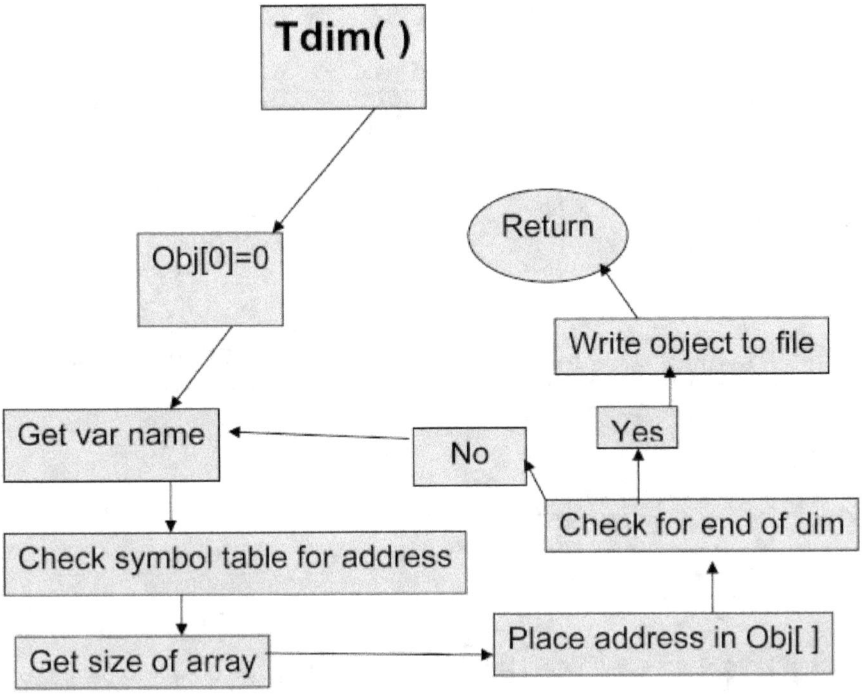

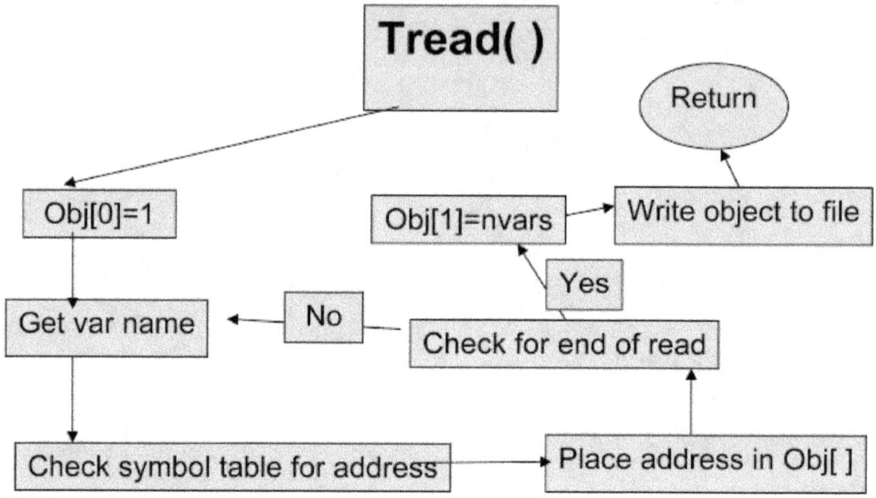
Tread( )
Return
Obj[0]=1
Obj[1]=nvars
Write object to file
Yes
Get var name
No
Check for end of read
Check symbol table for address
Place address in Obj[ ]

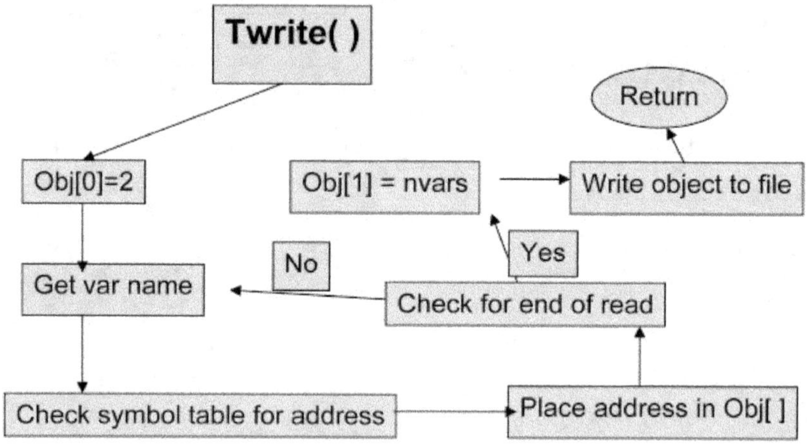
Twrite( )
Return
Obj[0]=2
Obj[1] = nvars
Write object to file
Yes
No
Get var name
Check for end of read
Check symbol table for address
Place address in Obj[ ]

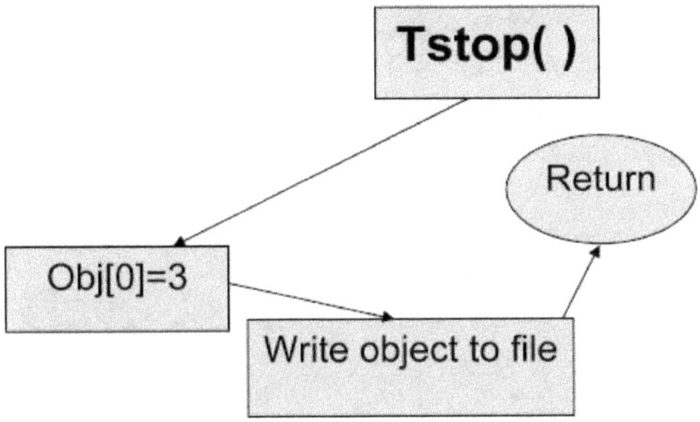
Tstop( )
Return
Obj[0]=3
Write object to file

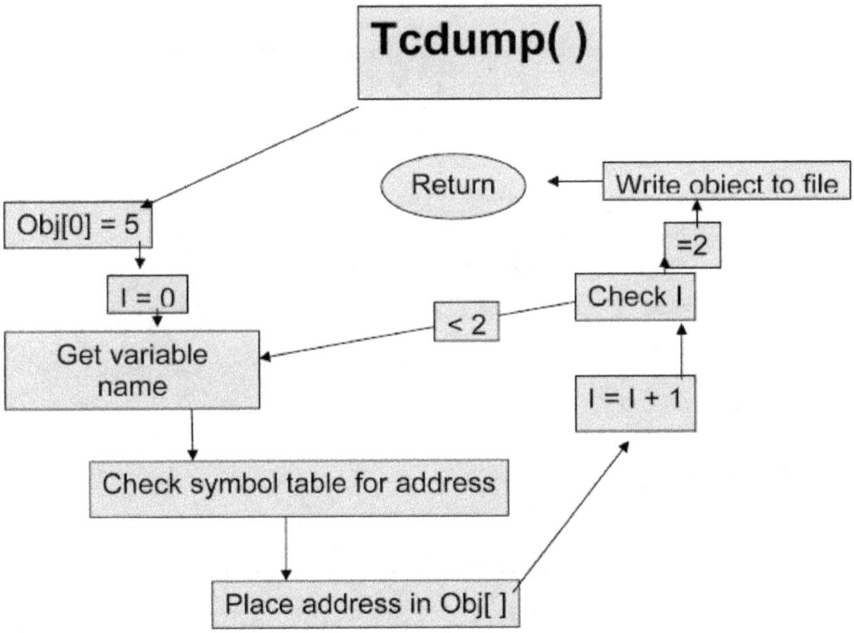
Tcdump( )
Return
Write object to file
Obj[0] = 5
=2
I = 0
Check I
< 2
Get variable name
I = I + 1
Check symbol table for address
Place address in Obj[ ]

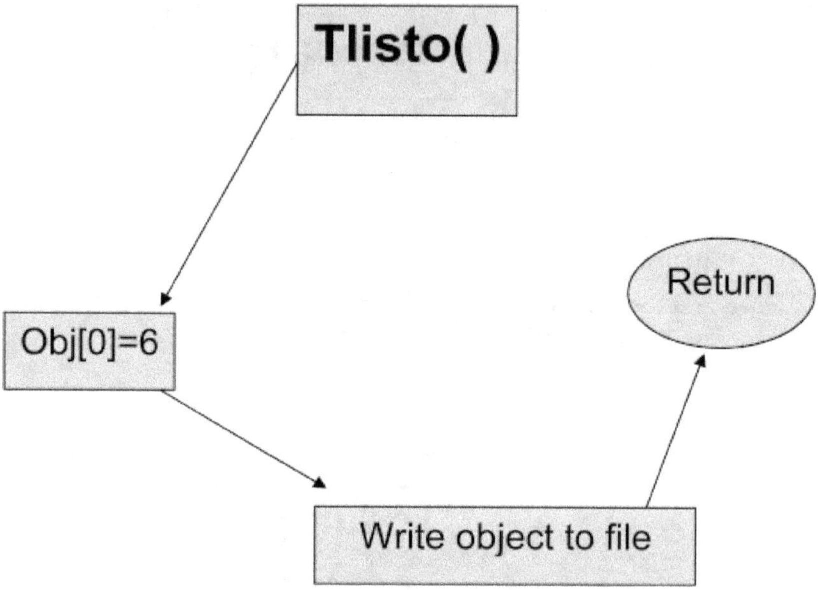
Tlisto( )
Obj[0]=6
Return
Write object to file

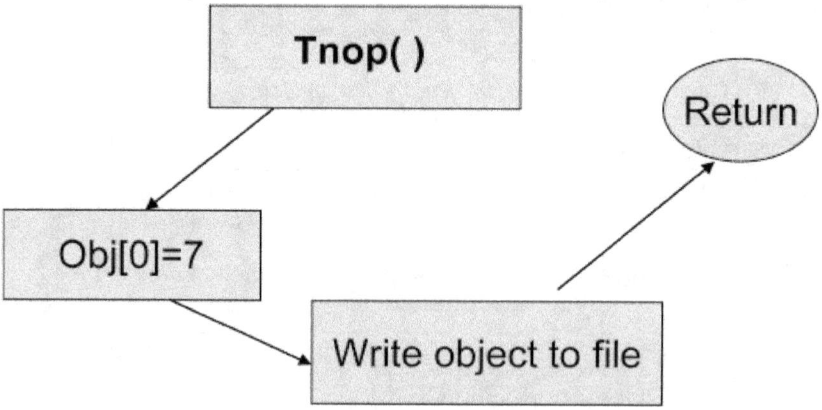
Tnop( )
Return
Obj[0]=7
Write object to file

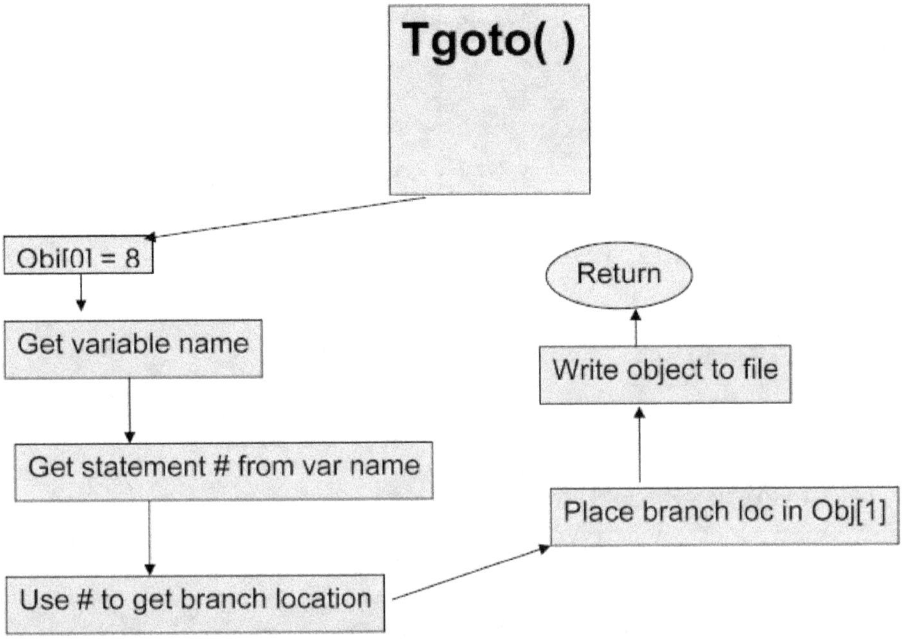
Tgoto( )
Obj[0] = 8
Get variable name
Get statement # from var name
Use # to get branch location
Place branch loc in Obj[1]
Write object to file
Return

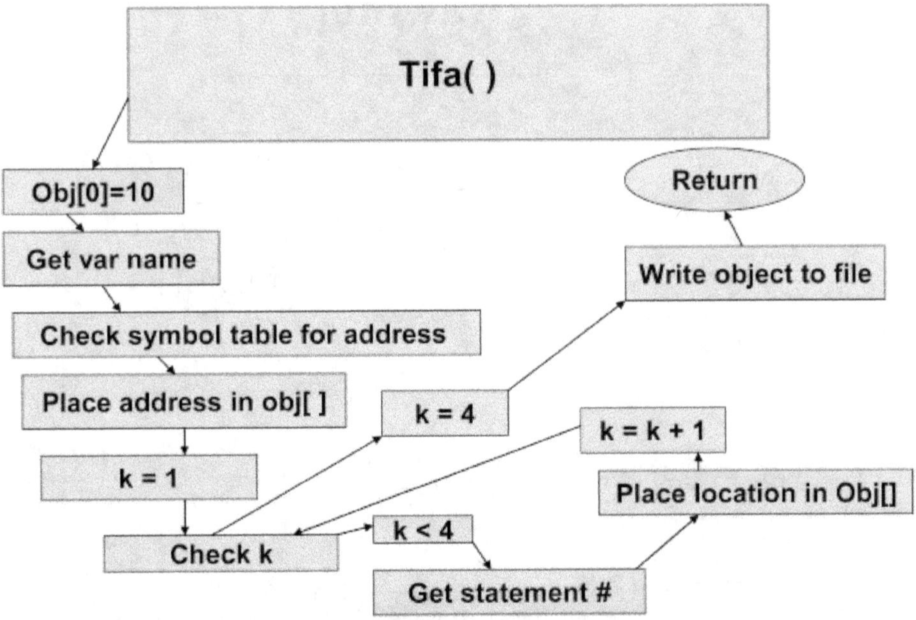
Tifa( )
Obj[0]=10
Get var name
Check symbol table for address
Place address in obj[ ]
k = 1
Check k
k = 4
k < 4
Get statement #
Place location in Obj[]
k = k + 1
Write object to file
Return

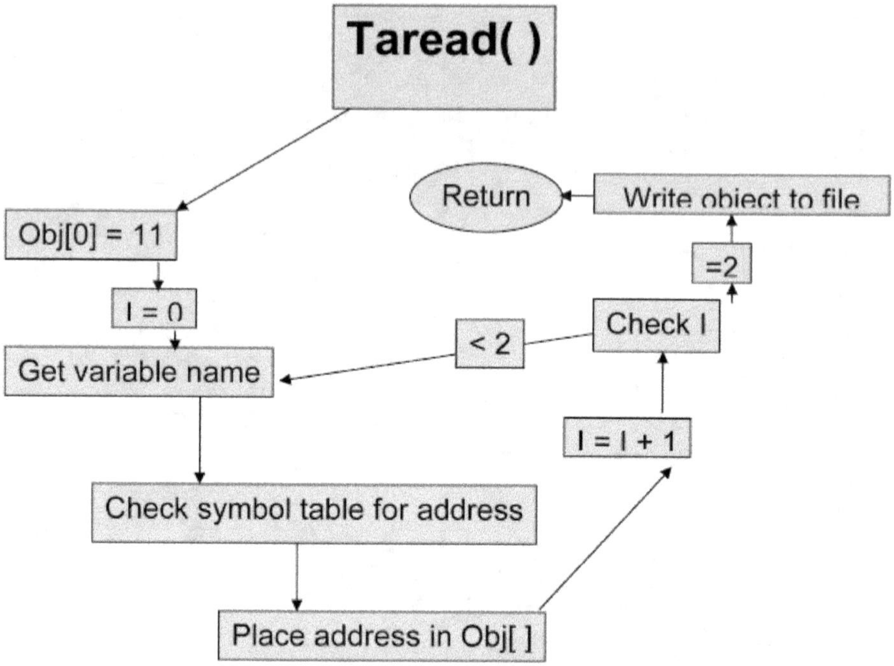
Taread( )
Return
Write object to file
Obj[0] = 11
=2
I = 0
Check I
< 2
Get variable name
I = I + 1
Check symbol table for address
Place address in Obj[ ]

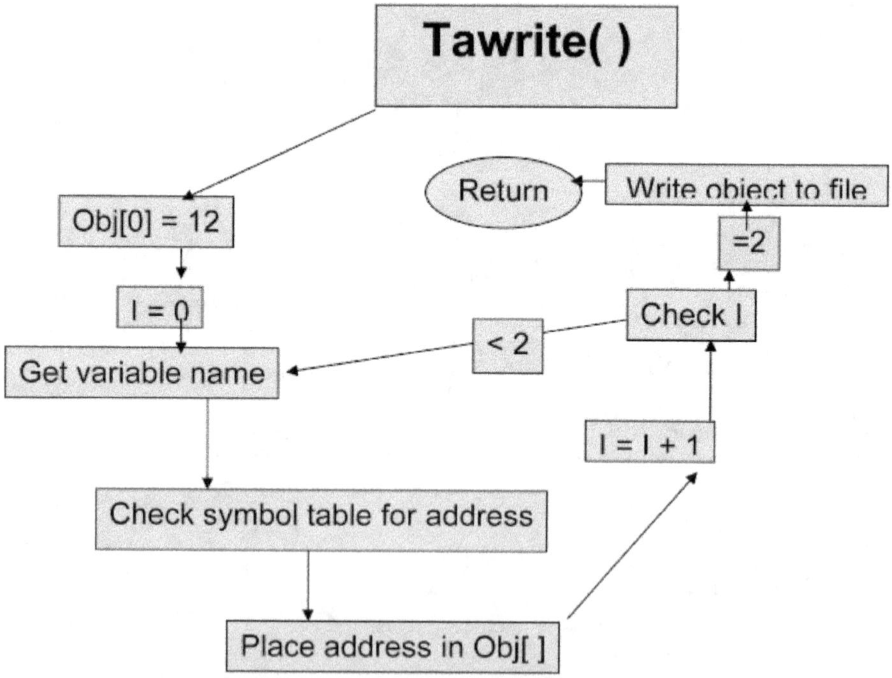
Tawrite( )
Return
Write object to file
Obj[0] = 12
=2
I = 0
Check I
< 2
Get variable name
I = I + 1
Check symbol table for address
Place address in Obj[ ]

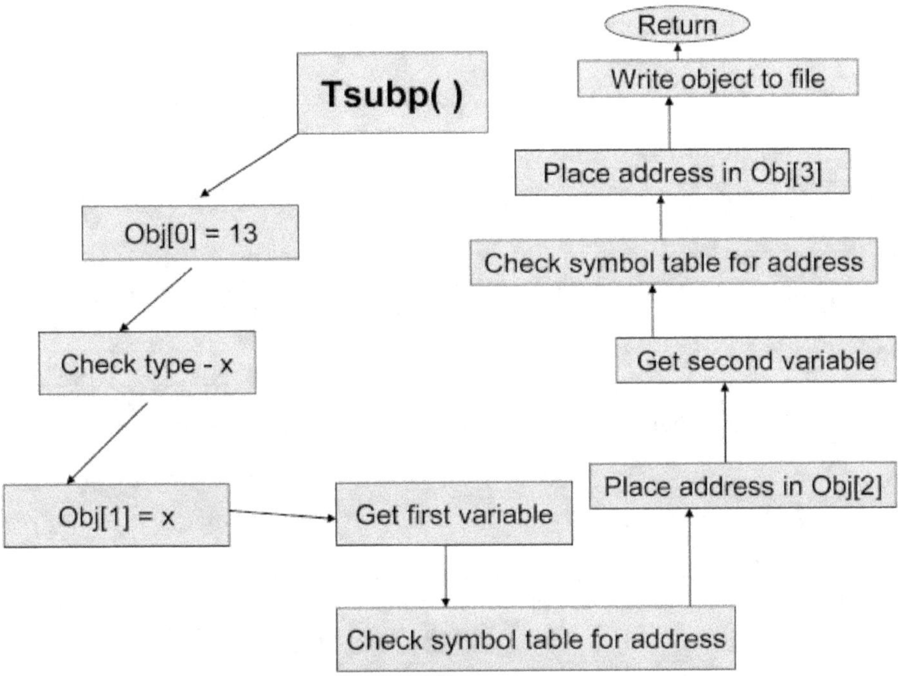
Return
Tsubp( )
Write object to file
Place address in Obj[3]
Obj[0] = 13
Check symbol table for address
Check type - x
Get second variable
Place address in Obj[2]
Obj[1] = x
Get first variable
Check symbol table for address

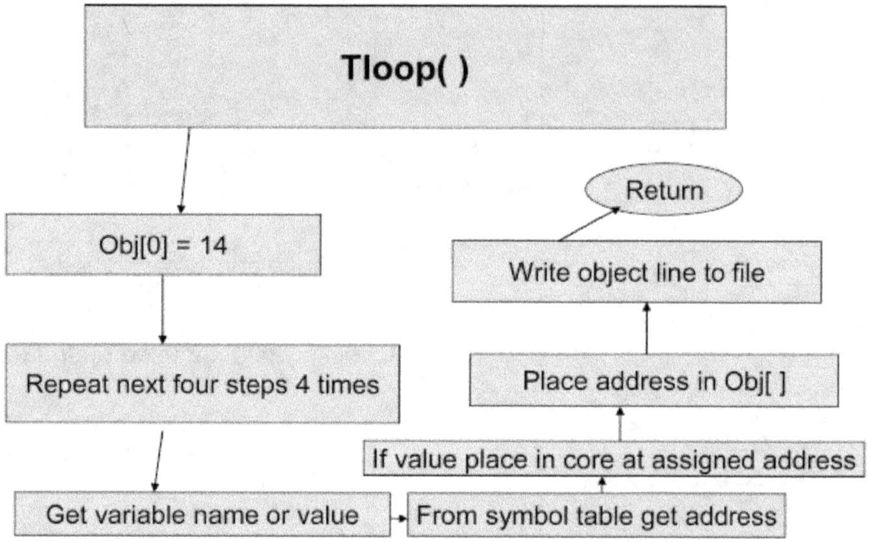
Tloop( )
Return
Obj[0] = 14
Write object line to file
Repeat next four steps 4 times
Place address in Obj[ ]
If value place in core at assigned address
Get variable name or value
From symbol table get address

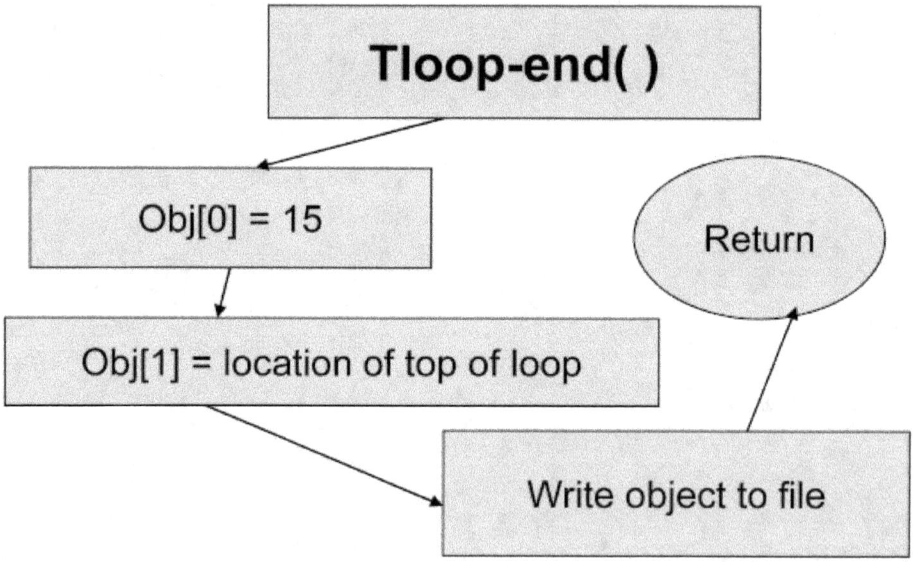
Tloop-end( )
Obj[0] = 15
Return
Obj[1] = location of top of loop
Write object to file

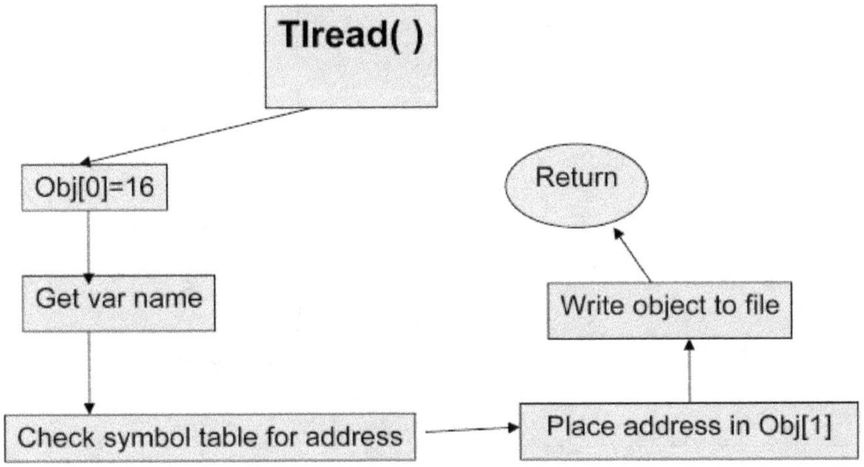
Tlread( )
Obj[0]=16
Get var name
Check symbol table for address
Place address in Obj[1]
Write object to file
Return

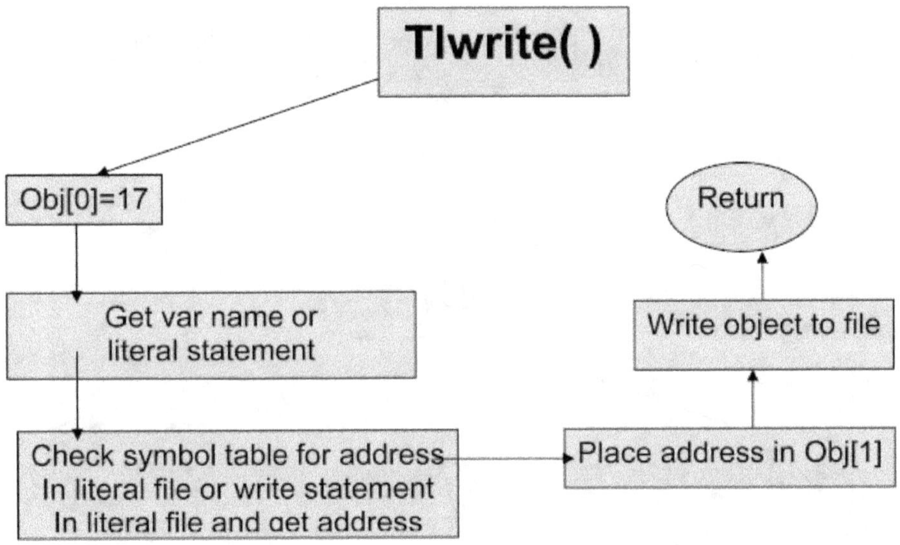
Tlwrite( )
Obj[0]=17
Get var name or
literal statement
Check symbol table for address
In literal file or write statement
In literal file and get address
Place address in Obj[1]
Write object to file
Return

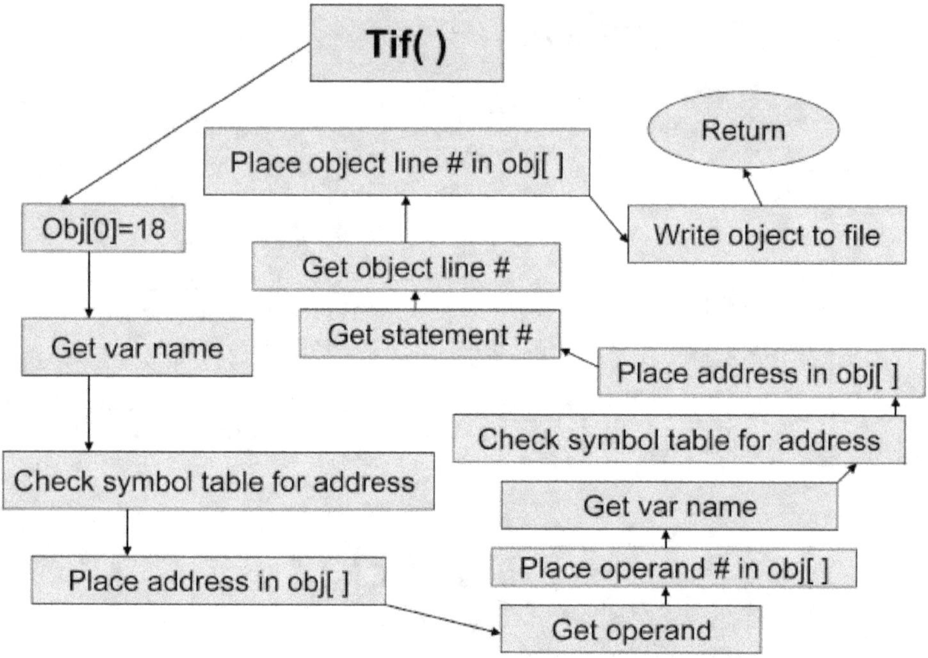
Tif( )
Obj[0]=18
Get var name
Check symbol table for address
Place address in obj[ ]
Get operand
Place operand # in obj[ ]
Get var name
Check symbol table for address
Place address in obj[ ]
Get statement #
Get object line #
Place object line # in obj[ ]
Write object to file
Return

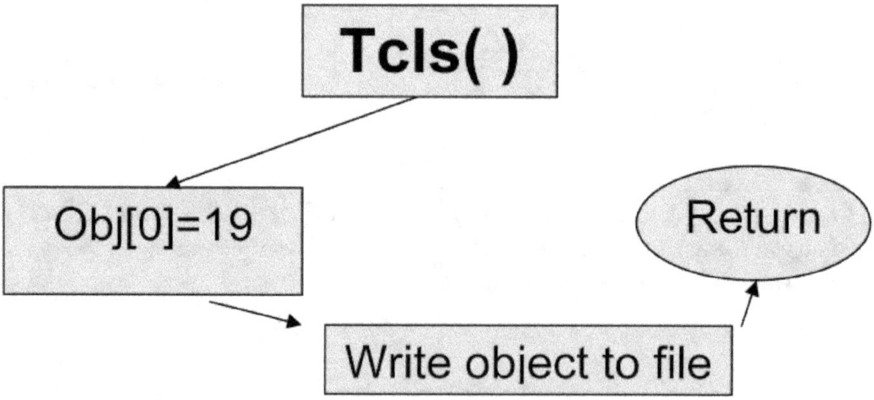
Tcls( )
Obj[0]=19
Write object to file
Return

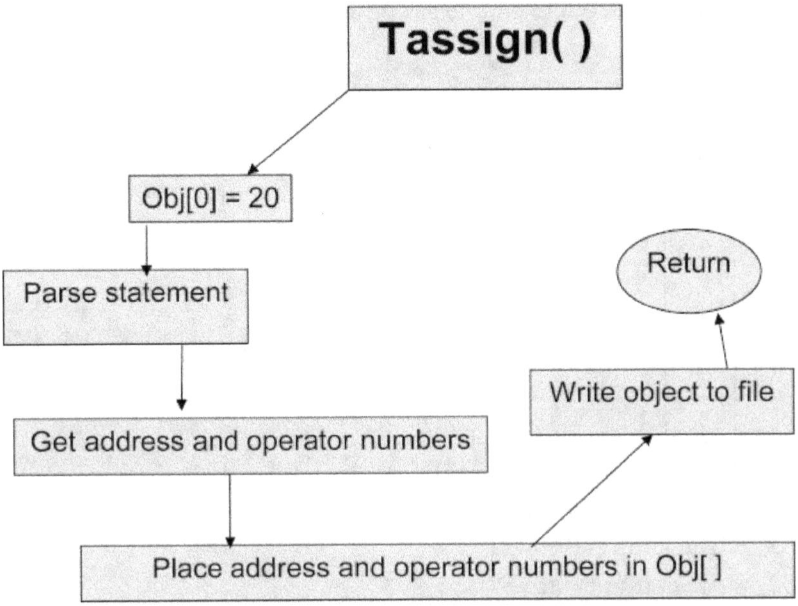

7.6 Parsing the Assignment Statement

The standard mathematical notation used in assignment statements is called **infix** notation, because each operator has an operand before and after it. This results in backward and forward scanning and the creation of nested partial results as can be seen in the expression:

A=(A-B/A*5)+3

the B/A is nested within the expression, yet it is a partial result that must be obtained first. How are we to simplify the expression so that partial results may be obtained as we move from left to right? We must use postfix notation (a form of Polish notation introduced by the logician, Lukasiewicz) to overcome the problem of nesting. A postfix expression is one in which all operators follow the operands reading from left to right. They are of the form OPERAND OPERAND OP. The infix notation is converted to postfix. The postfix is then used to generate a machine language statement for the given source language statement.

The infix-to-postfix algorithm is called a transducer, because it converts an input into an output of different form. The transducer is guided by a precedence table as shown below:

INPUT SYMBOL

		Identifier	=	+,-	*,/	(	)	[	]	|
	Null	S1	S2	E	E	E	E	E	E	E
TOP OF	=	S1	E	S2	S2	S2	E	S1	U4	U3
S2	+,-	S1	E	U1	S2	S2	U2	S1	U4	U3
	*,/	S1	E	U1	U1	S2	U2	S1	U4	U3
	(	S1	E	S2	S2	S2	U2	S1	U4	U3
	)	S1	E	E	E	E	E	E	E	E
	[	S2	S2	S2	S2	S2	S2	E	E	E
	]	E	E	E	E	E	E	E	E	E

S1 = stack input onto S1
S2 = stack input onto S2
E = error occurred, input not valid
U1 = unstack S2 to S1, stack input onto S2(one element)
U2 = unstack S2 to S1 repeatedly until (is encountered; discard (
U3 = unstack S2 to S1 until S2 is empty
U4 = unstack S2 to S1 repeatedly until [is encountered, place [
onto S1, discard]
| = End of Statement

Two stacks are operated by the transducer; stack S1 is a push-down stack which stores the output of the machine, and stack S2 is a temporary 'scratch pad' memory used by the transducer during operation. For simplicity, only operands in the form of identifiers, operators [=,+,-,*,/], and parentheses will be allowed as input. The output set will consist of all of the above except parentheses.

The table will be encoded into an array which 'drives' the transducer by telling it what to do with each input symbol.

The given transducer will transform the statement (string):

Z = A + B

into the string

ZAB+=

If only simple variable names such as A0...A9, ...,Z0...Z9 are permitted then a detailed **symbol table** is not necessary. A mathematical formula can be developed to assign each variable name an address in core (loc = (first character – 'A') *10 + (second character – '0')). However, if one chooses to use more general variable names, then a symbol table will be essential. Array names will be defined in the same manner as non-array variables: at most eight characters in length (preferred but not fixed), no special characters (again preferred but not fixed) other than '_' and starting with 'a' ... 'z'.

The table to encode the transducer to parse the assignment statement is given below:

INPUT

TOP OF S2

-10	-1	-6	-7	-4	-5	-2	-3	-8	-11	-12
0	1	2	2	2	2	2	2	2	2	2
-1	2	1	1	1	1	1	2	5	1	6
-6	2	3	3	1	1	1	4	5	1	6
-7	2	3	3	1	1	1	4	5	1	6
-4	2	3	3	3	3	1	4	5	1	6
-5	2	3	3	3	3	1	4	5	1	6
-2	2	1	1	1	1	1	4	5	1	6
-3	2	2	2	2	2	2	2	2	2	2
-11	1	1	1	1	1	1	1	2	2	2
-12	1	1	1	1	1	1	1	1	1	1

OPERATOR/GRID ELEMENT

= / -1	S2=1
(/ -2	E=2
) / -3	U1=3
* / -4	U2=4
/ / -5	U3=5
+ / -6	U4=6
- / -7	
| / -8	
[/ -11	
]/ -12	

EXAMPLE:

The infix expression

A = C + D / E - 14.76 * G * (C + E)

when converted to postfix by the above transducer becomes

A C D E / 14.76 G * C E + * – + =

with the following addresses assigned

A(1), C(2), D(3), E(4), 14.76(5), G(6)

The object code for the expression becomes

20 1 2 3 4 -5 5 6 -4 2 4 -6 -4 -7 -6 -1

The leading 20 implies that this object line is an assignment statement. The flow diagrams and transducer given above are used to convert each Transy_source statement to a Transy_object statement. Any high-level programming language could be used to make this conversion; however, here most of our illustrations are with the language C++. The checks necessary to determine syntax errors are left as programming exercises for the reader.

The notation in this text will be that the source statement with keyword READ will have the corresponding C++ function TREAD( ) that translates the source statement to object. Similarly, for the keyword LOOP, the C++ function TLOOP() will translate the source statement to object.

7.7 Programming Projects Used in Translation Conversion

The following 13 projects will take the Transy_source statements and convert to Transy_object statements.

Programming project #1. This programming project is part of the "front-end" of the compiler and is used to take the source file as input and output a new source file with all blanks suppressed and all characters to lower case (upper or lower case at compiler writer's option).

Write a subprogram to input a file of characters, line by line, suppress all blanks from each line, convert to lower case and then write new line to a second file.

Example of input:

C* this line will be a comment line in our language
Dimension will be used to specify arrays
This is line one of input.
1234 Line two of input is very similar to line one.
This would be easy if I knew what was asked of me.

Output:

c*thislinewillbeacommentlineinourlanguage
dimensionwillbeusedtospecifyarrays
thisislineoneofinput.
1234linetwoofinputisverysimilartolineone.
thiswouldbeeasyifIknewwhatwasaskedofme.

Calling sequence for the function with function header line is:

suppblnk( ); void suppblnk(void)

Programming project #2. This programming project is part of the "front-end" of the compiler and is used to remove statement labels from each source statement and remove all comment lines from the source file.

Write a subprogram that will take the suppressed blanks file, created in project #1 and remove all leading numbers (labels) from the file. Place the numbers or labels and the line in the file that the numbers were found into arrays sna[], sla[] – these arrays will be of integer type. Also, keep track of the number of statement labels – nsn. If any line starts with C*, do not increase the line number count for these lines. Write the new source lines with the numbers (labels) missing into a new file. Do not write any C* lines into the new file.

<u>Example of input:</u>

c*thislinewillbeacommentlineinourlanguage
dimensionwillbeusedtospecifyarrays
thisislineoneofinput.
1234linetwoofinputisverysimilartolineone.
thiswouldbeeasyifIknewwhatwasaskedofme.

<u>Output:</u>

dimensionwillbeusedtospecifyarrays
thisislineoneofinput.
linetwoofinputisverysimilartolineone.
thiswouldbeeasyifIknewwhatwasaskedofme.

nsn = 1
sna[0] = 1234 sla[0] = 2

Calling sequence for the function with function header line is:

nsn=stripnums(sna,sla); int stripnums(int sna[],int sla[])

Programming Project #3. This programming project will determine the keyword of each statement.

Write a function that takes as input a string and then checks the beginning of the string with a set of sub-strings for a match. Each sub-string will be at most 12 characters in length. The set of sub-strings will be ordered 0 thru 20. If a match is found, return the order number, otherwise return 20.

Strings:
int gettoken(char stng[ ]);
char *tokens[21] = {“dim”, “read”, “write”, “stop”, “xxx”, “cdump”,
“listo”,”nop”, “goto”, “xxx”, “ifa”, “aread”,
“awrite”, “subp”, “loop”, “loop-end”, “lread”,
“lwrite”, “if”, “cls”,”xxx”};

<u>Example of input:</u>

writea,b,c,d

<u>Value returned from function call</u>:

2

Programming Project #4. This programming project will get a token (variable name, operator, etc.) from a string.

Write a function that takes as input a string and an integer pointer (‘is’). Check the string starting at the position pointed to by the pointer (‘is’) for one of several delimiters. If a delimiter is found, and it should be, call the position that the delimiter was found, ‘ie’. Move the string from ‘is’ to ‘ie – 1’ to a sub-string called tempv, place an end of string marker at the end of tempv and return tempv to the calling program. Also, reset the pointer ‘is’ to the position the delimiter was found.

Delimiters and calling sequence:

void getvarn(char stng[], char tempv[], int &fav)
{
char delim[] = {‘,’,’+’,’-’,’*’,’/’,’)’,‘(’,’]’,’[’,’=’,’|’,’\0’};

Example of string passed:

abby=cabby+doggy/horsie

If the pointer passed, pointed to position 0 of stng[ ], then tempv, when returned would contain 'Abby' and the pointer would be to position 4.

Programming Project #5. This programming project will build a symbol table.

Write a function that takes the sub-string returned from programming project #4 (tempv) and build an array of unique sub-strings. This array of sub-strings combined with an integer array pointing to the memory locations assigned to tempv will constitute the symbol table. Also, keep a total of the unique sub-string and check the sub-string returned against those in the array and if not found then place tempv in the array and increase the number of unique sub-strings by one. Also update the integer array which contains the address in core assigned to the unique sub-string – the variable name. The core address will start with 0 and increase by one for each non-array name. If the variable name returned was an array name, then you will increase the position of the next core address by the size of the array and not by one, unless the size of the array was just one. If the variable is an array, you will need to get the size of the array to adjust the next location in core.

It is best to declare the following as global.

```
fstream sf;      // initial source file
fstream sfc;     // source file condensed
fstream  objf; // object file that will eventually be created

char *symbolt[] = {"    "",    "",    "",    ",
                    "    "",    "",    "",    "};
// will contain variable names and may want to open space for
//as many as 25 variables.

int locvar[25];   // will contain variable locations
```

```
int nvars = 0;   // number of variables
int nvloc = 0;   // next variables location in core, will be the same
                 // as nvars unless arrays have been declared.

// symbolt[ ] together with locvar[ ] will be your symbol table
// – nvars will be the
// number of unique variables in the symbol table and nvloc will
// point to the next variable location in core.
```

Example of input and output:

If the string passed to programming project #5 was

abby=cabby+doggy/horsie

and the pointer was 5, which points to "c" in cabby then tempv string returned should be cabby with the pointer now at 10 which points to "+" before doggy.

Assuming that abby had already been placed in the symbol table by a previous call and cabby was not in the symbol table then the status would now be:

symbolt[0] = "abby"
symbolt[1] = "cabby"

locvar[0] = 0
locvar[1] = 1

nvars = 2
nvloc = 2

Programming Project #6. This programming project will translate the READ, WRITE and STOP statements.

a)Write a function that takes the source string
reada,bb,funfun12

and creates the object line

1 3 0 1 2

and then writes this object line to the object file.

b)Write a function that takes the source string
writea,bb,funfun12

and creates the object line

2 3 0 1 2

and then writes this object line to the object file.

c)Write a function that takes the source string
stop

and creates the object line

3

and then writes this object line to the object file.

The numbers 0, 1 and 2 in a) and b) will be dependent on core addresses assigned to variable names a, bb, funfun12 by the symbol table.

Programming Project #7. This programming project will translate the CDUMP, LISTO and NOP statements.

a)Write a function that takes the source string
cdumpstartd,enddump

and creates the object line

5 3 4
and then writes this object line to the object file.

b)Write a function that takes the string

listo

and creates the object line

6

and then writes this object line to the object file.

c)Write a function that takes the string

nop

and creates the object line

7

and then writes this object line to the object file.

The numbers 3 and 4 in a) will be dependent on core addresses assigned to variable names *startd* and *enddump* by the symbol table.

Programming Project #8. This programming project will translate the GO TO, DIM and IFA statements.

a)Write a function that takes the string:

goto20

and creates the object line:

8 22

and then writes this object line to the object file.

The 22 above is the line number in the object file of statement with label 20.

b)Write a function that takes the string:

dimaa[20]

and places the aa in the symbol table and increases the *next variable position* by 20.

Nothing needs to be written to the object file.

c)Write a function that takes the string:

ifa(var1)33,44,55

and creates the object line:

10   12 14 11 18

and then writes this object line to the object file.

The number 12 is the core address assigned to var1 in the symbol table. The numbers 14, 11 and 18 are the locations in the object file of statements with labels of 33, 44 and 55.

Programming Project #9. This programming project will translate the AREAD and AWRITE statements.

a)Write a function that takes the string:(any of these forms)

areadaa,n1,n2
areadaa,n1,15
areadaa,15,n2
areadaa,1,20

and creates the object line:

11   22 33 44

and then writes this object line to the object file.

The numbers 22, 33 and 44 are the core addresses assigned to the three arguments that follow the aread.

b)Write a function that takes the string:(any of these forms)

awriteaa,n1,n2
awriteaa,n1,15
awriteaa,15,n2
awriteaa,1,20
and creates the object line:

12 22 33 44

and then writes this object line to the object file.

The numbers 22, 33 and 44 are the core addresses assigned to the three arguments that follow the awrite.

Programming Project #10. This programming project will translate the SUBP and LOOP statements.

a) Write a function that takes the string:(any of these forms)

subpsin(a,b)	x below will have the value of 1
subpcos(a,b)	x below will have the value of 2
subpexp(a,b)	x below will have the value of 3
subpalg(a,b)	x below will have the value of 4
subpacg(a,b)	x below will have the value of 5
subpabs(a,b)	x below will have the value of 6
sybpsqr(a,b)	x below will have the value of 7

and creates the object line:

13 x 33 44

and then writes this object line to the object file.

The 33 and 44 above are the core addresses assigned by the symbol table to the arguments "a" and "b".

b) Write a function that takes the string (must allow for n2, n3 and n4 to be constants or variable names – n1 must be a variable name)

loopn1=n2,n3,n4

and creates the object line:

14 12 24 33 44

and then writes this object line the object file.

The 12, 24, 33 and 44 above are core addresses assigned by the symbol table to the arguments n1, n2, n3, n4.

Programming Project #11. This programming project will translate the LOOP-END, LREAD and LWRITE statements.

a)Write a function that takes the string:

loop-end

and creates the object line

15 7

and then writes this object line to the object file.

The 7 is the object file location of the loop statement that begins this loop.

b)Write a function that takes the string:

lreadla

and creates the object line:

16 1

and then writes this object line to the object file.

The la will be placed in the symbol table like other variables, but its value will point to the locations in the literal file where data string will be stored. The programmer will be alerted not to name literal variables the same as regular variables. The 1 is the location in the literal file that was assigned to la.

c) Write a function that takes the string:

lwritela *other form* lwrite"Input"

and creates the object line:

17 1

and then writes this object line to the object file.

The la will be placed in the symbol table or will be there already and its location in the literal file will be returned (for this example, the value of 1 was returned). If literal data is of form "Input" then "Input" must be written to the literal file at the location assigned by the symbol table. The assigned location in this example was 1.

Programming Project #12. This programming project will translate the IF and CLS statements.

a) Write a function that takes the string:

if(a|gt|b)then30

and creates the object line:

18 2 10 20 5

and then writes this object line to the object file.

The 'a' and 'b' will be placed in the symbol table, and in this instance they have been assigned addresses of 10 and 20. The 2 represents the token number for the relational operator > and the 5 represents the statement location in object file of the statement with label of 30.

The token numbers for the relational operators are:

1 < (|lt|), 2 > (|gt|), 3 = (|eq|), 4 <= (|le|), 5 >= (|ge|),
6 <> (|ne|)

b)Write a function that takes the string:

cls

and creates the object line:

19

and then writes this object line to the object file.

Programming Project #13. This programming project will translate the ASSIGNMENT statement.

a) Write a function that takes the source string:

A = C + D / E - 14.76 * G * (C + E)

and converts to postfix by the given transducer and then creates the proper object line and writes it to the object file.

The above source line becomes the following when placed in reverse-Polish

A C D E / 14.76 G * C E + * – + =

then with the assigned addresses

A(1), C(2), D(3), E(4), 14.76(5), G(6)

the object code for the expression becomes

1 2 3 4 -5 5 6 -4 2 4 -6 -4 -7 -6 -1

and the object code with 20 signifying an assignment statement

20 1 2 3 4 -5 5 6 -4 2 4 -6 -4 -7 -6 -1

the object line will then be written to the object file.

Note that the positive numbers after 20 will be for addresses in core and negative numbers are token numbers assigned to operators.

The following algorithm is a representation of how to implement the above transducer, however, use with caution (i.e. understand before using).

```
int S1 [25], S2[25], NS1 = 0, NS2 = 0;
char oper [13] = {'x', '=', '(',')', '*', '/', '+', '-', '\0', 'x', 'x', ' [', '] '};
```

→ get var place address in S1

→ check STNG[fav] against oper [I] → save found = i.
(fav is the position of next variable or operator)

Make VAL = (-1)*FOUND;
If VAL = -1 place VAL on S2

If VAL = -2 place VAL on S2

If VAL = -3 unstack S2 to S1 until -2 found (discard – 2)

If VAL = -4 or -5 If top S2 – 1, -2, -6, -7 place VAL on S2
If top S2 – 4, -5 take one value from S2 place on S1, place VAL on S2

If VAL = -6 or -7 top of S2-1 or -2 place VAL on S2
top of S2 – 4, -5, -6, -7
take one value from S2 place on S1, place VAL on S2

If VAL = -11 place VAL on S2

If VAL = -12 unstack S2 to S1 until –11 found, place –11 on S1, discard -12

→ if end of string place S2 to S1 until S2 empty

→ copy S1 to object line (place a 20 at the beginning of the object line).

CHAPTER 8

The Execution Phase of the Compiler

INTRODUCTION

The **execution phase** of the compiler takes as input the information generated from the translation phase of the compiler. If the translation was a success, then the execution phase will sequentially perform the steps of the original algorithm.

The **object file**, the **core file** and the **literal file** are all passed from the **translation phase** to the **execution phase**. The "**front-end**" segment of the execution phase will load the three files into memory. The core file is loaded first into a float array core[1001]. Position 1000 of core is then checked to determine if the translation was a success or failure. If core[1000] contains a 1, then the translation contained an **error(s)** and execution will terminate with the indication of error(s) in translation. Otherwise, the object file is loaded into a two-dimensional integer array obj[150][50]. Here we are specifying that the object will never contain more than 150 lines and the maximum length of any object line will be 50. The literal file is then loaded into an array of strings stng[50]. We are assuming that 50 will be the maximum number of literal strings in any program.

8.1 The Basic Statements of the Transy Language

The basic source and object statements for the Transy Language are:

SOURCE: DIM AA[10], AB[20]
Object code: 000 nn1 nn2 (if created)

SOURCE: READ A1,B1,C1
Object code: 001 nn1 nn2 nn3 nn4

SOURCE: WRITE A1,B1,C1,Z1
Object: 002 nn1 nn2 nn3 ...nn11

SOURCE: STOP
Object code: 003

SOURCE: CDUMP A1,B1
Object code: 005 nn1 nn2

SOURCE: LISTO
Object code: 006

SOURCE: NOP
Object code: 007

SOURCE: GO TO N1
Object code: 008 nn1

SOURCE: IFA(A1)3,5,7
Object code: 010 nn1 nn2 nn3 nn4

SOURCE: AREAD AA, N1, 7
Object code: 011 nn1 nn2 nn3

SOURCE: AWRITE AA,7,11
Object code: 012 nn1 nn2 nn3

SOURCE: SUBP FUN(A1,A2)
Object code: 013 nn1 nn2 nn3

SOURCE: LOOP A1=1,5,N1
Object code: 014 nn1 nn2 nn3 nn4 0

SOURCE: LOOP-END
Object code: 015 nn1

SOURCE: LREAD LA
Object code: 016 nn1

SOURCE: LWRITE LA or LWRITE "This_String"
Object code: 017 nn1

SOURCE: IF(A|gt|B) THEN ST #
Object code: 018 nn1 nn2 nn3 nn4

SOURCE: CLS
Object code: 019

SOURCE: END
Object code: none generated

SOURCE: Z = A * B / C ...
Object code: 020 nn1 nn2 nn3 ...

8.2 The Execution Process

EXECUTION PHASE:

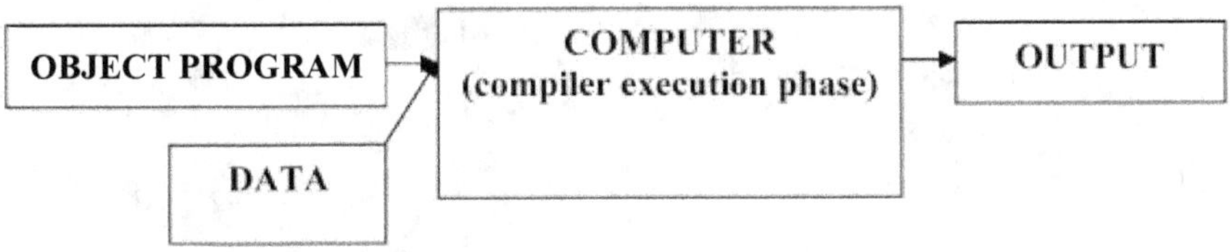

The following steps will be taken to execute the program:

1. Set object line pointers as follows: (LC – location counter) IP <-- 0, IC <-- 0, IN <-- 1 (IP previous object line executed, IC current object line – one to execute, IN next object line to execute after current).
2. Read object line --> IC.
3. Determine the type of object line and branch to specified function.
4. Execute object line --> If STOP OR ERROR then 7.
5. Redefine LC
   IP <-- IC, IC <-- IN OR B(L), IN <-- IC + 1
   B(L) – branch location.
6. Repeat 2.
7. Terminate with proper message.

8.3 The Execution Flow Diagrams

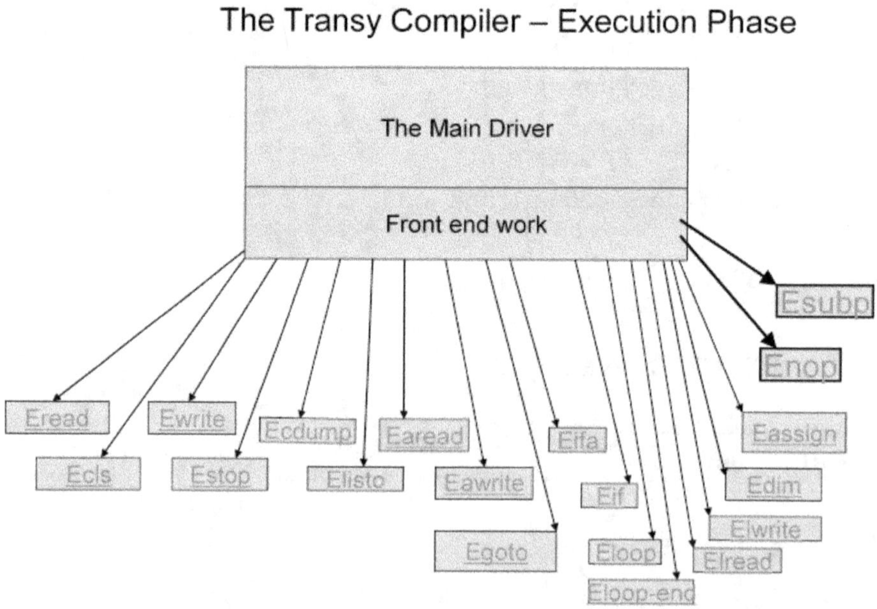

The main calling program for the execution phase has the following characteristics:

```
void main(void)
{
int tn;

lcore();   // load core into an array – global

if(core[1000] != 0)
 {
  cout<<"ERRORS IN TRANSLATION – EXECUTION
            TERMINATED"<<endl;
  exit;
  }
loadobj();   // load object file into an array obj[ ][ ] – global
lffl();      // load literal file into an array of strings fflit [ ] – global

while(obj[ic][0]!= 3)
 {

  tn = obj[ic][0];
  switch(tn)
   {
    case 0:
     edim();
     break;
    case 1:
     eread();
     break;
    case 2:
     ewrite();
     break;
    case 3:
     estop();
     break;
    case 4:
```

```
 eerrors();
 break;
case 5:
 ecdump();
 break;
case 6:
 elisto();
 break;
case 7:
 enop();
 break;
case 8:
 egoto();
 break;
case 9:
 eerrors();
 break;
case 10:
 eifa();
 break;
case 11:
 earead();
 break;
case 12:
 eawrite();
 break;
case 13:
 esubp();
 break;
case 14:
 eloop();
 break;
case 15:
 eloopend();
 break;
case 16:
 elread();
```

```
    break;
   case 17:
    elwrite();
    break;
   case 18:
    eif();
    break;
   case 19:
    ecls();
    break;
   case 20:
    eassgnn();
    break;
   }
  }
 cout<<endl;
 cout<<"EXECUTION HAS TERMINATED
          PROPERLY"<<endl;
}
```

The flow for each function in the **execution phase** follows:

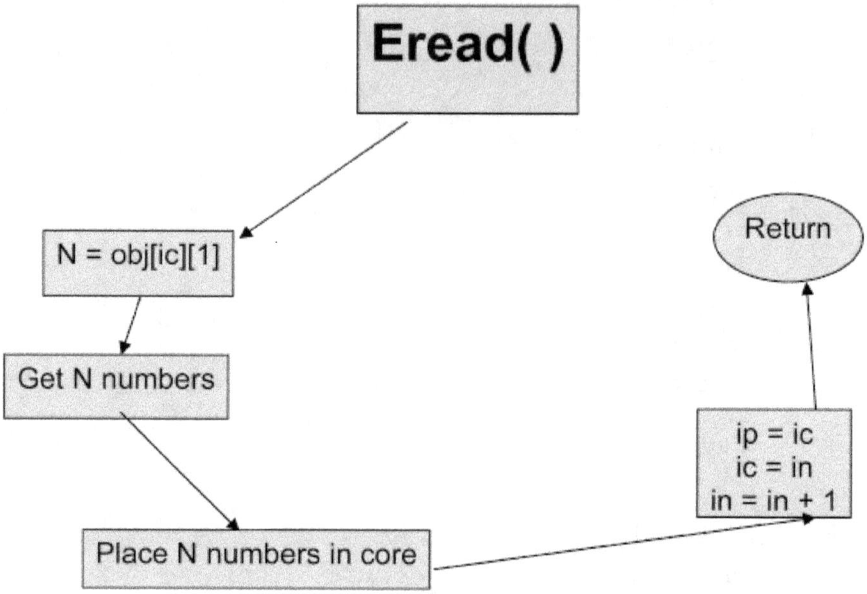

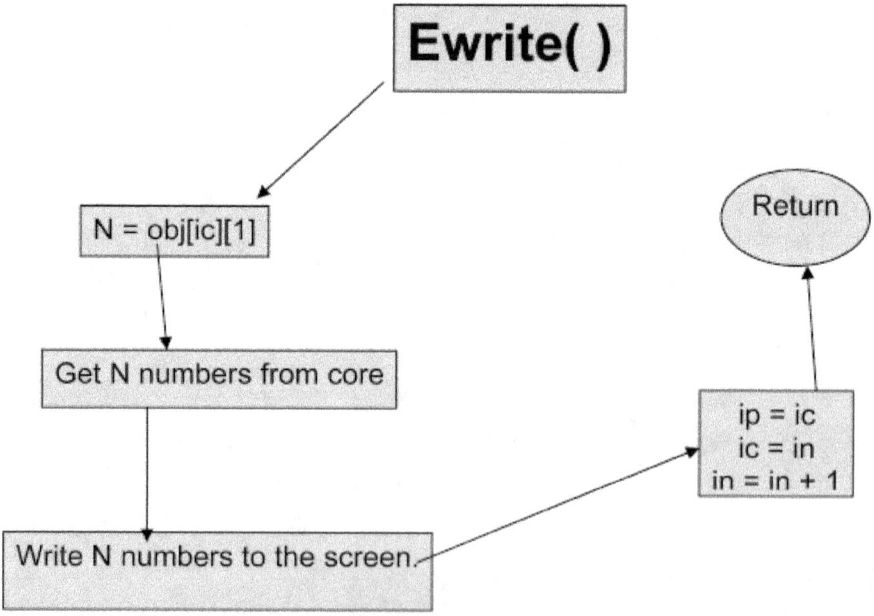

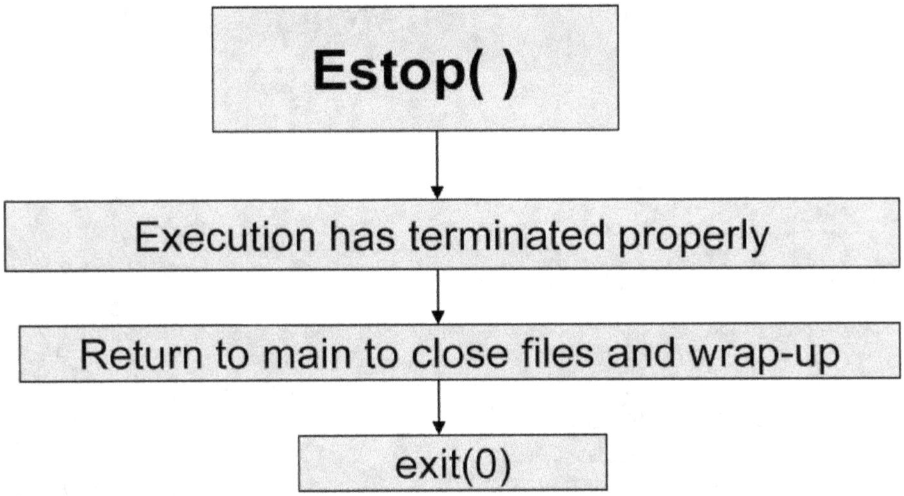
Estop( )
Execution has terminated properly
Return to main to close files and wrap-up
exit(0)

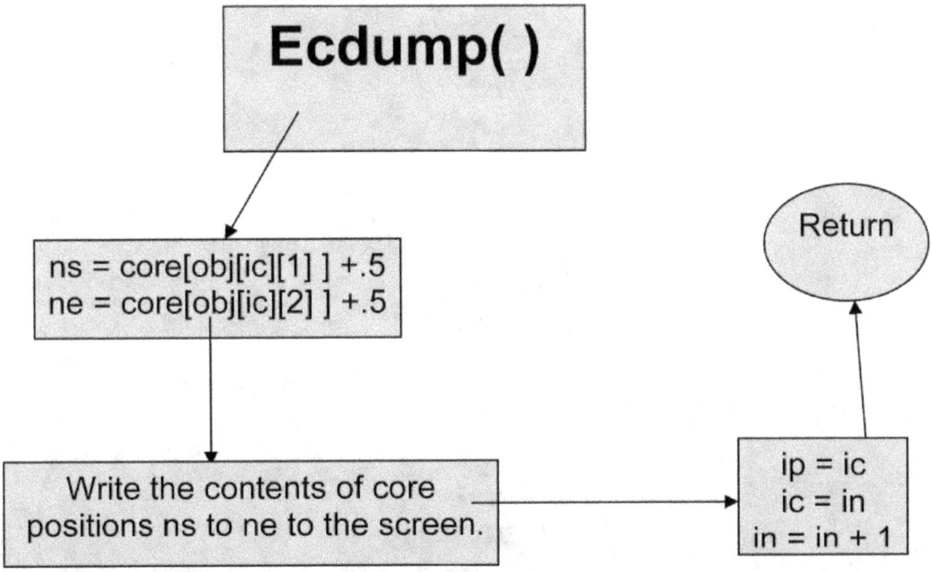
Ecdump( )
ns = core[obj[ic][1]] +.5
ne = core[obj[ic][2]] +.5
Write the contents of core positions ns to ne to the screen.
ip = ic
ic = in
in = in + 1
Return

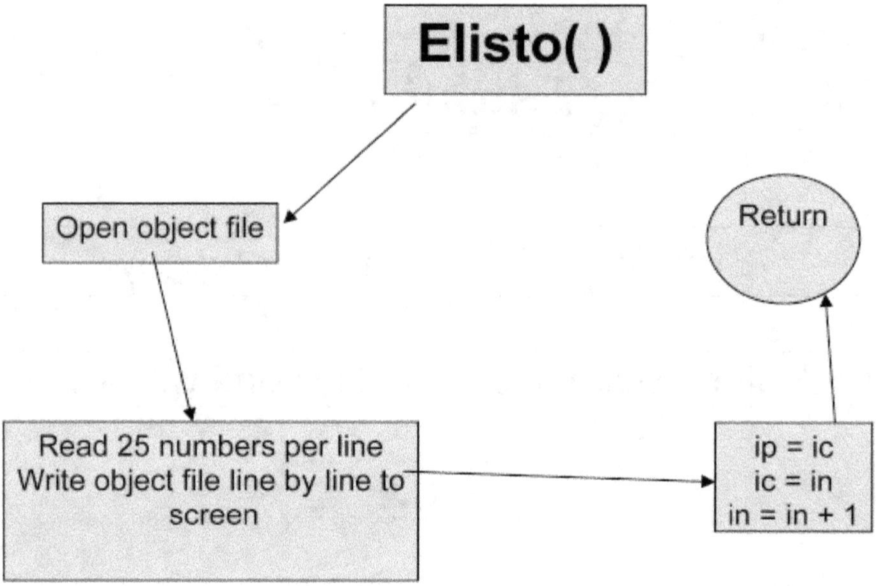
Elisto( )
Open object file
Read 25 numbers per line
Write object file line by line to screen
ip = ic
ic = in
in = in + 1
Return

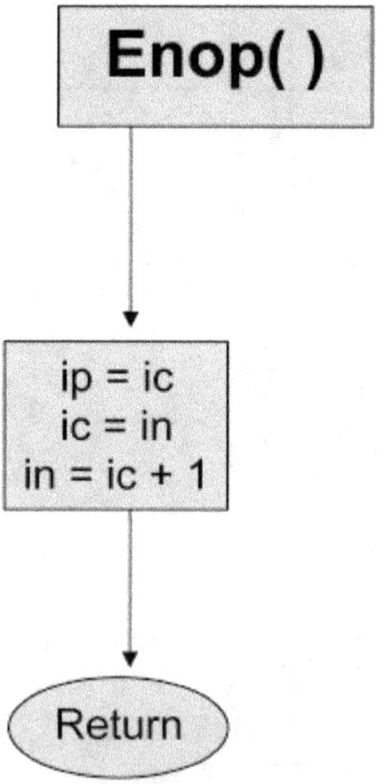
Enop( )
ip = ic
ic = in
in = ic + 1
Return

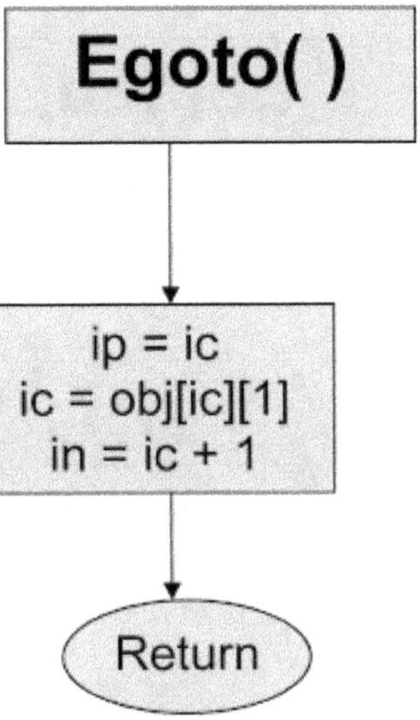
Egoto( )
ip = ic
ic = obj[ic][1]
in = ic + 1
Return

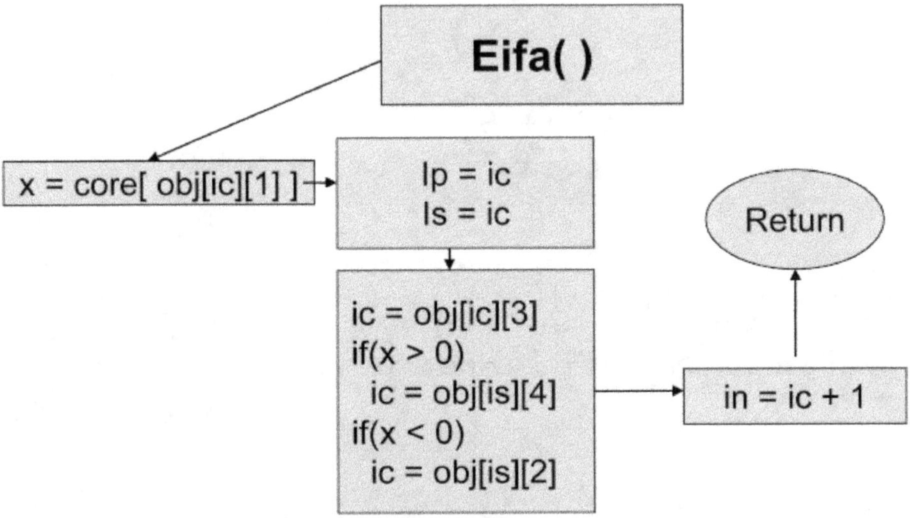
Eifa( )
x = core[obj[ic][1]]
Ip = ic
Is = ic
ic = obj[ic][3]
if(x > 0)
ic = obj[is][4]
if(x < 0)
ic = obj[is][2]
in = ic + 1
Return

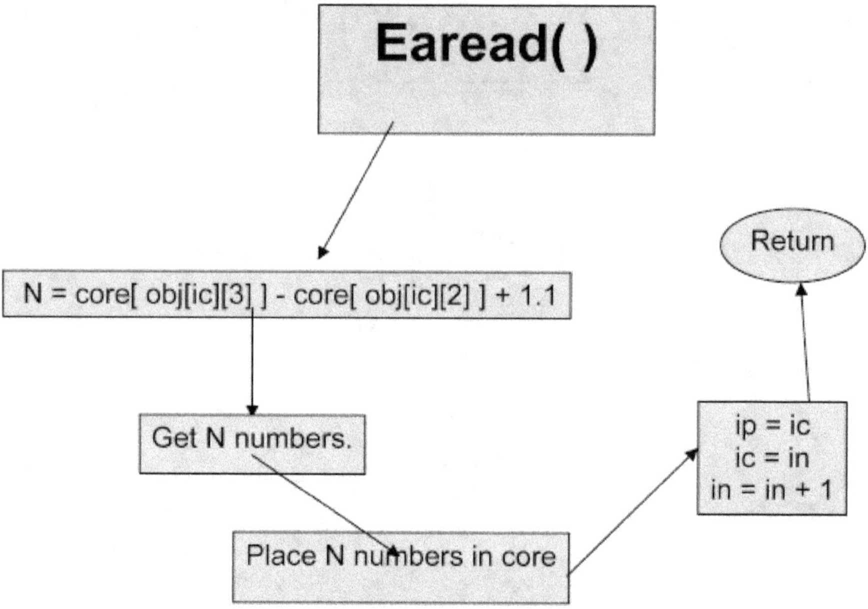
Earead( )
N = core[obj[ic][3]] - core[obj[ic][2]] + 1.1
Get N numbers.
Place N numbers in core
ip = ic
ic = in
in = in + 1
Return

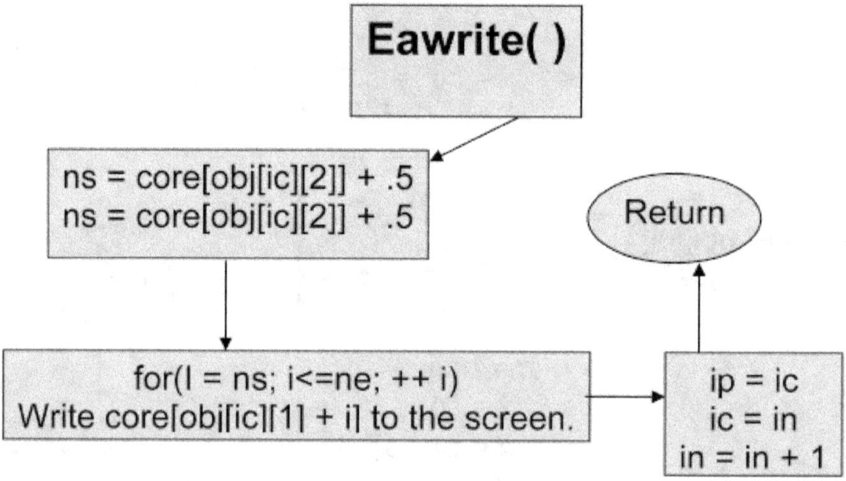
Eawrite( )
ns = core[obj[ic][2]] + .5
ns = core[obj[ic][2]] + .5
for(I = ns; i<=ne; ++ i)
Write core[obj[ic][1] + i] to the screen.
ip = ic
ic = in
in = in + 1
Return

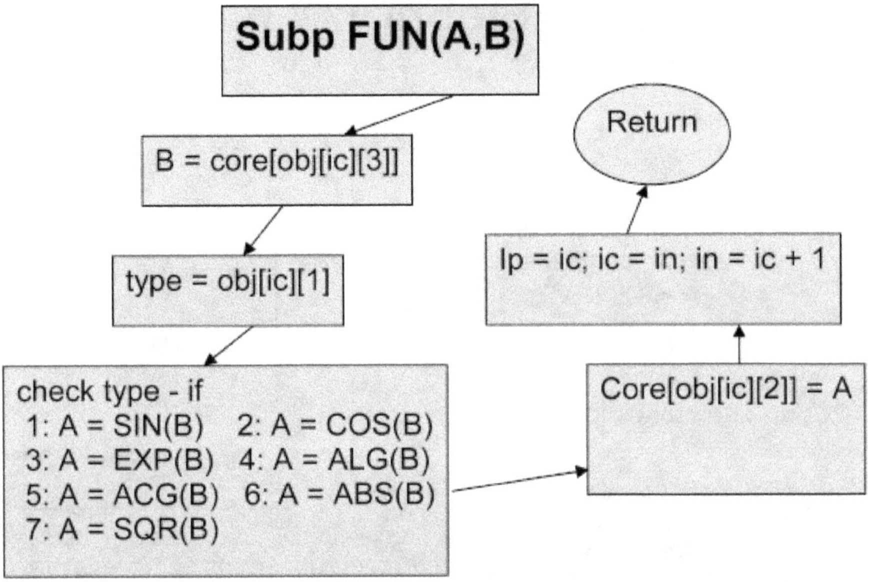
Subp FUN(A,B)
B = core[obj[ic][3]]
type = obj[ic][1]
check type - if
1: A = SIN(B) 2: A = COS(B)
3: A = EXP(B) 4: A = ALG(B)
5: A = ACG(B) 6: A = ABS(B)
7: A = SQR(B)
Core[obj[ic][2]] = A
Ip = ic; ic = in; in = ic + 1
Return

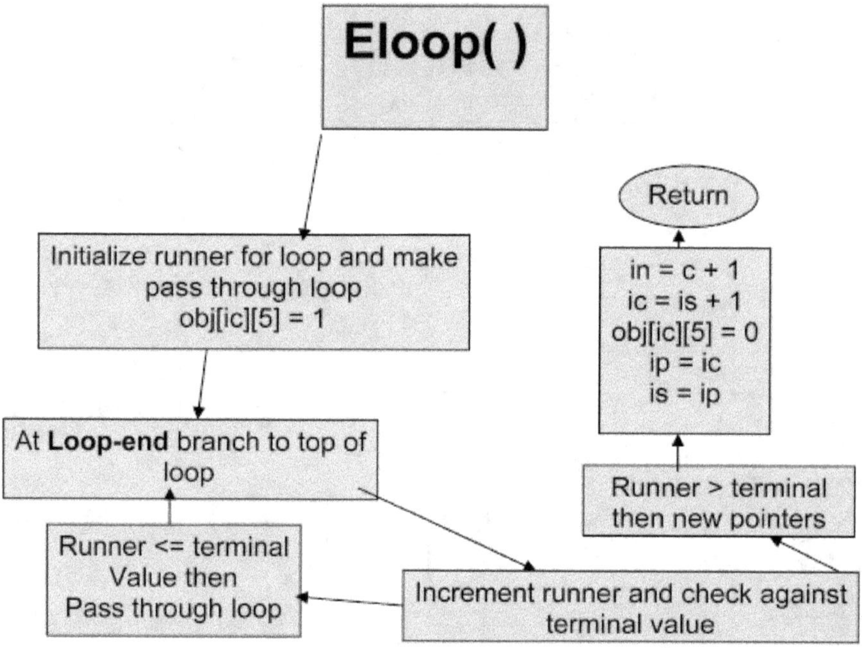
Eloop( )
Return
Initialize runner for loop and make pass through loop obj[ic][5] = 1
in = c + 1
ic = is + 1
obj[ic][5] = 0
ip = ic
is = ip
At **Loop-end** branch to top of loop
Runner > terminal then new pointers
Runner <= terminal Value then Pass through loop
Increment runner and check against terminal value

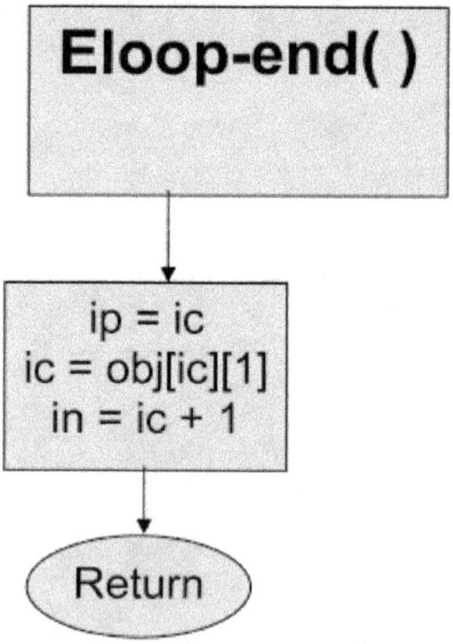
Eloop-end( )
ip = ic
ic = obj[ic][1]
in = ic + 1
Return

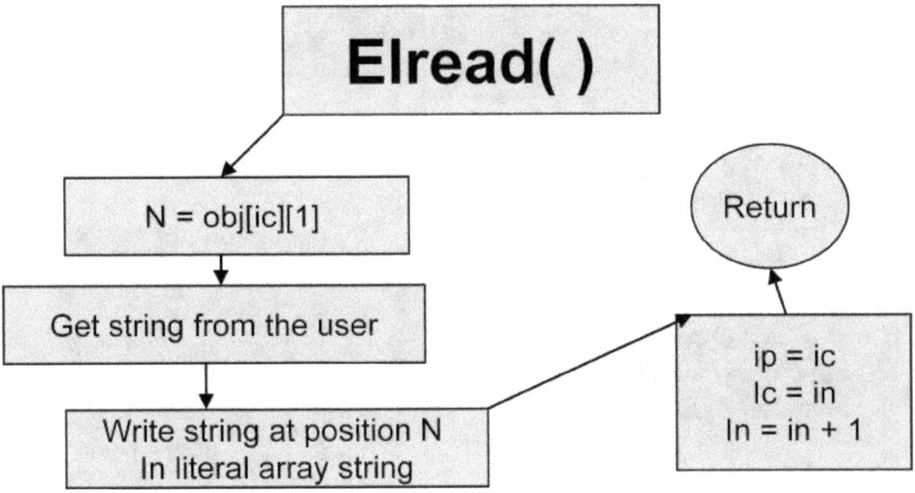
Elread( )
N = obj[ic][1]
Get string from the user
Write string at position N
In literal array string
Return
ip = ic
Ic = in
In = in + 1

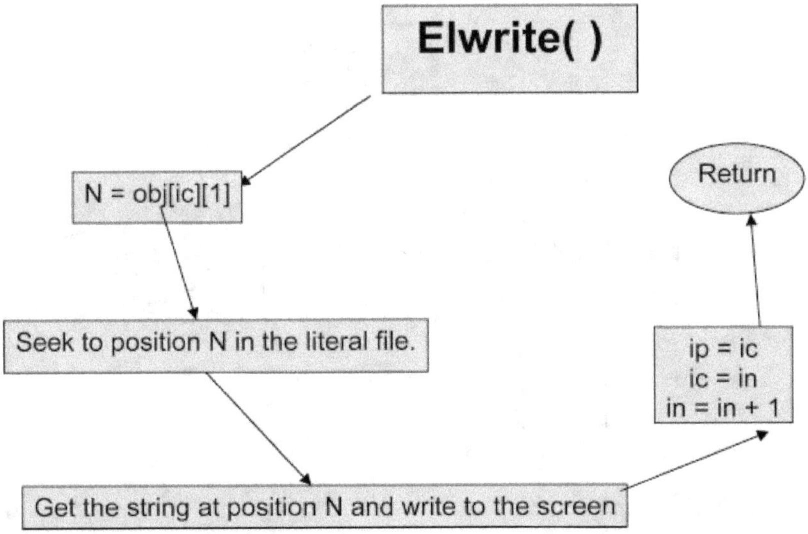
Elwrite( )
N = obj[ic][1]
Seek to position N in the literal file.
Get the string at position N and write to the screen
Return
ip = ic
ic = in
in = in + 1

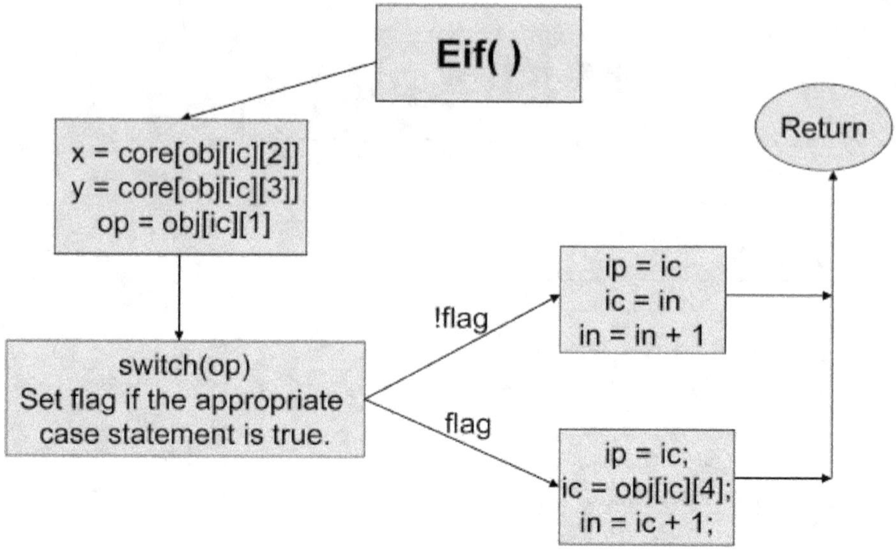
Eif( )
x = core[obj[ic][2]]
y = core[obj[ic][3]]
op = obj[ic][1]
switch(op)
Set flag if the appropriate case statement is true.
!flag
ip = ic
ic = in
in = in + 1
flag
ip = ic;
ic = obj[ic][4];
in = ic + 1;
Return

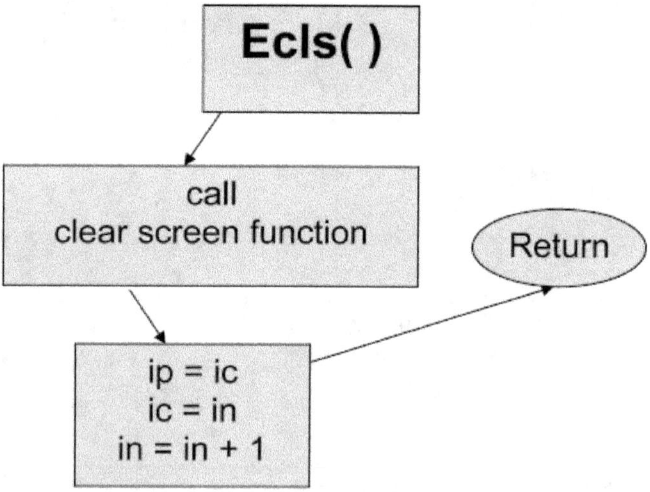
Ecls( )
call
clear screen function
ip = ic
ic = in
in = in + 1
Return

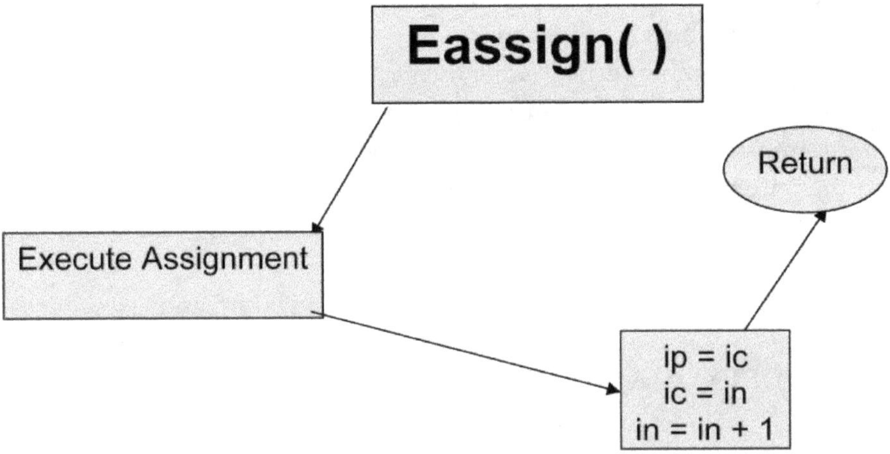

8.4 Programming Projects for the Execution Phase

The following projects will be used to perform the processes indicated by the flow diagrams given above.

Programming project #1.

Write a function to read a character string(s) then get 'N' numbers found in the string(s). The numbers can be integer mode or float mode (exponential or otherwise). The numbers will be separated by commas.

The calling sequence will be:

GETNOS(A, N);

A: a float array of at most 100 real numbers

N: an integer, which specifies the number of real numbers to get from the string(s) and return to the calling program

The function GETNOS will read character strings and get numbers from the string. It will check each string for end of line character (eoln) and if N numbers have not been read from the string when the eoln marker is found it will continue reading strings and getting numbers until N numbers have been read.

The numbers can be either integer or float mode and either positive or negative. Positive numbers will not be preceded by a + sign. Check for improper data and print an error message if improper data is found then prompt the operator to re-enter the line.

This function will perform essentially the same as INPUT performs for BASIC.

Example of call statement, data input and information stored in A:

```
GETNOS(A, 5);
```

Data:

```
12.45,-33.765,-444
.33e+02,44
```

```
A[0] = 12.45
A[1] = -33.765
A[2] = -444
A[3] = .33e+02
A[4] = 44
```

Programming project #2.

Write a program to execute the object line:

$1\ n\ a_1\ a_2\ a_3\ \ldots\ a_n$

The 1 represents that the object line is a READ line and 'n' is the number of numbers to input and the a_is are the addresses in core to place the n numbers.

Process:

1. place the object line ic (obj[ic][ ]) into a single array object[ ]
2. let n ← object[1]
3. call getnos(a,n)

4. let core[object[i+1]] ← a[i – 1], i =1 ... n
5. let ip ← ic; ic ← in; in← ic +1

Programming project #3.

Write a program to execute the object line:

2 n a_1 a_2 a_3 ... a_n

The 2 represents that the object line is a WRITE line and 'n' is the number of numbers to output and the a_is are the addresses in core of the numbers to output.

Process:

1. place the object line ic (obj[ic][ ]) into a single array object[ ]
2. let n ← object[1]
3. let add ← object[i +1]; fetch the contents of core at object[i+1] and output to screen, i =1, ... n
4. let ip ← ic; ic ← in; in ← ic +1

Programming project #4.

Write a program to execute the object line:

3

The 3 represents that the object line is a STOP line or terminate execution statement.

Process:

1. print a message that the program has terminated properly
2. call the system exit command

Programming project #5.

Write a program to execute the object line:

5 a_1 a_2

The 5 represents that the object line is a CORE DUMP line and a_1 and a_2 are the addresses in core that contain the start and end position of the core dump.

Process:

1. let $a1 \leftarrow obj[ic][1]$; $a2 \leftarrow obj[ic][2]$
2. let $n1 = core[\ a1]$; $n2 = core[\ a2]$
3. output to screen $core[i], i = n1 \ldots n2$
4. let $ip \leftarrow ic$; $ic \leftarrow in$; $in \leftarrow ic + 1$;

Programming project #6.

Write a program to execute the object line:

6

The 6 represents that the object line is a LISTO line.

Process:

1. open object file, list line-by-line to screen
2. let $ip \leftarrow ic$; $ic \leftarrow in$; $in \leftarrow ic + 1$;

Programming project #7.

Write a program to execute the object line:

7

The 7 represents that the object line is a NOP line.

Process:

1. let ip ic; $ic \leftarrow in$; $in \leftarrow ic + 1$;

Programming project #8.

Write a program to execute the object line:

8 nn1

The 8 represents that the object line is an unconditional GO TO line and the nn1 is the object line to branch to or the next line to execute.

Process:
1. let ip ← ic; ic ← obj[ic][1]; in ← ic +1;

Programming project #9.

Write a program to execute the object line:

10 a_1 nn1 nn2 nn3

The 10 represents that the object line is an ARITHMETIC IF line and a_1 is the address in core of the value to test and nn1 is branch line if core[a_1] is negative, nn2 is branch line if core[a_1] is zero and nn3 is branch line if core[a_1] is positive.

Process:
1. let value ← core[obj[ic][1]]
2. if value = 0 let ip ← ic; ic ← obj[ic][3]; in ← ic +1;
3. if value <0 let ip ← ic; ic ← obj[ic][2]; in ← ic +1;
4. if value >0 let ip ← ic; ic ← obj[ic][4]; in ← ic +1;

Programming project #10.

Write a program to execute the object line:

11 a_1 a_2 a_3

The 11 represents that the object line is an AREAD line and a_1 is the starting address of the array to store the items and a_2 is the address in core of the initial augment and a_3 is the address in core of the final augment.

Process:
1. let n1 ← core[obj[ic][2]]; let n2 ← core[obj[ic][3]]
2. let n ← n2 – n1+1
3. call getnos(a,n)
4. let core[obj[ic][1] + i] ← a[0], i = 0,n-1
5. let ip ← ic; ic ← in; in ← ic +1;

Programming project #11.

Write a program to execute the object line:

12 a_1 a_2 a_3

The 12 represents that the object line is an AWRITE line and a_1 is the starting address of the array and a_2 is the address in core of the initial augment and a_3 is the address in core of the final augment.

Process:
1. let n1 ← core[obj[ic][2]]; let n2 ← core[obj[ic][3]]
2. output core[obj[ic][1] + i −1] to screen; i = n1 ... n2
3. let ip ← ic; ic ← in; in ← ic +1

Programming project #12.

Write a program to execute the object line:

13 nn1 a_1 a_2

The 13 represents that the object line is a SUBP line and the nn1 is the subprogram type and a_1 is the address in core to store the results of the operation and a_2 is the address in core to find the value that the function will act on.

Process:
1. let n ← obj[ic][1]
2. let b ← core[obj[ic][3]]
3. let add ← [obj[ic][2]]
4. let core[add] ← funn (b)
5. let ip ← ic; ic ← in; in ← ic +1

Programming project #13.

Write a program to execute the object line:

14 a_1 a_2 a_3 $a_4$0

The 14 represents that the object line is a LOOP line and a_1 is the address of the runner of the loop, a_2 is the address of the initial value of the loop, a_3 is the address of the terminal value of the loop and a_4 is the address of the loop increment. The 0 at the end of the object line was placed there at translation and is used during execution. The LOOP statement is a post-test loop.

Process:

1. if obj[ic][5] = 0; let core[obj[ic][1]] ← core[obj[ic][2]] ; let ip ← ic; ic ← in; in ← ic +1; obj[ic][5] = 1
2. if obj[ic][5] = 1 and core[obj[ic][1]] + core[obj[ic][4]] < = core[obj[ic][3]] then let ip ← ic; ic ← in; in ← ic +1
3. if obj[ic][5] = 1 and core[obj[ic][1]] > core[obj[ic][3]] then is ← ic, ic ← ip +1; ip ← is; in ← ic +1; obj[ic][5] = 0

Programming project #14.

Write a program to execute the object line:

15 nn1

The 15 represents that the object line is a LOOP-END line and the nn1 is the object line of the corresponding loop start statement.

Process:

1. let ip ← ic; ic ← obj[ic][1]; in ← ic +1

Programming project #15.

Write a program to execute the object line:

16 nn1

The 16 represents that the object line is an LREAD line and the nn1 represents the location in the literal file that the input will be stored.

Process:

1. prompt the operator to input a string
2. input the string

3. write the string at location obj[ic][1] of the literal file
4. let ip ← ic; ic ← in; in ← ic +1

Programming project #16.

Write a program to execute the object line:

17 nn1

The 17 represents that the object line is an LWRITE line and the nn1 is the location in the literal file that the string to write is found.

Process:

1. read a string from the literal file at location obj[ic][1]
2. print the string to the screen
3. let ip ← ic; ic ← in; in ← ic +1

Programming project #17.

Write a program to execute the object line:

18 n1 a_1 a_2 n2

The 18 represents that the object line is a logical IF line and the n1 is a number that tells the type of relational operator and a_1 and a_2 are the addresses in core that contain the values to compare. The n2 is the object line to branch if the relational expression is true.

Process:

1. let A ← core[obj[ic][2]]; B ← core[obj[ic][3]]
2. check A with B using the relational operator defined by obj[ic][1];
   if true – let ip ← ic; ic ← obj[ic][4]; in ← ic +1
   if false – let ip ← ic; ic ← in; in ← ic + 1

Programming project #18.

Write a program to execute the object line:

19

The 19 represents that the object line is a CLS line

Process:

1. call the system command to clear the screen
2. let ip ← ic; ic ← in; in ← ic + 1

Programming project #19.

Write a program to execute the object line:

20 a_1 a_2 a_3 ...

The 20 represents that the object line is an assignment statement.

Process:

1. use a stack process to execute the statement line
2. let ip ← ic; ic ← in; in ← ic + 1

Chapter 9

Testing the Transy Compiler

Introduction

Testing a compiler can be an endless task. An exhaustive test requires testing a sufficient number of cases that include all possible combinations of the basic statements of the language. Even with a compiler with as few as 20 statements, the number of tests necessary to exhaust all possible cases will be larger than time permits for a project of this type.

A compiler is first tested with examples for which the output is known. Once the compiler passes the test of generating the correct output for known cases, then some confidence is given the compiler and more general and robust tests are made.

Since the object code for the Transy compiler is somewhat easy to follow, the compiler can be tested for correct object code generation as well as correct output for the coded algorithm.

In this chapter, programs selected somewhat randomly are written in the Transy_source language to test the array of statements presented in various order, then translated and executed using the Transy compiler.

9.1 Examples to Test the Correctness of the Compiler

Example #1 A program to test input and output

```
C* program to input 3 numbers, then output in reverse order
C*  of input.
   read a,b,c
   write c,b,a
   stop
   end
```

The following program was compiled by the Transy Compiler

Statement Number Statement

```
0:-----  C* program to input 3 numbers, then output in reverse order
1:-----   C*  of input.
2:-----      read a,b,c
3:-----      write c,b,a
4:-----      stop
5:-----      end
No errors in translation

Object code generated:
1 3 0 1 2 0 0 0 0 0 0 0 0 0 0 0 0 0 0 0 0 0 0 0 0
2 3 2 1 0 0 0 0 0 0 0 0 0 0 0 0 0 0 0 0 0 0 0 0 0
3 0 0 0 0 0 0 0 0 0 0 0 0 0 0 0 0 0 0 0 0 0 0 0 0
```

Start of execution:

```
input 3 numbers, one or many per line, separated by a comma,
end each input with a comma
22,33,44
The output follows

44
33
22
EXECUTION HAS TERMINATED PROPERLY
```

Example #2 A program to test an assignment statement

```
C* Program to input 3 numbers, then output sum
   read a,b,c
   s = a + b + c
   write s
   stop
   end
```

The following program was compiled by the Transy Compiler

Statement Number Statement

```
0:----- C* Program to input 3 numbers, then output sum
1:-----    read a,b,c
2:-----    s = a + b + c
3:-----    write s
4:-----    stop
5:-----    end
```

No errors in translation

Object code generated:

```
1 3 0 1 2 0 0 0 0 0 0 0 0 0 0 0 0 0 0 0 0 0 0 0 0
20 3 0 1 -6 2 -6 -1 0 0 0 0 0 0 0 0 0 0 0 0 0 0 0 0 0
2 1 3 0 0 0 0 0 0 0 0 0 0 0 0 0 0 0 0 0 0 0 0 0 0
3 0 0 0 0 0 0 0 0 0 0 0 0 0 0 0 0 0 0 0 0 0 0 0 0
```

Start of execution:

input 3 numbers, one or many per line, separated by a comma, end each input with a comma

2,4,6

The output follows

12

EXECUTION HAS TERMINATED PROPERLY

Example #3 A program to test an IF statement

```
C* Program to input 2 numbers, then output the larger
C* of the two numbers.
   read a,b
   if(b|gt|a)then 20
    write a
    stop
 20 write b
    stop
   end
```

The following program was compiled by the Transy Compiler

Statement Number Statement

```
0:-----  C* Program to input 2 numbers, then output the larger
1:-----  C* of the two numbers.
2:-----     read a,b
3:-----     if(b|gt|a)then 20
4:-----      write a
5:-----      stop
6:-----   20 write b
7:-----      stop
8:-----     end
```

No errors in translation

Object code generated:

```
1 2 0 1 0 0 0 0 0 0 0 0 0 0 0 0 0 0 0 0 0 0 0 0 0
18 2 1 0 4 0 0 0 0 0 0 0 0 0 0 0 0 0 0 0 0 0 0 0 0
2 1 0 0 0 0 0 0 0 0 0 0 0 0 0 0 0 0 0 0 0 0 0 0 0
3 0 0 0 0 0 0 0 0 0 0 0 0 0 0 0 0 0 0 0 0 0 0 0 0
2 1 1 0 0 0 0 0 0 0 0 0 0 0 0 0 0 0 0 0 0 0 0 0 0
3 0 0 0 0 0 0 0 0 0 0 0 0 0 0 0 0 0 0 0 0 0 0 0 0
```

Start of execution:

input 2 numbers, one or many per line, separated by a comma, end each input with a comma

15,22

The output follows

22
EXECUTION HAS TERMINATED PROPERLY

Example #4 A program to test the LOOP and LOOP-END statements

```
C* Program to input 10 numbers, then output the largest
C* of the 10
   read largest
   loop i = 1, 9, 1
    read x
     if(x|lt|largest)then 10
      largest = x
 10 loop-end
   write largest
   stop
   end
```

The following program was compiled by the Transy Compiler

```
Statement Number           Statement

  0:-----  C* Program to input 10 numbers, then output the largest
  1:-----  C* of the 10
  2:-----     read largest
  3:-----     loop i = 1, 9, 1
  4:-----      read x
  5:-----       if(x|lt|largest)then 10
  6:-----        largest = x
  7:-----   10 loop-end
  8:-----     write largest
  9:-----     stop
  10:-----      end
```

No errors in translation

Object code generated:

```
1 1 0 0 0 0 0 0 0 0 0 0 0 0 0 0 0 0 0 0 0 0 0 0 0
14 1 2 3 2 0 0 0 0 0 0 0 0 0 0 0 0 0 0 0 0 0 0 0 0
1 1 4 0 0 0 0 0 0 0 0 0 0 0 0 0 0 0 0 0 0 0 0 0 0
18 0 5 6 6 0 0 0 0 0 0 0 0 0 0 0 0 0 0 0 0 0 0 0 0
20 0 4 -1 0 0 0 0 0 0 0 0 0 0 0 0 0 0 0 0 0 0 0 0 0
15 1 0 0 0 0 0 0 0 0 0 0 0 0 0 0 0 0 0 0 0 0 0 0 0
2 1 0 0 0 0 0 0 0 0 0 0 0 0 0 0 0 0 0 0 0 0 0 0 0
3 0 0 0 0 0 0 0 0 0 0 0 0 0 0 0 0 0 0 0 0 0 0 0 0
```

Start of execution:

input 1 numbers, one or many per line, separated by a comma, end each input with a comma
22
input 1 numbers, one or many per line, separated by a comma, end each input with a comma
33
input 1 numbers, one or many per line, separated by a comma, end each input with a comma
44
input 1 numbers, one or many per line, separated by a comma, end each input with a comma
55
input 1 numbers, one or many per line, separated by a comma, end each input with a comma
66
input 1 numbers, one or many per line, separated by a comma, end each input with a comma
77
input 1 numbers, one or many per line, separated by a comma, end each input with a comma
22
input 1 numbers, one or many per line, separated by a comma, end each input with a comma
33
input 1 numbers, one or many per line, separated by a comma, end each input with a comma
44

input 1 numbers, one or many per line, separated by a comma,
end each input with a comma
55
The output follows

77

EXECUTION HAS TERMINATED PROPERLY

Example #5 A program to further test the assignment statement

```
C* Program to input 5 numbers, then output the value of the
C* expression  a + b / c – d * f
   read a,b,c,d,f
   x = a + b / c – d * f
   write x
   stop
   end
```

The following program was compiled by the Transy Compiler

Statement Number   Statement

```
0:-----  C* Program to input 5 numbers, then output the value of the
1:-----  C* expression  a + b / c – d * f
2:-----     read a,b,c,d,f
3:-----     x = a + b / c – d * f
4:-----     write x
5:-----     stop
6:-----     end
```

No errors in translation

Object code generated:
1 5 0 1 2 3 4 0 0 0 0 0 0 0 0 0 0 0 0 0 0 0 0 0 0
20 5 0 1 2 -5 3 4 -4 -7 -6 -1 0 0 0 0 0 0 0 0 0 0 0 0 0
2 1 5 0 0 0 0 0 0 0 0 0 0 0 0 0 0 0 0 0 0 0 0 0 0
3 0 0 0 0 0 0 0 0 0 0 0 0 0 0 0 0 0 0 0 0 0 0 0 0

```
Start of execution:
input 5 numbers, one or many per line, separated by a comma,
end each input with a comma
2,3,4,5,6
The output follows

-27.25

EXECUTION HAS TERMINATED PROPERLY
```

Example #6 A program to test the AREAD, AWRITE and DIM statements

```
C* Write a program to input an array of 10 numbers, then
C* print the numbers in reverse order of input
   dim a[11]
C*
   aread a, 1, 10
C*
   x = 10
   loop i = 1, 10, 1
    awrite a, x, x
    x = x–1
   loop-end
   stop
   end
```

The following program was compiled by the Transy Compiler

```
Statement Number          Statement

 0:-----  C* Write a program to input an array of 10 numbers, then
 1:-----  C* print the numbers in reverse order of input
 2:-----     dim a[11]
 3:-----  C*
 4:-----     aread a, 1, 10
 5:-----  C*
 6:-----     x = 10
```

```
7:-----     loop i = 1, 10, 1
8:-----      awrite a, x, x
9:-----      x = x – 1
10:-----      loop-end
11:-----      stop
12:-----      end
```

No errors in translation

Object code generated:
0 0 0 0 0 0 0 0 0 0 0 0 0 0 0 0 0 0 0 0 0 0 0 0 0
11 0 11 12 0 0 0 0 0 0 0 0 0 0 0 0 0 0 0 0 0 0 0 0 0
20 13 12 -1 0 0 0 0 0 0 0 0 0 0 0 0 0 0 0 0 0 0 0 0 0
14 14 11 12 11 0 0 0 0 0 0 0 0 0 0 0 0 0 0 0 0 0 0 0 0
12 0 13 13 0 0 0 0 0 0 0 0 0 0 0 0 0 0 0 0 0 0 0 0 0
20 13 13 11 -7 -1 0 0 0 0 0 0 0 0 0 0 0 0 0 0 0 0 0 0 0
15 3 0 0 0 0 0 0 0 0 0 0 0 0 0 0 0 0 0 0 0 0 0 0 0
3 0 0 0 0 0 0 0 0 0 0 0 0 0 0 0 0 0 0 0 0 0 0 0 0

Start of execution:
input 10 numbers, one or many per line, separated by a comma,
end each input with a comma
10,20,30,40,50,60,70,80,90,100
100
90
80
70
60
50
40
30
20
10

EXECUTION HAS TERMINATED PROPERLY

Example #7 A program to test the DIM, LOOP, LOOP-END, AWRITE, IFA, LREAD, LWRITE, SUBP and GO TO statements

```
C* A general program to test the compiler
C*
C* Use the following data
C* 2, 44.44, -63
C* b_is_greater_than_zero_OK
  dim aa[10], ab[5], ac[5]
  read a,b,c
  write a,b,c
  aa[1] = a
  ab[1] = a + aa[1]
  ac [1] = a + aa[1] + ab[1]
  loop i = 1, 1, 1
   awrite aa, i, i
   awrite ab, i, i
   awrite ac, i, i
  loop-end
  ifa(c)7,9,9
 7 lwrite "C_is_less_than_zero_OK"
  go to 11
 9 lwrite "C_is_greater_than_or_equal_zero???"
11 lread la
  if (b |gt| 0.0) then 20
   lwrite "b_is_less_than_zero???"
  go to 30
20 lwrite la
30 subp exp (d,a)
  lwrite "Is_the_output_7.389_should_be"
  write d
  aa[1] = 2
  ab[1] = 4
  ac[1] = 2*aa[1]/ab[1] + (4 + a)/(ab[1] + 2)
  c = ac[1]
  write c
  lwrite "Was_the_output_2?"
  stop
  end
```

The following program was compiled by the Transy Compiler:

```
Statement Number        Statement

0:-----   C*  A general program to test the compiler
1:-----   C*
2:-----   C* Use the following data
3:-----   C* 2, 44.44, -63
4:-----   C* b_is_greater_than_zero_OK
5:-----     dim aa[10], ab[5], ac[5]
6:-----     read a,b,c
7:-----     write a,b,c
8:-----     aa[1] = a
9:-----     ab[1] = a + aa[1]
10:-----     ac [1] = a + aa[1] + ab[1]
11:-----      loop i = 1, 1, 1
12:-----        awrite aa, i, i
13:-----        awrite ab, i, i
14:-----        awrite ac, i, i
15:-----      loop-end
16:-----      ifa(c)7,9,9
17:-----    7  lwrite "C_is_less_than_zero_OK"
18:-----      go to 11
19:-----    9  lwrite "C_is_greater_than_or_equal_zero???"
20:-----   11  lread la
21:-----      if (b |gt| 0.0) then 20
22:-----        lwrite "b_is_less_than_zero???"
23:-----      go to 30
24:-----   20  lwrite la
25:-----   30  subp exp (d,a)
26:-----      lwrite "Is_the_output_7.389_should_be"
27:-----      write d
28:-----      aa[1] = 2
29:-----      ab[1] = 4
30:-----      ac[1] = 2*aa[1]/ab[1] + (4 + a)/(ab[1] + 2)
31:-----      c = ac[1]
32:-----      write c
```

```
33:-----    lwrite "Was_the_output_2?"
34:-----    stop
35:-----    end
No errors in translation
```

Start of execution:

```
input 3 numbers, one or many per line, separated by a comma,
end each input with a comma
2,44.44,-63
The output follows

2
44.44
-63
2
4
8
c_is_less_than_zero_ok
Input a string of at most 60 characters
My_String
My_String
is_the_output_7.389_should_be
The output follows

7.38906
The output follows

2
was_the_output_2?

EXECUTION HAS TERMINATED PROPERLY
```

Example #8 A program that will test most statements in The Transy_ source language

```
C* A general program to test the compiler
C*
C* 5, -15.55
```

```
C* 2, 4, 6, 8, 10
C* 3, 1, -1,-3, -5
C* Was_the_output_2.71828?
C*
   dim aa[10], ab[10]
   read a,b
   aread aa, 1, 5
   aread ab, 1, 5
   s = 0
   loop i = 1,5,1
    s = s + aa[i] + ab[i]
    write i, s
   loop-end
   lwrite "The_value_of_s_after_loop_is_25?"
   write s
   ifa(a)20, 30, 30
 20 lwrite "A_is_negative_wrong!!"
   go to 40
 30 lwrite "A_is_zero_or_positiv_right?"
 40 nop
   zz = 17.7
   a1 = zz/17.7
   a2 = a/5
   a3 = 15.55/b
   x = a1 + a2 – a3 + 22.22*(a – 4 )
   write x
   lwrite "Was_the_output_25.22?"
   lread la
   subp exp(z,1)
   write z
   lwrite la
   if(4 |eq| 7) then 55
    lwrite "Four_is_not_equal_to_seven"
   go to 60
 55 lwrite "Four_is_equal_to_seven-really?"
 60 stop
   end
```

The following program was compiled by the Transy Compiler:

```
Statement Number          Statement

  0:-----  C*  A general program to test the compiler
  1:-----  C*
  2:-----  C*  5, -15.55
  3:-----  C*  2, 4, 6, 8, 10
  4:-----  C*  3, 1, -1,-3, -5
  5:-----  C*  Was_the_output_2.71828?
  6:-----  C*
  7:-----    dim aa[10], ab[10]
  8:-----    read a,b
  9:-----    aread aa, 1, 5
 10:-----    aread ab, 1, 5
 11:-----    s = 0
 12:-----    loop i = 1,5,1
 13:-----      s = s + aa[i] + ab[i]
 14:-----      write i, s
 15:-----    loop-end
 16:-----    lwrite "The_value_of_s_after_loop_is_25?"
 17:-----    write s
 18:-----    ifa(a)20, 30, 30
 19:-----  20 lwrite "A_is_negative_wrong!!"
 20:-----    go to 40
 21:-----  30 lwrite "A_is_zero_or_positiv_right?"
 22:-----  40 nop
 23:-----    zz = 17.7
 24:-----    a1 = zz/17.7
 25:-----    a2 = a/5
 26:-----    a3 = 15.55/b
 27:-----    x = a1 + a2 – a3 + 22.22*(a – 4 )
 28:-----    write x
 29:-----    lwrite "Was_the_output_25.22?"
 30:-----    lread la
 31:-----    subp exp(z,1)
 32:-----    write z
```

```
33:-----     lwrite la
34:-----     if(4 |eq| 7) then 55
35:-----      lwrite "Four_is_not_equal_to_seven"
36:-----     go to 60
37:-----  55 lwrite "Four_is_equal_to_seven-really?"
38:-----  60 stop
39:-----     end
```

No errors in translation

Start of execution:
input 2 numbers, one or many per line, separated by a comma, end each input with a comma
5,-15.55
input 5 numbers, one or many per line, separated by a comma, end each input with a comma
2,4,6,8,10
input 5 numbers, one or many per line, separated by a comma, end each input with a comma
3,1,-1,-3,-5
The output follows

1
5
The output follows

2
10
The output follows

3
15
The output follows

4
20
The output follows

```
5
25
the_value_of_s_after_loop_is_25?
The output follows
25
a_is_zero_or_positiv_right?
The output follows

25.22
was_the_output_25.22?
Input a string of at most 60 characters
Was_the_output_2.71828
The output follows

2.71828
Was_the_output_2.71828
four_is_not_equal_to_seven

EXECUTION HAS TERMINATED PROPERLY
```

Example #9 A program for random testing of the Transy_source language

```
C* A general program to test the compiler
C* The program should not generate any errors
C* data
C* 1,-1,14.4
C* 1,2,3,4
C* 5,4,3,2
   dim aa[10], ab[5], ac[5]
   read a,b,c
2  write c,b,a,c
   aread aa,1,4
   aread ab,1,4
   loop i = 1,4,1
    ac[i] = aa[i] + ab[i]
   loop-end
   lwrite "Is_the_output_6_6_6_6?"
   awrite ac,1,4
```

```
3  ifa(a)4,4,6
4  lwrite "a_is_negative_or_zero_wrong"
   go to 8
6  lwrite "a_is_positive_right"
8  nop
   lwrite "Is_the_following_output_5?"
   z = a + b *(a – b) / (a – b) + ac[3]/ac[1]*5
   write z
   if(z |lt| 9) then 200
   write z
   go to 300
200  z = z + 5
   write z
300  stop
   end
```

The following program was compiled by the Transy Compiler:

```
Statement Number          Statement

0:-----   C* A general program to test the compiler
1:-----   C* The program should not generate any errors
2:-----   C* data
3:-----   C* 1,-1,14.4
4:-----   C* 1,2,3,4
5:-----   C* 5,4,3,2
6:-----      dim aa[10], ab[5], ac[5]
7:-----      read a,b,c
8:-----   2  write c,b,a,c
9:-----      aread aa,1,4
10:-----      aread ab,1,4
11:-----      loop i = 1,4,1
12:-----        ac[i] = aa[i] + ab[i]
13:-----      loop-end
14:-----      lwrite "Is_the_output_6_6_6_6?"
15:-----      awrite ac,1,4
16:-----   3  ifa(a)4,4,6
```

```
17:-----  4  lwrite "a_is_negative_or_zero_wrong"
18:-----     go to 8
19:-----  6  lwrite "a_is_positive_right"
20:-----  8  nop
21:-----     lwrite "Is_the_following_output_5?"
22:-----     z = a + b *(a – b) / (a – b) + ac[3]/ac[1]*5
23:-----     write z
24:-----     if(z |lt| 9) then 200
25:-----     write z
26:-----     go to 300
27:-----  200  z = z + 5
28:-----     write z
29:-----  300  stop
30:-----     end
```

No errors in translation

Start of execution:
input 3 numbers, one or many per line, separated by a comma, end each input with a comma
1,-1,14.4
The output follows

14.4
-1
1
14.4
input 4 numbers, one or many per line, separated by a comma, end each input with a comma
1,2,3,4
input 4 numbers, one or many per line, separated by a comma, end each input with a comma
5,4,3,2
is_the_output_6_6_6_6?
6
6
6
6

```
a_is_positive_right
is_the_following_output_5?
The output follows

5
The output follows

10

EXECUTION HAS TERMINATED PROPERLY
```

Example #10 A program for more random testing of the Transy_ source language

```
C* A general program to test the compiler
C*
C* It will test most statements
C*
C* Use the following as input
C* -22, 33, 14.76
C* 4,5,6,7
   dim aa[10]
   read a,b,c
10 read x,y,z,p
   write a,b,x,y
   cls
C* Use the following input
C* This_will_test_lread_lwrite
   lread la
   go to 20
   cdump 0,4
   cdump z,p
20 listo
   ifa(a)30,40,40
30 write a,b,c
40 nop
C* Use the following as input
C* 10,9,8,7,6
```

```
C*
  aread aa, 1, 5
  awrite aa, 1, 5
C* Test the assignment statement
  c = a + b/c + aa[1] + aa[2]/aa[3] * 12.6
  write c
  s = 0
  loop i = 1, 5, 1
   s = s + aa[i]
   write i, s
  loop-end
  write s
C*
  subp sin(a,1.5708)
   write a
  subp exp(a, 1.0)
   write a
  subp abs(a, -22.4)
   write a
  subp sqr(a, 16.0)
   write a
  loop i = 1, 5, 1
   awrite aa, i, i
  loop-end
  if(a |gt| 2.0) then 120
  lwrite "This_statement_should_be_passed"
120 lwrite "The_output_from_la_is_next"
  lwrite la
  stop
```

The following program was compiled by the Transy Compiler

```
Statement Number          Statement
  1:-----  C* A general program to test the compiler
  2:-----  C*
  3:-----  C* It will test most statements
```

```
C*
C* Use the following as input
C* -22, 33, 14.76
C* 4,5,6,7
    dim aa[10]
    read a,b,c
10 read x,y,z,p
    write a,b,x,y
    cls
C* Use the following input
C* This_will_test_lread_lwrite
    lread la
    go to 20
    cdump 0,4
    cdump z,p
20 listo
    ifa(a)30,40,40
30 write a,b,c
40 nop
C* Use the following as input
C* 10,9,8,7,6
C*
    aread aa, 1, 5
    awrite aa, 1, 5
C* Test the assignment statement
    c = a + b/c + aa[1] + aa[2]/aa[3] * 12.6
    write c
    s = 0
    loop i = 1, 5, 1
      s = s + aa[i]
      write i, s
    loop-end
    write s
C*
    subp sin(a,1.5708)
      write a
```

```
40:-----    subp exp(a, 1.0)
41:-----     write a
42:-----    subp abs(a, -22.4)
43:-----     write a
44:-----    subp sqr(a, 16.0)
45:-----     write a
46:-----    loop i = 1, 5, 1
47:-----     awrite aa, i, i
48:-----    loop-end
49:-----    if(a |gt| 2.0) then 120
50:-----    lwrite "This_statement_should_be_passed"
51:-----  120 lwrite "The_output_from_la_is_next"
52:-----    lwrite la
53:-----    stop
```

No errors in translation

Start of execution:

```
Input a string of at most 60 characters
This_will_test_lread_lwrite
0 0 0 0 0 0 0 0 0 0 0 0 0 0 0 0 0 0 0 0 0 0 0 0 0
1 3 10 11 12 0 0 0 0 0 0 0 0 0 0 0 0 0 0 0 0 0 0 0 0
1 4 13 14 15 16 0 0 0 0 0 0 0 0 0 0 0 0 0 0 0 0 0 0 0
2 4 10 11 13 14 0 0 0 0 0 0 0 0 0 0 0 0 0 0 0 0 0 0 0
19 0 0 0 0 0 0 0 0 0 0 0 0 0 0 0 0 0 0 0 0 0 0 0 0
16 0 0 0 0 0 0 0 0 0 0 0 0 0 0 0 0 0 0 0 0 0 0 0 0
8 9 0 0 0 0 0 0 0 0 0 0 0 0 0 0 0 0 0 0 0 0 0 0 0
5 17 18 0 0 0 0 0 0 0 0 0 0 0 0 0 0 0 0 0 0 0 0 0 0
5 15 16 0 0 0 0 0 0 0 0 0 0 0 0 0 0 0 0 0 0 0 0 0 0
6 0 0 0 0 0 0 0 0 0 0 0 0 0 0 0 0 0 0 0 0 0 0 0 0
10 10 11 12 12 0 0 0 0 0 0 0 0 0 0 0 0 0 0 0 0 0 0 0 0
2 3 10 11 12 0 0 0 0 0 0 0 0 0 0 0 0 0 0 0 0 0 0 0 0
7 0 0 0 0 0 0 0 0 0 0 0 0 0 0 0 0 0 0 0 0 0 0 0 0
11 0 19 20 0 0 0 0 0 0 0 0 0 0 0 0 0 0 0 0 0 0 0 0 0
12 0 19 20 0 0 0 0 0 0 0 0 0 0 0 0 0 0 0 0 0 0 0 0 0
20 12 10 11 12 -5 0 19 -11 -6 0 21 -11 0 22 -11 -5 23 -4 -6 -6 -1 0 0 0
```

```
2 1 12 0 0 0 0 0 0 0 0 0 0 0 0 0 0 0 0 0 0 0 0
20 24 17 -1 0 0 0 0 0 0 0 0 0 0 0 0 0 0 0 0 0 0 0 0 0
14 25 19 20 19 0 0 0 0 0 0 0 0 0 0 0 0 0 0 0 0 0 0 0 0
20 24 24 0 25 -11 -6 -1 0 0 0 0 0 0 0 0 0 0 0 0 0 0 0 0 0
2 2 25 24 0 0 0 0 0 0 0 0 0 0 0 0 0 0 0 0 0 0 0 0 0
15 18 0 0 0 0 0 0 0 0 0 0 0 0 0 0 0 0 0 0 0 0 0
2 1 24 0 0 0 0 0 0 0 0 0 0 0 0 0 0 0 0 0 0 0 0
13 1 10 26 0 0 0 0 0 0 0 0 0 0 0 0 0 0 0 0 0 0 0 0 0
2 1 10 0 0 0 0 0 0 0 0 0 0 0 0 0 0 0 0 0 0 0 0
13 3 10 27 0 0 0 0 0 0 0 0 0 0 0 0 0 0 0 0 0 0 0 0 0
2 1 10 0 0 0 0 0 0 0 0 0 0 0 0 0 0 0 0 0 0 0 0
13 6 10 28 0 0 0 0 0 0 0 0 0 0 0 0 0 0 0 0 0 0 0 0 0
2 1 10 0 0 0 0 0 0 0 0 0 0 0 0 0 0 0 0 0 0 0 0
13 7 10 29 0 0 0 0 0 0 0 0 0 0 0 0 0 0 0 0 0 0 0 0 0
2 1 10 0 0 0 0 0 0 0 0 0 0 0 0 0 0 0 0 0 0 0 0
14 25 19 20 19 0 0 0 0 0 0 0 0 0 0 0 0 0 0 0 0 0 0 0 0
12 0 25 25 0 0 0 0 0 0 0 0 0 0 0 0 0 0 0 0 0 0 0 0 0
15 31 0 0 0 0 0 0 0 0 0 0 0 0 0 0 0 0 0 0 0 0 0
18 2 10 30 36 0 0 0 0 0 0 0 0 0 0 0 0 0 0 0 0 0 0 0 0
17 1 0 0 0 0 0 0 0 0 0 0 0 0 0 0 0 0 0 0 0 0 0
17 2 0 0 0 0 0 0 0 0 0 0 0 0 0 0 0 0 0 0 0 0 0
17 0 0 0 0 0 0 0 0 0 0 0 0 0 0 0 0 0 0 0 0 0 0 0
3 0 0 0 0 0 0 0 0 0 0 0 0 0 0 0 0 0 0 0 0 0 0 0
```

The output follows

```
-22
33
14.76
input 5 numbers, one or many per line, separated by a comma,
end each input with a comma
10,9,8,7,6
10
9
8
7
6
```

The output follows

4.41077
The output follows

1
10
The output follows

2
19
The output follows

3
27
The output follows

4
34
The output follows

5
40
The output follows

40
The output follows

1
The output follows

2.71828
The output follows

22.4
The output follows

```
4
10
9
8
7
6
the_output_from_la_is_next
This_will_test_lread_lwrite

EXECUTION HAS TERMINATED PROPERLY
```

Bibliography

Aho, A.V., Sethi, R. and Ullman, J.D. (1986) *Compilers: Principles, Techniques and Tools*, Addison- Wesley, Reading, MA.

Alblas, H. and Nymeyer, A. (1996) *Practice and Principles of Compiler Building with C*, Prentice-Hall, Hemel Hempstead, England.

Barrett, W. A., et.al. (1986) *Compiler Construction, Theory and Practices* Chicago:Science Research Associates.

Barron, D.W. (ed) (1981) *Pascal - the Language and its Implementation*, Wiley, Chichester, England.

Bennett, J.P. (1990) *Introduction to Compiling Techniques: a First Course using ANSI C, LEX and YACC*, McGraw-Hill, London.

Bergmann, S. (1994) *Compiler Design Theory, Tools, and Examples*, Wm. C. Brown Publishers, Iowa.

Brinch Hansen, P. (1985) *On Pascal Compilers*, Prentice-Hall, Englewood Cliffs, NJ.

Cichelli, R.J. (1980) *Minimal perfect hash functions made simple, Communications of the ACM*, 23(1), 17- 19.

Cohen, D.I.A.(1986) *Introduction to Computer Theory* New York: Wiley.

Cooper, D. (1983) *Standard Pascal Reference Manual*, Norton, New York.

Dobler, H. and Pirklbauer, K. (1990) *Coco-2 - a new compiler-compiler*, ACM SIGPLAN Notices, 25(5), 82- 90.

Ellis, M.A. and Stroustrup, B. (1990) *The Annotated C++ Reference Manual*, Addison-Wesley, Reading, MA.

Ensley, Douglas E.; & Crawley, J. Winston (2006), *Discrete Mathematics: Mathematical Reasoning and Proof with Puzzles, Patterns, and Games* (Hoboken, NJ: John Wiley & Sons).

Epp, Susanna S. (2004), *Discrete Mathematics with Applications, Third Edition* (Belmont, CA: Brooks/Cole—Thomson Learning).

Feil, Todd; & Krone, Joan (2003), *Essential Discrete Mathematics for Computer Science* (Upper Saddle River, NJ: Pearson/Prentice Hall).

Fischer, C.N. and LeBlanc, R.J. (1991) *Crafting a Compiler with C*, Benjamin Cummings, Menlo Park, CA.

Gerstin, Judith L. (2007), *Mathematical Structures for Computer Science: A Modern Approach to Discrete Mathematics, Sixth Edition* (New York: W.H. Freeman).

Gough, K.J. (1988) *Syntax Analysis and Software Tools*, Addison-Wesley, Wokingham, England.

Hein, James L. (2002), *Discrete Structures, Logic, and Computability, Second Edition* (Sudbury, MA: Jones & Bartlett).

Holmes, J. (1995) *Object-Oriented Compiler Construction*, Prentice-Hall, Englewood Cliffs, NJ.

Holub, A.I. (1990) *Compiler Design in C*, Prentice-Hall, Englewood Cliffs, NJ.

Hopcroft, J.E., and J.D. Ullman (1979) *Introduciton to Automata Theory, Languages and Computation Reading*, Ma: Addison Wesley.

Hunter, R.B. (1985) *The Design and Construction of Compilers with Pascal*, Wiley, New York.

Johnsonbaugh, Richard (2005), *Discrete Mathematics, Sixth Edition* (Upper Saddle River, NJ: Pearson/Prentice Hall).

Johnson, S.C. (1975) *Yacc - Yet Another Compiler Compiler, Computing Science Technical Report* 32, AT&T Bell Laboratories, Murray Hill, NJ.

Kamin, S.N. (1990) *Programming Languages: An Interpreter Based Approach Reading*, Ma: Addison Wesley.

Kernighan, B.W. and Ritchie, D.M. (1988) *The C Programming Language (2nd edn)*, Prentice-Hall, Englewood Cliffs, NJ.

Knuth, D.E. (1973) *The Art of Computer Programming, Sorting and Searching, Vol. 3*, Addison-Wesley, Reading Ma.

Lee, J.A.N. (1972) *The formal definition of the BASIC language, Computer Journal*, 15, 37-41.

Lemone, K.A. (1992) *Fundamentals of Compilers: An Introduction to Computer Language Translation* Boca Raton, Fl: CRC.

Louden, K.C. (1997) *Compiler Construction Principles and Practice* PWS, Boston, Ma.

Mak, R. (1991) *Writing Compilers and Interpreters: an Applied Approach*, John Wiley, New York.

McGettrick, A.D. (1980) *The Definition of Programming Languages*, Cambridge University Press, Cambridge, England.

Parr, T.J., Dietz, H.G. and Cohen W.E. (1992) *PCCTS 1.00: The Purdue Compiler Construction Tool Set, ACM SIGPLAN Notices*, 27(2), 88-165.

Parsons, T. W. (1992) *Introduction to Compiler Construction*, New York: Freeman.

Pittman, T. and Peters, J. (1992) *The Art of Compiler Design*, Prentice-Hall, Englewood Cliffs, NJ.

Rees, M. and Robson, D. (1987) *Practical Compiling with Pascal-S*, Addison-Wesley, Wokingham, England.

Rosen, Kenneth H. (2007), *Discrete Mathematics and Its Applications, 6th Edition* (New York: McGraw-Hill).

Ross, Kenneth A.; & Wright, Charles R.B. (2003), *Discrete Mathematics, Fifth Edition* (Upper Saddle River, NJ: Pearson/Prentice Hall).

Schreiner, A.T. and Friedman, H.G. (1985) *Introduction to Compiler Construction with UNIX*, Prentice-Hall, Englewood Cliffs, NJ.

Sethi R. (1989) *Programming Languages Concepts and Constructs*, Addison-Wesley Reading, Ma.

Stroustrup, B. (1993) *The Design and Evolution of C++*, Addison-Wesley, Reading, MA.

Tremblay, J.P. and Sorenson, P.G. (1985) *Theory and Practice of Compiler Writing*, McGraw-Hill, New York.

Waite, W.M. and Goos, G. (1984) *Compiler Construction*, Springer, New York.

Watt, D.A. (1991) *Programming Language Syntax and Semantics*, Prentice-Hall, Hemel Hempstead, England.

Wirth, N. (1976) *Algorithms + Data Structures = Programs*, Prentice-Hall, Englewood Cliffs, NJ.

Wirth, N. (1996) *Compiler Construction*, Addison-Wesley, Wokingham, England.

Index

www.ingramcontent.com/pod-product-compliance
Lightning Source LLC
LaVergne TN
LVHW022003060526
838200LV00003B/81